Thomas North

# The church bells of Leicestershire

Their inscriptions, traditions and peculiar uses

Thomas North

**The church bells of Leicestershire**
*Their inscriptions, traditions and peculiar uses*

ISBN/EAN: 9783337259570

Printed in Europe, USA, Canada, Australia, Japan

Cover: Foto ©Lupo / pixelio.de

More available books at **www.hansebooks.com**

# THE CHURCH BELLS

OF

# *LEICESTERSHIRE :*

Their Inscriptions, Traditions, and Peculiar Uses;

WITH

CHAPTERS ON BELLS AND THE LEICESTER

BELL FOUNDERS.

BY THOMAS NORTH,

Honorary Secretary of the Leicestershire Architectural and Archæological
Society, and Member of the Royal Archæological Institute
of Great Britain and Ireland.

WITH ILLUSTRATIONS.

LEICESTER: SAMUEL CLARKE.
1876.

# SUBSCRIBERS.

HIS GRACE THE DUKE OF RUTLAND, K.G., Lord Lieutenant of the County.

THE RIGHT REVEREND THE LORD BISHOP OF THE DIOCESE.

THE WORSHIPFUL THE MAYOR OF LEICESTER.
(William Barfoot, Esq.)

The Venerable HENRY FEARON, B.D., Archdeacon of Leicester.
The Venerable F. H. THICKNESSE, M.A., Archdeacon of Northampton.
The Venerable the LORD ALWYNE COMPTON, M.A., Archdeacon of Oakham.
The Right Honourable the EARL OF GAINSBOROUGH, Exton Park, Oakham.
Sir GEORGE HOWLAND BEAUMONT, Bart., Coleorton Hall.
Sir WILLIAM DE CAPEL BROOKE, Bart., M.A., The Elms, Market Harborough.
Sir HENRY EDWARD LEIGH DRYDEN, Bart., M.A., Canon's Ashby.
Sir FREDERICK THOMAS FOWKE, Bart., Lowesby Hall, Leicester.
Sir GEOFFREY PALMER, Bart., M.A., Carlton.

ADCOCK, William, Esq., Melton Mowbray.
Addison, the Rev. Leonard, M.A., Leicester.
Agar, Thomas, Esq., Leicester.
Argles, the Rev. Canon, M.A., Barnack Rectory.
Armitage, W., Esq., Lownfield House, Altringham.

BAINES, Mr. F. J., Leicester.
Baker, Charles, Esq., Leicester.
Barnard, Thomas, Esq., Leicester.
Barrow, Mr. Joseph, Long Eaton.
Barwell, Mr. James, Birmingham.
Bean, Miss, Garnstone Villa, Burnt Ash, Lee, Kent.

Beedham, B. H., Esq., Ashfield House, Kimbolton.
Bellairs, the Rev. G. S., M.A., Goadby Marwood Rectory.
Bellairs, Major, Leicester.
Benfield, T. W., Esq., Leicester.
Berridge, R. B., Esq., Leicester.
Bigge, the Rev. H. J., M.A., Rockingham Rectory.
Billson, Wm., Esq., Leicester.
Billson, Wm., jun., Esq., Leicester.
Bird, James, Esq., Leicester.
Blackwood, Mrs., Woodhall, Port Glasgow. (2 copies).
Bland, Mr. Thomas, Leicester.

*b.*

Bleasdall, the Rev. John, B.A., Ashton-under-Lyne.

Blews, Messrs. W. and Sons., Birmingham.

Bloxam, Matthew Holbeche, Esq., F.S.A., Rugby.

Bonser, the Rev. J. A., M.A., Bottisham Lode Vicarage.

Boulter, H. C., Esq., F.S.A., Hull.

Bradshaw, the Rev. H., M.A., Breedon, Ashby-de-la-Zouch.

Bragge, Wm., Esq., F.S.A., Shirle Hall, Sheffield.

Bridges, the Rev. F. B. H., M.A., Brunting-thorpe Rectory.

Brook, Miss, Pencraig, Enderby.

Brooks, Thomas, Esq., Barkby Hall (2 copies).

Brooksbanks, Miss M., The Bailey, Durham.

Brown, Miss, Shoby House (2 copies).

Browne, Mr. T. C., Leicester.

Bruxner, the Rev. G. E., M.A., Thurlaston Rectory.

Burdett, Chas., Esq., Lutterworth (2 copies).

Burnaby, Colonel E. S., Baggrave Hall.

CATTEL, James, Esq., Peterborough.

Chaplin, C. W., Esq., Market Harborough.

Charlesworth, Mr. Thomas, Leicester.

Charters, Robert jun., Esq., Leicester.

Chataway, the Rev. T. E., M.A., Peckleton Rectory.

Chester, Mrs., Halstead Grange.

Clarence, L. B., Esq., Deputy Queen's Advocate, Colombo, Ceylon.

Clark, G. T., Esq., F.S.A., Dowlais House, Dowlais.

Clark, the Rev. J., M.A., Kegworth Rectory.

Clarke, the Rev. J. Erskine, M.A., 6, Atten-bury Gardens, Clapham Common, London, (2 copies).

Clephan, Edwin, Esq., Leicester.

Clephan, James, Esq., Newcastle-on-Tyne.

Coleman, J. S., Esq., Leicester.

Coltman, Mr. T., jun., Leicester.

Cooper, J. H., Esq., Manor House, Rotherby.

Cooper, Alfred, Esq., Wigston Magna.

Corah, Edwin, Esq., Leicester.

Corrance, the Rev. H. F., M.A., King's Walden.

Cox, J. C., Esq., Chevin House, Belper.

Crick, Thomas, Esq., Rupert's Rest, Glen Magna.

Crossley, C. R., Esq., Leicester.

Crossley, J. S., Esq., Barrow-on-Soar.

DALBY, the Rev. Robert, M.A., R.D., Staunton Harold.

Day, Miss, Wymondham House.

Day, John, Esq., Wymondham House.

Day, Robert, Esq., Wymondham House.

Deakins, Mr. Superintendent, Leicester.

Denton, the Rev. John, M.A., Ashby-de-la-Zouch Vicarage.

Disney, the Rev. W. H., M.A., Hinckley Vicarage.

Dodds, the Rev. H. L., M.A., Glen Magna Vicarage.

Donisthorpe, A. R., Esq., Oadby.

Dunkin, E. H. W., Esq., 14, Kidbrooke Park Road, Blackheath.

EDMONDS, J. R., Esq., Mountsorrel.

Elmhirst, the Rev. E., B.A., Shawell Rectory.

Ellacombe, the Rev. H. T., M.A., F.S.A., Clyst S. George Rectory, Devon.

Ellis, Alfred, Esq., Belgrave.

Ellis, James, Esq., Gynsills, Leicester.

Ellis, Miss Lucy, Belgrave.

Evans, John, Esq., F.R.S., F.S.A., 65, Old Bailey, London.

FARMER, the Rev. J., S.C.L., New Walk, Leicester.

Farmer, W. G., Esq., Hinckley.

Fawcett, Josh., Esq., Sheffield.

Fenwicke, the Rev. G. C., B.A., Stockerstone Rectory.

Fisher, the Rev. H., M.A., Higham Rectory.

Fisher, E., jun., Esq., Over Seile.

Fitz-Gerald, Edward Ryvers, Esq., Blackrock, Co. Dublin.

Fletcher, W. G. Dimock, Esq., S. Edmund's Hall, Oxford.

Flude, Mr. John, Leicester.

Foster, Richard, Esq., Lanwithan, Lostwithiel.

Fowler, the Rev. J. F., M.A., F.S.A., Hatfield Hall, Durham.

Freer, C. T., Esq., The Coplow, Billesdon.

Freer, Wm. J., Esq., Stonygate, Leicester.

Freestone, Mr. Henry, Market Harborough.

GILL, Miss, Hoton, Loughborough.

Gill, Miss, Princess Street, Leicester.

Gill, Miss Alice J., Princess Street, Leicester.

Gill, Elliott J. Esq., Princess Street, Leicester.

Gillett and Bland, Messrs., Croydon (2 copies).

Gimson, Wm. Esq., Ashby-de-la-Zouch.

Goddard, Joseph, Esq., F.R.I.B.A., Leicester.

Goddard, Mr. T. C., Leicester.

Godson, The Rev. J., M.A., Ashby-Folville Vicarage.

Goodacre, R. J., Esq., Leicester.

Goodacre, Mrs., 27, Belsize Crescent, Hampstead.

Grieveson, H. J., Esq., Nevill Holt, Market Harborough.

Grundy, Chas., Esq., 26, Budge Row, London.

HACKET, Miss, Langdale Lodge, Clapham Park, Surrey.

Hambly, C. H. Burbidge-, Esq., Barrow-on-Soar.

Hanbury, the Rev. Thos., M.A., Church Langton Rectory.

Hancock, Mr. J. H., Leicester.

Hardy, Mrs. W., jun., Thistleton.

Harris, Joseph, Esq., Westcotes (2 copies).

Harris, the Rev. Joseph, M.A., Shepey Magna Rectory.

Harris, John Dove, Esq., Ratcliffe Hall.

Harris, G. Shirley, Esq., Stonygate, Leicester.

Hart, Mr. John, Leicester.

Herrick, W. Perry-, Esq., Beaumanor Park.

Heude, Mrs., Barrow-on-Soar.

Hickson, Thomas, Esq., Melton Mowbray.

Holdich, the Rev. C. W., M.A., Knipton.

Holyland, Mr. Thomas, Leicester.

Hoskyns, the Rev. H. J., M.A., Blaby Rectory.

Hunt, John, Esq., Thurnby.

Hunt, Mrs. Stonygate, Leicester.

INGRAM, the Rev. R., M.A., Chatburn, Clitheroe.

Ingram, Thomas, Esq., Hawthorn Field, Wigston Magna (2 copies).

JACKSON, James, Esq., Leicester.

James, Miss, Theddingworth (2 copies).

Jee, T. W., Esq., Peckleton Hall.

Jenks, Wm., Esq., Upper Penn, Wolverhampton.

Jerram, Mr. J. R., Sutton Bridge, Lincoln.

Jessop, Mr. Joseph, Leicester.

Johnson, Wm., Esq., Saddington.

Jones, H. S., Esq., Stonygate, Leicester.

Jones, W. H., Esq., Uppingham.

Jones, Mr. Thomas, Leicester.

Jones, Miss, Lowesby Vicarage.

Jones, the Rev. T. Henry, M.A., Ashwell Rectory.

KECK, Harry Leycester Powys-, Esq., Stoughton Grange.

Kelly, Wm., Esq., Leicester.

Kempson, Wm., Esq., Leicester.

King, Miss L., Thurnby House.

Kirk, Charles, Esq., Sleaford.

Knight, Colonel, Glen Parva Manor.

Knowles, the Rev. C., M.A., Wintringham Rectory.

LAKIN, the Rev. J. M., M.A., Gilmorton Rectory.

Langley, the Rev. Wm., M.A., Leicester.

Latham, Wm., Esq., Melton Mowbray (2 copies).

Lee, the Rev. George, D.C.L., F.S.A., All Saints' Vicarage, Lambeth.

Lynam, C., Esq., Stoke-on-Trent.

Lloyd, R., Esq., S. Albans.

Luck, Richard, Esq., Plâs Llanfair, Llanfairfechan (2 copies).

MACAULAY, W. H., Esq., Leicester.

Mallaby, Mr. Thomas, Masham, Bedale, Yorkshire.

Marriott, Chas., Esq., Cotesbach Hall.

Marris, Mr. W. H., Kibworth.

Marshall, Mr. Governor, Borough Gaol, Leicester.

Martin, R. F., Esq., Somerset House, Whitehaven (2 copies).

Miles, E. P., Esq., Kirby Muxloe.

Mitchell, the Rev. T., M.A., Long Clawson Vicarage.

Molesworth, Mr. J., Leicester.

Moore, the Rev. W. B., Evington Vicarage.

Moore, Miss M. J., Evington.

Moore, Miss C. L., Evington.

Morley, F. R., Esq., Stonesby House, Leicester.

Mowbray, Major, Grangewood House, Over Seile.

Murdin, Mr. J. G., Leicester.

NEEDHAM, H. W., Esq., Syston.

Nevile, the Rev. Gerard, M.A., Somerset Place, Bath.

Nevinson, Thomas, Esq., Leicester (2 copies).

Newby, Mr. W. T., Leicester.

Nickolds, the Rev. W., O.S.D., Holy Cross, Leicester.

Norman, Mrs. George, Goadby Marwood Hall.

OAKLEY, the Rev. W. H., M.A., Wyfordby Rectory.

Ord, Mrs. J. E., Langton Hall (6 copies).

Osborn, the Rev. M. F., R.D., Kibworth Rectory.

Ottley, the Rev. F. J., M.A., Thorpe Acre Vicarage.

Overton, Robert, Esq., Stonygate, Leicester.

Owen, the Rev. T. M. N., B.A., F.G.H.S., Middleton, Manchester.

PACKER, the Rev. George, M.A., Thurmaston Vicarage.

Paget, Thos., Esq. (the late) Queniborough.

Paget, Thomas Tertius, Esq., Humberstone.

Paget, Alfred, Esq., Leicester.

Paget, A. H., Esq., Leicester.

Palmer, Captain, Withcote Hall.

Parry, Thomas, Esq., Sleaford.

Peacock, Edward, Esq., F.S.A., Bottesford Manor, Brigg.

Pilling, the Rev. W., M.A., West Beach, Lytham.

Powell, Miss M. (the late), Bitteswell (2 copies).

Power, the Rev. J. P., M.A., Barkestone Vicarage.

Pownall, the Rev. Assheton, M.A., F.S.A., Honorary Canon of Peterborough, South Kilworth Rectory.

RABBETTS, the Rev. F. D., M.A., Buckminster Vicarage.

Redfern, Henry, Esq., Shoby House.

Redfern, Charles, Esq., Grove House, Ventnor, I. W.

Rendell, the Rev. A. M., M.A., Coston Rectory.

Rice, J. S., Esq., Leicester.

Richards, W., Esq., Belgrave.

Richardson, the Rev. H. K., M.A., R.D., Leire Rectory.

Richardson, J. G. F., Esq., Stonygate, Leicester.

Roberts, J., jun., Esq., Stonygate, Leicester.

Robinson, G. A., Esq., The Elms, Melton Road, Leicester.

Robinson, T. W. U., Esq., Houghton-le-Spring, Fence Houses, Durham.

SALT, W. H., Esq., Mapplewell, Loughborough.

Sankey, Charles, Esq., M.A., Marlborough College.

Sarson, Mr. T. F., Leicester.

Shaw, George, Esq., M.D., Leicester.

Shirley, Evelyn P., Esq., F.S.A., Lower Estington Park, Warwickshire.

Small, the Rev. N. P., M.A., Market Bosworth Rectory (3 copies).

Smythies, the Rev. E., B.A., Hathern Rectory.

Spencer, C. Alfred, Esq., Leicester.

Sperling, the Rev. J. H., M.A., Ramsgate.

Stainbank, W. L., Esq., 267, Whitechapel Road, London.

Staples, Mrs., Leicester.

Stevenson, George, Esq., Leicester.

Stone, S. F., Esq., Leicester.

Stretton, Mrs., Dane Hill House, Leicester (2 copies).

Stretton; Albert, Esq., Leicester.

Swithenbank, G. E., Esq., Pyemont Lodge, Annerley.

TAYLER, Mrs., Rothwell.

Taylor, Mr. J. W., Loughborough (2 copies).

Terrot, Mrs., Wispington Vicarage, Horncastle.

Thompson, Charles, Esq., M.D., Leicester.

Thomson, C. S., Esq., Leicester.

Tilley, H. T., Esq., Caius College, Cambridge.

Titley, the Rev. R., M.A., Barwell Rectory.

Tucker, C., Esq., F.S.A., Marlands, Exeter.

Turner, the Rev. T. A., M.A., Drayton Paislow, Bletchley.

Twells, the Rev. H., M.A., Waltham Rectory.

Tyssen, John R. Daniel-, Esq., F.S.A., 9, Lower Rock Gardens, Brighton.

VAUGHAN, Mrs., All Saints, Leicester.

Vaughan, the Rev. C. J., D.D., Master of the Temple, London.

Vialls, George, Esq., 24, Doughty Street, London.

Venables, the Rev. George, S.C.L., Great Yarmouth Vicarage.

WALES, the Worshipful Wm., Chancellor of the Diocese of Peterborough, Uppingham Rectory.

Ward, the Rev. Henry, M.A., Aldwinkle S. Peter's, Thrapstone.

Warner, Mr. Thomas, Leicester Abbey.

Warner, Messrs. J. and Sons, Cripplegate, London.

Wartnaby, Mrs., Market Harborough.

Watson, G. L., Esq., Rockingham Castle.

Watson, the Rev. J. S., M.A., Cotesbach Rectory.

Watts, Henry, Esq., Leicester.

Webster, J. D., Esq., F.R.I.B.A., Sheffield.

Webster, Mrs., Scalford.

Whitby, Captain, Leicester.

White, George, Esq., S. Briavel's, Epsom.

Whitlock, T. O., Esq., Loughborough.

Wigram, the Rev. W., M.A., Furneaux Pelham Vicarage, Herts.

Wild, the Rev. J., M.A., Tetney Vicarage, Grimsby.

Willcox, Mr. W., Melton Mowbray.

Williams, J. H., Esq., Leicester.

Wing, Vincent, Esq., Melton Mowbray.

Woodd, Mrs. Charles H. L., Roslyn House, Hampstead.

Woodhouse, J. T., Esq., Over Seile.

Woolley, W. J., Esq., Loughborough.

Woodward, the Rev. G. J., Kibworth.

### LIBRARIES, SOCIETIES, &c.

The Bedfordshire Architectural Society.

The Leicestershire Architectural and Archæological Society.

The Leicester Literary and Philosophical Society.

The Leicester Permanent Library.

The Lincoln Diocesan Architectural Society.

The Dean and Chapter of Lincoln.

The Newcastle-upon-Tyne Literary and Philosophical Society.

The Architectural Society of the Archdeaconry of Northampton.

# PREFACE.

Twenty years ago I contributed two articles to a local Antiquarian Magazine—"The Midland Counties' Historical Collector "—on *Campanology in Leicester*. Those articles (among my first essays in Archæological research) were brief, and, in one or two particulars, inaccurate. I then saw that the subject was one worthy of further investigation, and one that promised to reward the industry of any antiquary who could devote sufficient time to carry his investigations through the county, as well as through the town, of Leicester. I also saw that a careful record of the Inscriptions on the Church Bells of Leicestershire, illustrated by accurate drawings of the Founders' Marks, Crosses and Stops, would be a useful contribution towards that reprint of our great County History, which all students of local antiquities hope, in due time, to see.

Apart from this aspect of the value of such an investigation, the study of Campanology has lately taken a not unimportant place in the estimation of Archæologists. The Inscriptions on the Church Bells of several counties have been diligently placed on record, and their Founders traced. Bellfounding, as a prominent art in the middle ages (with all the interest by which it was surrounded), has been

carefully enquired into and described. It was therefore
evident that a description, such as I have referred to, of the
Leicestershire Bells, accompanied by such an account of
the Leicester Founders as could be gathered from Local
and National Records, would be a fitting chapter in that
History of Campanology in England which antiquaries, in
its various counties, are gradually compiling.

Want of leisure, and stronger claims upon my time,
however, prevented me from attempting to follow the path
I have indicated. It was not until I found, in the enforced
partial retirement from the active duties of life, consequent
upon severe illness, that leisure, which calling for occasional
occupation, brought to my remembrance my former desire to
prosecute my enquiries into the Campanology of Leicestershire further than I was then enabled to do.

Distance from the county, and inability to climb its
bell-chambers and turrets, did not seem promising circumstances in preparing the Work I had in view. I determined,
however, to apply to the clergy, and to my archæological
and other friends in the county, for their assistance, in
procuring for me Rubbings of the Inscriptions, and Casts
of the Founders' Marks, Initial Crosses and Stops. Right
willingly and heartily have they helped me. I being unable
to go to the bells, have had the bells (as it were) brought
to me. My kind helpers have overcome almost every
difficulty, for it is only in one or two insignificant instances
where I am obliged to be content to mark a bell-turret as
"inaccessible." To one and all I offer my most grateful
thanks. Without their ready help this work could not have

been undertaken. I sincerely trust that the care I have attempted to bestow upon the compilation of that part specially devoted to the description of the Leicestershire Bells will show that I am not unmindful of the labour undertaken by my many helpers and correspondents on my behalf. May the music of our Church Bells sound joyously in their ears for many years to come!

My thanks are tendered to John Robert Daniel-Tyssen, Esq., F.S.A., to the Rev. H. T. Ellacombe, F.S.A., and to Llewellyn Jewitt, Esq., F.S.A., for the loan of several wood-cuts, also to the following ladies and gentlemen (referred to above) who have helped me by procuring rubbings, or casts, from bells, in the parishes placed against their names.

| | |
|---|---|
| ADAMS, Rev. S. | Bagworth, Thornton. |
| Armstrong, Rev. C. E. | Stonton Wyville. |
| Astley, Rev. B. B. G, | Cadeby. |
| Atkinson, Rev. A. W. | Thurmaston. |
| BARRETT, Rev. D. W. | Eastwell, Eaton, Scalford, Stathern, Stonesby, Waltham. |
| Baker, Chas., Esq. | Wigston's Old Hospital. |
| Badcock, Rev. T. | Fleckney. |
| Beaumont, Rev. W. | Coleorton. |
| Bennie, Rev. J. N. | Glenfield. |
| Bellairs, Rev. S. G. | Caldwell, Goadby Marwood. |
| Berry, Rev. W. | Peatling Magna, Peatling Parva, Willoughby Waterless. |
| Belgrave, Rev. C. W. | North Kilworth. |
| Bown, Mr. T. P. | Aylestone, Glen Magna, Houghton, Leicester (All Saints', S. Margaret's, and S. Mary's), Thurcaston, Wigston Magna, Wistow. |

*c*

| | |
|---|---|
| Bowmar, Rev. H. | Kirby Muxloe. |
| Bridges, Rev. F. B. H. | Bruntingthorpe. |
| Brooks, John, Esq. | Croft, Frolesworth, Narborough, Thurlaston. |
| Bullivant, Rev. H. E. | Foxton, Lubenham. |
| Burfield, Rev. Canon | S. Mark's, Leicester. |
| | |
| CAREY, Rev. A. H. | Owston. |
| Chataway, H. M., Esq. | Peckleton. |
| Cherry, Mr. C. | Cranoe, Glooston. |
| Clark, Rev. J. | Kegworth. |
| Cooke, Rev. C. F. | Diseworth. |
| Cooper, J. H., Esq. | Rotherby, |
| Colyer, Rev. J. E. | Fenny Drayton. |
| Cole, Rev. W. G. | Newbold Verdon. |
| Cox, Rev. Thos. | Norton-by-Twycross. |
| Cox, Rev. T. | Kimcote. |
| Corah, E., Esq. | S. John's, Leicester. |
| Coalbank, Rev. S. | Old Dalby. |
| Crick, Thos., Esq. | Burton Overy, Glen Magna. |
| | |
| DAWES, Mr. C. J. | S. Mark's, Leicester. |
| Dalby, Rev. R., R.D. | Breedon, Staunton Harold, Worthington. |
| Day, John, Esq. | Birstall, Buckminster, Cossington, Dalby Parva, Edmonthorpe, Garthorpe, Leicester (All Saints'), Lockington, Nailstone, Narborough, Sproxton, Wanlip, Wyfordby, Wymondham. |
| Drake, Rev. T. | Mountsorrell. |
| Drummond, Rev. J. | Galby. |
| | |
| EASTBURN, Rev. C. F. | Medbourne. |
| Ebsworth, Rev. G. S. | Croxton Kerrial. |
| Emberlin, H. E., Esq. | Oadby. |
| Everett, Rev. E. | Theddingworth. |
| | |
| FENWICKE, Rev. G. C. | Stockerstone. |
| Fisher, W. P., Esq. | Dalby Magna, Hungarton, Loseby, Thorpe Satchville, Twyford. |
| Fisher, Rev. John | Cossington. |
| Fisher, Rev. Henry | Higham-on-the-Hill. |

Fletcher, W. G. Dimock, Esq. .. .. Loughborough.
Foster, Rev. John .. .. .. The Oaks.
Freer, S. C., Esq. .. Carlton Curlieu, Houghton, Illston, King's Norton.
Fry, Rev. L. G. .. .. .. Belgrave.
Furnival, Rev. James .. .. Muston.

GARDNER, Rev. W. .. .. .. Coalville.
Gatty and Freestone, Messrs. .. .. Bowden Magna, Market Harborough.
Gallwey, Rev. T. G. .. .. Birstall.
Gimson, Wm., Esq. .. .. Ashby-de-la-Zouch (Holy Trinity).
Gill, E. J., Esq. .. .. .. Melton Mowbray.
Glenn, Mr. .. .. .. Hose.
Godson, Rev. J. .. .. Beeby, Cold Overton, Dalby Parva, Grimstone, Long Clawson, Pickwell.
Gordon, Rev. J. W. .. .. Knighton.
Green, C. N., Esq. .. .. .. Blackfordby, Normanton-le-Heath.
Gresley, Messrs. R. and S. .. Seile (Nether and Over).

HARRIS, Rev. Joseph .. .. Ratcliffe Culey, Shepey Magna.
Hassall, Rev. T. .. .. Rearsby.
Hall, Rev. R. E. .. .. .. Congerstone.
Harrington, Rev. H. Duke .. Knossington.
Hanbury, Rev. T. .. .. Church Langton, Thorpe Langton, Tur Langton.
Hazlerigg, Rev. W. G. .. Nosely.
Halford, Rev. J. F. .. Wistow.
Henton, Geo., Esq. .. .. Holy Trinity, Leicester.
Holdich, Rev. C. W. .. .. Branstone, Knipton, Redmile.
Hoskyns, Rev. H. J. .. .. Blaby, Countesthorpe.
Holyland, Mr. T. .. .. S. Martin's, Leicester.
Homan, Rev. J. F. .. Aston Flamville, Broughton Astley, Burbage, Claybrooke, Cosby, Dadlington, Hinckley, Narborough, Sapcote, Wibtoft, Wigston Parva.
Homer, Rev. H. .. .. .. Barlestone.
Hodgson, Rev. W. E. .. .. .. Swepstone.
Hunt, John, Esq. .. .. Illston, Keyham, Scraptoft, Thurnby.
Hynde, Rev. W. .. .. .. Cosby.

INGRAM, Thos., Esq. ..     ..   Wigston Magna.
Isaacs, Rev. A. A.     .. ..   Christ Church, Leicester.

JACKSON, Rev. J.     ..   Shearsby
Johnson, W., Esq.     .. ..   Saddington.
Johnson, R. W., Esq.     ..   Harby, Plungar.
Jones, Miss    ..     .. ..   Ashby Folville, Billesdon, Burrough, Gad-
                  desby, Somerby, South Croxton.

KNIGHT, Colonel     ..   Aylestone.

LAW and Sons, Messrs.    ..     .. ..   Lutterworth.
Lewis, Rev. M.     ..     ..   Ashby Parva, Bitteswell, Catthorpe, Cottes-
                  bach, Gilmorton, Husband's Bosworth,
                  Lutterworth, Misterton, Peatling Parva,
                  Shawell, Swinford.
Loveday, Mr. Arthur ..     ..   Gumley, Illston, Kibworth, Laughton, New-
                  ton Harcourt.

MASON, Rev. J.    ..     ..   S. Paul's, Leicester.
Middleton, Rev. C. G     .. ..   Belton.
Millington, Rev. T. C.     ..   Woodhouse Eaves.
Moore, Rev. W. B.     .. ..   Evington, Stoughton, Stretton Magna, Stret-
                  ton Parva.

NEWBY, Rev. R. J.     ..   Whetstone.
Neale, G. C., Esq.     .. ..   Billesdon, Loddington, Skeffington, Tugby.
Nevile, Rev. G.    ..     ...   Tilton.
Newham, W. E., Esq.     ..   Barrow-on-Soar, Hoton, Prestwold, Quorn-
                  don, Seagrave, Sileby, Walton-on-the-
                  Wolds, Woodhouse.
Noble, Rev. Jno. (the late)     ..   Nether Broughton.
Norman, Rev. Canon    ..     ..   Bottesford.
Norris, Rev. T.    ..     ..   Goadby, East Norton, Rolleston.

OAKLEY and Wilder, Messrs.     ..   Ab-Kettleby, Brentingby, Burton Lazars,
                  Freeby, Garthorpe, Saltby, Saxby, Sprox-
                  ton, Stapleford, Thorpe Arnold, Wyfordby.
Osborne, Rev. M. F., R.D.     ..   Kibworth.
Ottley, Rev. F. J.    ..     ... ..   Dishley.

PAGE, Rev. T. Douglas .. Sibstone.

Packe, Rev. H. V. .. .. Shankton.

Palmer, Captain .. Withcote.

Pearson, Mr. M. .. .. .. Barkby, Beeby, Brooksby, Castle Donington, Frisby, Gaddesby, Holwell, Hungarton, Kirby Belers, Kegworth, Long Whatton, Nether Broughton, Old Dalby, Queniborough, Rotherby, Ragdale, Saxelby, Seagrave, Sysonby, Thrussington, Walton Isley, Wartnaby, Welby.

Peake, Rev. T. C. .. .. .. Hallaton.

Phillipps, Rev. C. L. M. (the late).. .. Sheepshed.

Pilling, Rev. W. .. .. Arnesby.

Piercy, Rev. J. M. W. .. Slawston.

Power, Rev. J. P. .. .. Barkeston.

Pownall, Rev. Canon .. .. South Kilworth.

Pughe, Rev. K. M. .. .. Market Bosworth, Shenton, Sutton Cheney.

RABBITTS, Rev. F. B. .. .. Sewstern.

Rendell, Rev. A. M. .. .. Coston.

Reeves, Mr. S. .. .. .. Ansty.

Reynard, Rev. W. .. .. .. Lockington.

Richardson, Rev. H. K., R.D. .. .. Leire.

SARGENT, Mr. J. R. .. .. .. Humberstone.

Sankey, Rev. Jno. (the late) .. .. Stoney Stanton.

Serjeant, Rev. J. S. .. .. Twycross.

Smythies, Rev. E. .. Hathern.

Syers, Rev. H. S. .. Syston.

TAYLOR, Mr. W. .. .. .. Ashby-de-la-Zouch, Packington.

Thomas, Rev. A. F. .. .. Witherley.

Titley, Rev. R. .. .. .. Barwell, Potter's Marston.

Townson, Rev. W. .. Carlton.

Tower, Rev. E. .. .. Earl's Shilton, Elmsthorpe.

Tomkins, H. B., Esq .. .. Orton-on-the-Hill.

Traylen, J. C., Esq. .. .. Leicester (S. Nicolas'), Queniborough.

Tronsdale, Rev. R. .. .. Ratby.

UPCHER, Rev. H. B. .. .. Allexton.

| | | |
|---|---|---|
| WAYTE, Mr. .. | .. | Ibstock. |
| Watts, Rev. R. .. | .. .. | Nailstone. |
| Watson, Rev. H. L. .. | .. | Sharnford. |
| Welchman, H. J. P., Esq. .. | .. .. | Rothley. |
| Welby, Rev. W. H. E. | .. | Harston. |
| Whitby, Captain .. | .. .. | Desford, Enderby, Groby, Hoby, Huggles-cote, Kirkby Mallory, Markfield, Newtown Linford, Ratcliffe-on-the-Wreake, Ragdale, Saxelby, Snibstone, Snareston, Shacker-ston, Thrussington, Whitwick, Wymeswold. |
| Wing, Rev. Chas. .. | .. | Foston. |
| Wing, Arthur S., Esq. | .. .. | Asfordby. |
| Willes, Rev. Canon .. | .. | Ashby Magna. |
| Woodhouse, Rev. T. E. .. | .. | Braunstone. |
| Woodward, Rev. G. J. | .. | Blaston S. Michael, Bringhurst, Great Easton, Holt, Horninghold, Kibworth, Welham. |
| Wright, W., Esq. | .. .. | Wanlip. |

I have pleasure in adding that Mr. Utting has most carefully engraved for me, from casts taken direct from the bells, a large number of the woodcuts which illustrate the following pages.

T. N.

LEICESTER, *January,* 1876.

\*\*\* In order to complete an account of the Campanology of the Diocese of Peterborough, this volume may be succeeded by similar accurate descriptions of the Church Bells of the counties of Northampton and Rutland.

# CONTENTS.

———

# ILLUSTRATIONS.

# CHURCH BELLS.

M UCH has been written, and might be repeated here, upon the Origin and Antiquity of Bells.

In the oldest existing writings—those of Moses—we find mention of the bells which were ordered to be placed upon the hem of the ephod of the High Priest,* and which, we are told by the son of Sirach,† made a noise that might be heard in the temple, when he went in, and when he came out of the holy place.‡ They were used also as appendages to their royal robes, by the ancient Persians. The Greeks and the Romans used them (more, perhaps, in the shape of gongs) to call people to the baths and to the markets. Mr. Layard mentions the discovery, in the palace of Nimroud, of about eighty small bells of bronze with iron tongues.§ They appear to have been used in very early times in

---

* *Exod.* xxviii. 33.

† *Ecclus.* xlv. 9.

‡ According to Justyn Martyr these bells (twelve in number) which tinkled on the garments of the High Priest, were a symbol that the sound of the Apostles was to go forth into all lands. Vide *Blunt's Church in the First Three Centuries*, p. 131.

§ *Discoveries at Nineveh*, &c. Second Series, p. 177.

B

Hindoo temples. They have been found in Egypt.* The Chinese have bells, and probably had them long ages ago. Most, if not all, of these, however, were so small and insignificant that they have been more correctly described as " metallic rattles," rather than as bells.

Leaving these precursors of the Church Bell, and referring all who are interested in pursuing their history further to the researches of the many competent writers on the subject, I offer by way of introduction to the pages which follow, a few remarks upon the Bell as used in the Christian Church. In doing so I have little to add to the few historical facts which have become the common property of all writers on this branch of archæology. I should have hesitated to reproduce some of these here if the following pages were only intended for the reading of campanists, and as a chapter in the history of the Church Bells of this country. This work may, however, fall into the hands of some who may wish for a sketch of the origin of those musical ornaments of our churches which they so often hear, but so seldom see. I trust therefore to be pardoned for treading in the footsteps of several learned predecessors, and for availing myself, occasionally, of their researches.

The early Christians, in consequence of the persecutions to which, from time to time, they were exposed, would be very unlikely to use any noisy summons to their meetings

---

* I am indebted to J. R. Daniel-Tyssen, Esq. for the use of the two woodcuts of Bells from Egypt. They are supposed to belong to the Ptolemean period, two hundred years B.C.

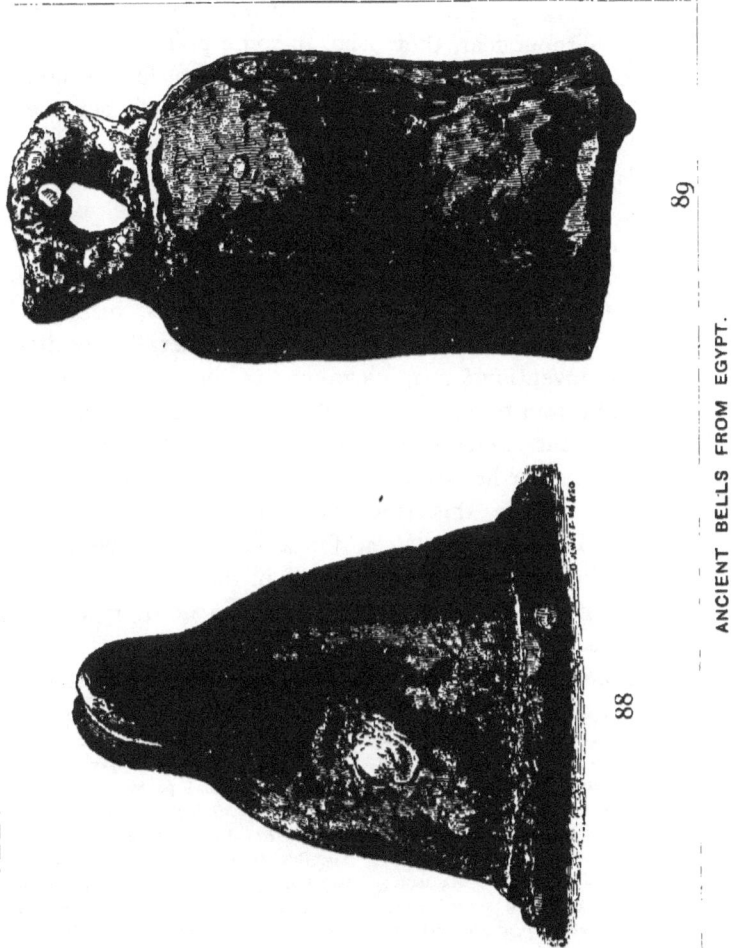

89

88

ANCIENT BELLS FROM EGYPT.

for prayer and praise. So soon as they were able to meet publicly, without fear, they used, in some places, trumpets, like the Jews of old.* S. Ephrem (*circa* 370) further mentions the *Signum*—a clapper or tablet—as the call then used to Holy Communion.†

Bells do not appear to have been introduced into the Christian Church until the fifth century. The earliest Christian writer who refers to them is thought to be Saint Jerome, who in the *Regula Monachorum* (*circa* 422) mentions their use as a call to matins, &c.‡ Paulinus, bishop of Nola, in Campania (A.D. 400), has been generally credited with their invention,§ but, inasmuch, as there is extant an epistle from him to Severus, in which he minutely describes his church, but makes no mention of either tower or bells, we must consider he was ignorant, at least at that time, of their use.‖ From this tradition, however, we have the mediæval Latin name, *Nola*, for a small hand-bell, and *Campana* for the larger bell hanging in the church tower or turret. Church Bells are also called *Signa* in mediæval documents.

It is not proposed—as being foreign to this work—to attempt a description of the *Nola* or *Tintinnabulum*, as the

---

* Bingham's *Antiq.*, Bk. viii., c. 7. Tin Trumpets preserved at Willoughton and Thorney are said to have been used to call the congregation together. Walcott's *Sac. Arch.*, p. 70.

† *Parænesi* xliii. The Rev. Mackenzie E. C. Walcott, F.S.A., to whom I am indebted for this reference, so interprets the "sign."

‡ Quoted by *Rocca, De Campanis*. Opera. Romæ, 1719. Vol. I. p. 156.

§ Dupin's *Eccl. Hist. Ninth Cent.*, p. 166.

‖ *The Bell*, by Rev. Alfred Gatty, p. 13. The Rev. H. T. Ellacombe in his *Bells of the Church*, p. 338, gives an engraving of an ancient bell "supposed to have been invented or adopted by Paulinus, *circa* 420, for church purposes."

early portable hand-bell was called. Several of these, of great antiquity, are still extant in Ireland, North Wales, and Scotland. Some of them are very elaborately ornamented, and are accompanied by covers of exquisite workmanship. They are frequently formed of a sheet of metal hammered into shape, and rivetted at the side. There does not appear to be any clue as to the precise original use of these curious bells, which in many instances were, until recently, held in high reverence, and even in superstitious dread, by the ignorant peasantry. Some antiquaries think they are relics of the early founders of Christianity in these Islands, and have been, as such, carefully preserved in Religious Houses founded at the time by the saints themselves.*

Pope Sabinian (A.D. 604) having ordered the hours to be sounded on the bells,† is thought by others to have introduced the use of the *Campanæ* or *Signa*, as the large bells were called, into churches. He, however, more probably found bells in partial use, and recognizing their beauty and value, encouraged their general adoption, as it is soon after his time that we read of their use in this country. They are mentioned in the *Ordo Romanus* about this date, as being used to announce Tierce, Mass, and Processions, and S. Owen in the life of S. Eloy (*circa* 650) speaks of the *Campana*.‡

---

* A very full and profusely illustrated account of these bells will be found in *The Bells of the Church*, a *Tome* lately put forth by my venerable friend The Rev. H. T. Ellacombe, F.S.A.
† Walcott's *Sac. Arch.*, p. 96.
‡ Walcott's *Sac. Arch.*, p. 66.

Bede mentions the existence of a bell at Streanæshalch (Whitby) in the year 680, which was used to awake, and to call the nuns to prayer.* The second excerption of Egbert, issued about the year 750, commands every priest, at the proper hours, to sound the bells of his church, and then to go through the sacred offices of God. In the tenth century we trace the existence of bells in one of the illuminations in S. Æthelwold's *Benedictional*, a gorgeous manuscript, certainly executed before the close of that century: an open campanile appears in which are suspended four bells.†　About the same time, if we may trust Ingulph, we find a ring of bells at Croyland Abbey. Turketil, who was made abbot of that House about 946, had "one very large bell" cast, called Guthlac; to that one bell his successor, Egelric the elder (who died in 984) added six more—two large ones, which he called Bartholomew and Bettelm, two of medium size, which he named Turketil and Tatwin, and two small ones to which he gave the names of Pega and Bega. The chronicler adds, that when all these seven bells were rung "an exquisite harmony was produced thereby, nor was there such a peal of bells in those days in all England."‡　From this we may infer that single bells, if not rings, were then well known in this country. Neither were the abbots of Croyland the only ecclesiastics of that period whose names are handed down to us as founders of bells. S. Dunstan "the chief of monks," an expert worker in metals, cast a bell, which for many ages after his death hung in Canterbury

---

* *Eccl. Hist.*, Book IV. c. xxiv. (Gidley's Translation).

† *Archaeologia* xxiv. plate 32.

‡ *Ingulph's Chron.*, Bohn's Ed., p. 107.

Cathedral; two bells cast under his direction were at Abingdon, where also were other two the work of its founder S. Æthelwold.* Indeed there is every reason for believing that at the Norman Conquest the art of bellfounding was well understood, and carried to great perfection in this country. The grand old Norman towers of our churches clearly point to the large and heavy bells which they were built to contain.

The first Englishman who followed bellfounding as a trade at present known by name, is Roger de Ropeforde of Paignton, who, in 1284, was employed to make four bells for the north tower of Exeter Cathedral.†

In the thirteenth century we meet with constant mention of bells as of things not in the least extraordinary or rare. Matthew Paris writes as if, at least, every church of note, possessed one bell or more.‡ He tells us that Otto the Legate was received with processions, and the music of bells.§ That upon the return of Henry the Third, from Gascony, in 1243, when he had come to Winchester, he gave orders that all the bells in the place should resound with joy ;‖ and he further tells that in 1250, the Canons of S. Bartholomew, London, received the Archbishop Boniface of Canterbury "amidst the ringing of bells."¶ In 1239, Henry the Third directed a bell-turret to be made for the

---

* Rock's *Church of our Fathers.* iii., Part 2, p. 57.

† Ellacombe's *Bells of Exeter Cathedral,* p. 3. See also *Notes and Queries,* 5th, s. iii., p. 77, for an interesting account of the casting of a bell in the same year (1284).

‡ Bohn's Ed. vol. iii. p. 51.

§ Vol. i. p. 55.

‖ Vol. i. p. 455.

¶ Vol. ii. p. 346.

chapel of S. Thomas, in the castle of Winchester;* and
the same monarch, in 1243, commanded a stone turret to
be built in front of the King's chapel at Windsor, in which
three or four bells might be hung.† In 1273 we hear of the
bell of the church of S. Benedict, Cambridge, being used
to convene the clerks to extraordinary lectures.‡

The following century (the fourteenth) furnishes the
earliest mention of the existence of church bells in Leicester
that I have met with. Mr. James Thompson in his History
of the town,§ incidentally proves the existence of a bell at
the now destroyed church of S. Peter, in the year 1306;
and Nichols‖ says:—"Mr. Samuel Carte noticed in the
archiepiscopal register at Lambeth, an article relative to the
taking away one of the bells from S. Nicholas' Church
(Leicester), in 1321."

In the middle ages, when roads were bad, and locomo-
tion difficult, bells were frequently cast within the precincts
of Religious Houses, and in churchyards, the clergy or
monks standing round, and reciting prayers and chanting
psalms. Southey says:—"The brethren stood round the
furnace, ranged in processional order, sang the 150th Psalm,
and then, after certain prayers, blessed the molten metal,
and called upon the Lord to infuse into it His grace, and
overshadow it with His power, for the honour of the saint to
whom the bell was to be dedicated, and whose name it was

---

* Turner's *Dom. Arch.*, vol. i. p. 193.
† Ibid, p. 259. See also an article
contributed by the writer to *The Midland
Counties Historical Collector*, vol. i. p. 228.
‡ *Church Bells of Cambridgeshire*, p. 3.
§ *Hist. Leicester*, p. 108.
‖ *Hist. Leicestershire*, vol. i. part 2, p. 608.

to bear."* During excavations in the churchyard of Scalford, Leicestershire, some years ago, indications of the former existence of a furnace for the casting of the church bells there were discovered, and a mass of bell-metal was found, which had clearly been in a state of fusion on the spot. Until quite recently the bellfounders occasionally acted in the same manner. "Great Tom" of Lincoln was cast in the minster yard in 1610;† and the great bell of Canterbury was cast in the cathedral yard in 1762.‡ We also find instances (at Kirkby Malzeard, Yorkshire, and Haddenham, in the Isle of Ely,) where a furnace was erected, and bells recast within the walls of the church itself.§ The founders, too, sometimes itinerated with the implements of their craft to a central spot, where they set up their furnace, and did what business they could with the neighbourhood around. This was done at Winterton, in Lincolnshire, by Daniel Hedderly, of Bawtry, in 1734; and although the elaborate ceremonial of the middle ages no longer attended upon the casting of the modern bell, still the founder and his men did not always neglect to ask God's blessing upon their work at the critical moment of running the metal into the mould. Thomas Hedderly, a founder at Nottingham, in the last century, is said to have joined in prayer with his men before any important casting, and in Messrs. Blew's foundry at Birmingham, similar observances are said to be used at the present time.‖

---

* *Southey's Doctor*, vol. i. p. 296.
† *Hist. Lincoln* (1816), p. 75.
‡ *Bells and Bell-ringing*, by Rev. J. T. Fowler, F.S.A.

§ *Bells of the Church*, p. 287. *Notes and Queries*, 5th. s. ii. 147.
‖ *Bells and Bell-ringing*, by Rev. J. T. Fowler, F.S.A.

C

It may be well to state here that the composition of bell-metal may be roughly said to be one portion of tin to three of copper. Mr. E. B. Denison states that "four parts of tin to thirteen of copper produce a very hard elastic and strong bell-metal."* Mr. Gatty remarks: "Some people talk as familiarly of sweetening the tone of bell-metal by the introduction of a little silver, as they would speak of sweetening a cup of tea, or a glass of negus, with a lump of sugar; but this is a dream. It is, however, a very popular error, and has led to many speculations on the great value of our old church bells, which have been supposed to contain large quantities of the more precious ores. The mistake has, no doubt, arisen from the ancient custom of casting a few coins into the furnace, which have become melted in the glowing mass; but no bellfounder can be deluded on this point, for silver, if introduced in any large quantity, would injure the sound, being in its nature more like lead as compared with copper; and therefore incapable of producing the hard, brittle, dense and vibratory amalgam called bell-metal. There are, nevertheless, various little ingredients, which the skilful founder employs to improve his composition; but these are the secrets of the craft, and peculiar to every foundry."†

After the bell was cast, and was made ready for its high

---

* Some of the ancient bells appear to have had a larger proportion of tin. In the *Liberate Roll,* 26 Hen. III., sec. 12, is an entry of 1050 lbs of copper and 500 lbs of tin, and the metal of an old bell, to be melted up with it to make three new bells for the church of the castle of Dover. Lukis' *Account of Church Bells,* p. 19. See *Notes and Queries,* 5th, s. iii. p. 77, for the composition of a Bell in A.D. 1284.

† *The Bell,* p. 30.

and airy chamber, it was set apart for its future use by a
solemn ceremonial, and by the recitation of an Office which
has been variously termed the Blessing, the Consecration,
and the Baptism of the Bell. The use of this Office, if not
coeval with the introduction of the church bell, is certainly
of great antiquity. Mr. L'Estrange, quoting the Abbé
Barraud, states, that since the year 800 the Order of the
prayers and rites employed in the Benediction of bells has
not varied much. "It appears from a Pontifical preserved
in the British Museum (*Cottonian MS. Vespasian D.i. p.* 127)
that the service commenced with the recital of the Litany,
and that whilst the choir sang the antiphon *Asperges me*, the
psalm *Miserere* and psalm 145, with the five following
psalms, and the antiphon *In civitate Domini clare sonant*, the
bell about to be blessed was washed with holy water, wiped
with a towel, and anointed by the bishop with the holy oil."*

The *De Benedictione Signi vel Campanæ* of the Roman
Pontifical enjoins the same ceremonies interspersed with
prayers, psalms, and antiphons. The bell washed by the
bishop with water, into which salt had been previously cast,
was then dried by his attendants with clean linen; the
bishop next dipped the thumb of his right hand in the holy
oil for the sick, and made the sign of the cross on the top of the
bell; he then marked the bell again both with the holy oil
for the sick and with chrism, saying the words :—

"*Sancti ✝ ficetur, et conse ✝ cretur, Domine signum istud : in nomine
Pa ✝ tris et Fi ✝ lii, et Spiritûs ✝ Sancti : in honorem Sancti N. Pax tibi.*"

---

* *Church Bells of Norfolk.* p. 17.

After which the inside of the bell was censed.* The
Pontifical of Egbert, Archbishop of York, and other Office
books, have similar services.

This Office bore so close a resemblance to that of Holy
Baptism, both in the ceremonial used, and in the giving of
a name to the bell,† as to be frequently considered synony-
mous with it.   That such was the case even in early times
we gather from the fact that Charlemagne issued, in the
year 789, an express injunction against the baptism of bells.
Learned liturgical writers of the Roman Church maintain
that the baptism of bells was not in ancient times, and is
not now, as used by them, such as confers remission of sins—
Southey quaintly observes "the original sin of a bell would
be a flaw in the metal, or a defect in the tone, neither of
which the priest undertakes to remove"—but the bells are
thereby set apart from all secular uses, and blessed or consecrated; and the hope is that (in accordance with the
prayers offered) by their sound the powers of demons may
be restrained, and the sources of storm, tempest, and
contagion, kept away.   Whilst this is no doubt quite true,
it must, nevertheless, be evident that the ceremony did
frequently, in mediæval times, surpass that of a consecration,
and, by an addition of other ceremonies to those enjoined
in the Pontificals just quoted, bore so close a resemblance
to baptism, as to present, at least to the eyes of the vulgar,
a too close and irreverent resemblance to that Holy

* See full copy of this service from
the Pontifical (Antwerp, 1627) in *Bells of
the Church*, p. 83.

† Pope John IV. gave his name to the
great bell of S. John Lateran in the seventh
century.

Sacrament. Le Sueur, an old French writer, shows this to have been the case. He says "that the imposition of the name, the godfathers and godmothers, the aspersion with holy-water, the unction, and the solemn consecration in the names of the Father, Son, and Holy Ghost, exceed in ceremonial splendour what is common at baptism, in order to make the blessing of bells more highly regarded by the people. Real baptism" he remarks, "may be administered by all kinds of persons, and the rite is simple; but in what is done to the bells there is much pomp. The service is long, the ceremonies are numerous, the sponsors are persons of quality, and the most considerable priest in the place, or even a bishop or archbishop officiates."* That this was the case in England, as well as in France, we learn from a curious entry made by the churchwardens of S. Lawrence, Reading, in their Accounts for the year 1499:

s. d.

"Itm. payed for haloweng of the grete bell namyd Harry  vj. viij.
And mem. that Sir Willm. Symys, Richard Clech
and maistres Smyth beyng godfaders and godmoder
at the consecracyon of the same bell, and beryng
all o'. costs to the suffrygan."†

This custom of blessing the bells before raising them to their place in the church tower points to the origin of bell inscriptions; the earliest inscriptions being simply the name of the saint placed upon the bell when it was cast, and ratified at its consecration. There is a singular proof of

---

* Quoted by Gatty, *The Bell*, p. 22.    † *Notes and Queries*, 3rd. s. vii. p. 90.

this in an unique inscription on a bell at Crostwight, Norfolk:

ASLAK JOH'ES JOH'EM ME NOI'AVIT

John Aslak being clearly the godfather at the benediction or baptism of the bell.*

When the mediæval form of consecration was done away with in this country at the Reformation, English churchmen, unfortunately, were not furnished with any form of dedication to supply its place. Consequently, the people in getting rid of the superstitious rite of their fathers, substituted, upon the advent of a new bell or ring of bells, indecorous conviviality similar to that which is described by White of Selborne, who tells us that when new bells were brought to his parish in 1735, the event was celebrated by fixing the treble bottom upwards, and filling it with punch. It is a matter for thankfulness that this profane "christening" is becoming a thing of the past, and that the church is again receiving bells within her towers with a dedication service, sanctioned and used by her bishops, which is joyous and reverent in tone, and calculated to give all, clergy and people, a fitting impression of the uses to which the Bells of the Church are intended to be put. After such a dedication they can scarcely be used, as they frequently have been in times past, upon most improper occasions—occasions when things had been enacted completely opposed to the honour of God, and utterly alien to the teaching of the church, whose fast and festival the bells

---

* *Church Bells of Norfolk,* p. 17.

are to mark, and whose summons to prayer and praise they are day by day to sound.

It is now time to turn to the bell itself, and to see what it has to say in elucidation of its past history. To do this we must ascend to the bell chamber in the church tower, or to the bell turret on the roof. This is not always, by any means, an easy, pleasant, or even a safe, thing to do. Some of the stone staircases in our Leicestershire church towers are so much worn that only a scant and precarious foothold is left, and some of the long ladders by which the bells are reached are almost perpendicular, and, occasionally, so decaying with age, as to render a climb up them a proceeding requiring great care, and some nerve. The floor of the bell chamber, too, is occasionally, found rotten and covered with filth. Once up, however, the slight difficulty or danger attending the ascent is forgotten; the ancient bells, so often heard, never, perhaps before seen, are looked upon with reverence, almost with awe. We think of the many changes which have taken place in all around—many of which they have noted with their solemn tolls or their joyous peals—since they were first placed there. Our reverie, however, is broken by the cold wind rushing through the louvre boards in the windows, so we hasten to complete our work—take our "rubbing" or our "squeeze," give one hasty glance through the openings at the grand peeps of the surrounding country, so well obtained in our elevated position, and then descend with much greater ease, and with much less trepidation, than we ascended.

The earliest bells do not generally tell us anything as to

the date when, or the locality in which, they were cast. They usually bear nothing more than the names of the saints in whose honour they were dedicated. Upon the tenor, or largest, bell is frequently found the name of the patron saint of the church; upon the smaller ones, perhaps, the names of the saints whose altars were formerly in the church below, or who were the patrons of ancient Guilds or Confraternities in the parish. We have already seen that the ancient bells at Croyland Abbey bore names; and from an ancient Roll at Ely we learn that when they cast four new bells for the Cathedral in 1346-7, they gave them the names of Jesus, John, Mary, and Walsyngham.* Bells of this class (though not necessarily of this early date) are found in Leicestershire, as will be seen when we treat of the bells of the county. We may mention now :—

IHESVS

at Wistow. Two or three early dated English bells have, however, been discovered. One (supposed to be the oldest dated bell in the kingdom) is at S. Chad's Church, Claughton, Lancashire, and is dated 1296, thus :—

+ ANNO  DNI · M · CC · NONO · AI .

the letter V being reversed.† Another has been found at Cold Ashby, Northamptonshire, dated 1317, thus :—

+ MARIA : VOCOR : ANO : DNI : M° : CCC° XVIJ°‡

---

* *Church Bells of Cambridgeshire*, p. 6.    † *Bells of the Church*, p. 250.
‡ For an inspection of a rubbing of this I am indebted to the Rev. T. M. Owen, F.G.H.S.

Two, richly ornaménted, dated 1323, are in the tower of S. Mary's Church, Somercotes, Lincolnshire.*

These early inscriptions are usually in stately Gothic capital letters, and in Latin—the language of the mediæval church.

We soon meet with a slight extension of the inscriptions such as—to quote Leicestershire examples :—

+ IN HONORE SANCTI LEONARDI at Sysonby.

HVIVS SCI PETRI at Saltby.

Bells cast in the fourteenth and fifteenth centuries though undated, have generally founders' marks, initial crosses, and other means of recognition by which they can be classified, and, in many cases, assigned to their respective dates and foundries. "These trade marks, however," as is well observed by Mr. Ellacombe, "are by no means infallible guides to the uninitiated in such matters; for foundries often went on for generations, and marks and stamps were, no doubt, handed down from father to son often for a century or more."† This is the case with several bells in our own county.

On bells of this date, and on to the period of the Reformation, we frequently find the invocation "*Ora pro nobis*" added to the name of the saint, thus:

SCA CATERINA ORA P NOBIS as at Aston Flamville.

+ SCE LEONARDE ORA PRO NOBIS as at Shenton.

---

* Associated Arch. Socs. Reports and Papers, vol. xii. p. 19.
† *Church Bells of Devon*, p. 226.

D

These invocations were taken from the Litany; and other inscriptions doubtless owe their origin to the various Offices of the mediæval church.   For instance a learned correspondent in *Notes and Queries* says the following inscription found on the tenor bell at Billesdon :

+ STELLA MARIA MARIS SUCURRE (*sic*) PIISSIMA NOBIS

is from the *Benedictiones de S. Maria* Sarum and York.*
Very many have the angelic salutation :

+ AVE MARIA as at Melton Mowbray.

+ AVE MARIA GRA PLENA as at Horninghold.

+ AVE MARIA GRACIA PLENA DOMINVS TECVM

as at Little Dalby and Wyfordby.

A common inscription of this period was :

IN MULTIS ANNIS RESONET CAMPANA IOHANNIS

This we find at Bottesford; and other inscriptions of a similar character will be found on other Leicestershire bells.

Occasionally we find figures of men and angels on bells of this date.  Examples are in Leicestershire at Thurcaston Welham and Wanlip.  English inscriptions though rare as early as the fourteenth and fifteenth centuries, were sometimes used.  At Long Sutton, near Odiham Hants., is a bell inscribed :

HAL MARI FVL OF GRAS

---

* *Notes and Queries*, 5th s. vol. i. p. 465.

At Gainford, Durham, is another with :—

HELP MARI QUOD ROGER OF KIRKEBY

that is Help Mary quoth, or saith, Roger of Kirkby, who was vicar 1401—1412.* And at Thurcaston, in this county, we shall see one :—

IN THE NAYM OF IHS SPED ME

The founder's name, too, occasionally appears, as at All Saints, Leicester, and at Sproxton; and the donor's, as at Aylestone.

At the date of which we are now speaking there was no such thing known as change-ringing : and, indeed it would seem that ringing rounds and chiming in " tune " were both impossible in the great majority of our country churches. In the Returns of the Commissioners for taking a list of the ornaments of the churches in the Hundred of Framland, Leicestershire, in the sixth year of King Edward the Sixth, we see that Coston, Saltby, and Stonesby, had each " iij bells *of a corde*," Croxton Kerrial " iiij bells *of a ryng*," and Muston " iiij bells *of one ryng ;*" meaning, I presume, that the notes of these bells were in musical sequence.† All the other churches are noted, simply, as possessing a certain number of bells, unfit, apparently, for musical chiming or ringing, but quite adequate to the custom of the time. This custom probably was in ordinary churches to have in addition to its own, or parish, bell, a bell for the Angelus,

---

* Sottanstall's *Campanologia.*

† Stow, describing S. Bartholomew's Church in Smithfield says, "This church having in the bell tower sixe Belles *in a tune*," &c. *Notes and Queries,* 3rd s. ii. 328.

and one for each of the several altars which were usually found there dedicated to different saints, and which was sounded when mass was about being said at its particular altar. Even now one bell is all that is required by the Rubric and (as now followed) the Canons to be provided, of necessity, in churches at the charge of the parish. Thus at Melton Mowbray we find the Churchwardens, in 1562, speaking of "our Lady Bell," that being either the bell used for the Angelus or Ave, or else the bell which had been wont to be used when mass was about being said at our Lady's altar which is known to have stood in that church. There is however no doubt that all the bells, notwithstanding their being unfitted for musical ringing or chiming, were used for Divine Service on Sundays. We find the Bell-master at Loughborough, in the time of Edward VI. or earlier, was obliged "to help to reng to sarvys if ned be." The custom in larger churches where the canonical hours were kept will be referred to hereafter. Towards the close of the sixteenth century care was sometimes taken when bells were recast to have them "in tune." An instance of this occurred at Loughborough, in 1586, when the churchwardens paid fourteenpence "to John Wever for his tow dayes chardges when he went to Nottingham for them that came to prove the tune of ye bells."

The Reformation introduced many changes in connection with bells, as it did with other "ornaments" of the church. The stately Gothic capital, and the quaint small "black letter," gradually gave place to clumsy Roman letters for the inscriptions. The beautiful initial cross, also, gradually disappeared. Figures of saint or angel were discarded. English, although it did not supplant Latin, gained a full share of use on the bells. The old forms of inscriptions were dropped, at first to give place to mottos of a reverent character, which soon, however, drifted, in many instances, into doggrel rhyme—stupid, frivolous, and thoroughly out of place, or into a bare list of names of vicar and church-wardens. Dates, in Arabic numerals, now appear on every bell; and founders' names abound. As specimens may be mentioned the third bell at Nether Broughton:

+ Jesvs be ovre spede

the first at Thorpe Arnold:

Cum cum and pray 1597

the first at Segrave:

+ God save.the Chvrch 1595

the first at Tilton on the Hill:

Praise the Lorde

the first at Fenny Drayton:

Hec Campana Sacra Fiat Trinitate Beata

a bell at Passenham Northants.:

A + trvsty + frende + ys + harde + to + fynde + 1585.

the third at Earl's Shilton:

+ Be · yt · knowne · to · all · that · doth · me · see
That · Newcombe · of · Leicester · made · mee

This was a common form which was not improved when used in the plural number, as at Himbleton Worcestershire:

> John Martin of Worcester he made wee
> Be it known to all that do wee see

On other bells are found these, and many similar inscriptions:

> Henry Pleasant did me run
> In the year 1701

> At proper time my voice I'll raise
> And sound to my subscribers' praise

> I'm given here to make a peal
> And sound the praise of Mary Neale

> John Eyer gave twenty pound
> To meck mee a losty sound 1703

The following refers to the recasting of an ancient tenor into two treble bells:

> We trebles came by small consent
> Our birth we hope will give content
> Twins from old Tenor, our lost old Dad
> Some we make merry and some are sad

Other bells bear the names of the donors, or commemorate some event of national interest, but these specimens will suffice to give an idea of the various kinds of inscriptions found on Post-Reformation bells. Bell inscriptions after the middle of the seventeenth century afford little interest. With the revival of Gothic art, and a clearer perception of the fitness of things, we may hope that our new bells, when they bear anything beyond the name of the founder, will have inscriptions befitting their position and their use.

There are comparatively few ancient bells now left in our church towers. Many reasons have been assigned for their disappearance; such as ordinary wear and tear, accidents to the fabric of the church entailing injury to the bells, the remodelling of rings of bells to adapt them for change-ringing, the spoliation of churches at the period of the Reformation, and the poverty or parsimony of churchmen in after times.

There are now in existence, unfortunately, only, so far as yet discovered, inventories of church goods for two of the Hundreds in Leicestershire taken in the reign of Edward VI. So far as can be learned from them the parish churches of Leicestershire, in common as it seems to me, with the parish churches throughout the country generally, suffered little from the hands of the spoiler in the sixteenth century. Indeed, I incline to think, the bells were too popular with the people to allow of their being seized with impunity. Neither were church towers falling with sufficient frequency to make an appreciable inroad upon our Pre-Reformation bells. Undoubtedly in the two hundred years succeeding the Reformation—and more especially in the eighteenth century—as churches fell into decay, in rural districts, a very common way of raising money to pay for the repairs, was to petition the Bishop to grant a faculty empowering the parishioners to sell some of the bells which they represented as being unnecessary, or as cracked, and so unfit for use. Happily it does not appear that the church bells of

Leicestershire have suffered in this way. It is therefore to
ordinary and (in some cases, not all,) unavoidable wear and
tear, and to the introduction of change ringing that we must
look as the causes of the loss of a great number of our
ancient bells. As to wear and tear:—when we remember
the nature of the metal of which bells are made—how easily
it may be cracked, and how reckless and ignorant, as a
body, have been the ringers, into whose charge the bells
have frequently been entirely left, we can well believe that
many of our ancient bells have from time to time succumbed
to their almost inevitable fate. They were cracked, and so
obliged to be recast, to fit them again for their work. In
this way, undoubtedly, many of them disappeared, to be
replaced by more modern ones.

The introduction, however, of change ringing in the
seventeenth century produced more havoc among our
ancient church bells than any of the causes already mentioned. Early in that century ringing increased in popularity.
The churchwardens of Loughborough, Leicestershire, charge
in 1616 :—

> "It.  spent in giveing entertainment to the gentlemen
>          strangers when they came to ringe       ...       ...   xjs."

Fabian Stedman, a printer, resident in Cambridge, is said
to have reduced change ringing to an art.* He published
his "*Tintinnalogia*" in 1668. Previously to the seventeenth
century the ringing in use, where anything of the kind was
attempted, was "rounds" or—as a slight advance upon

---

* *Church Bells of Cambridgeshire*, p. 37.

that—at most "call changes," that is, the bells were rung
"in one particular position for a great many pulls consecutively, and changed at some accustomed signal to a variation
called by a fugleman or chalked on the belfry wall."* These
must, in most cases, have been sorry performances, the bells
not being "tunable" and so unfit for the purpose. "With
change ringing proper the case"—to quote Mr. Ellacombe—
"is very different: here a change is made at each stroke;
the bells being never sounded twice in the same order; and
this is continued till the end of the peal, when the bells are
brought '*home*' to their regular places. This end is only to
be attained by each bell being made to follow a certain
course, and to change places with the other bells by the
evolution of certain rules or '*methods.*' To manage his bell
properly in this respect, and guide it up and down the maze,
making it strike now before, and now after, this or that other
bell, not only requires much practice and study, but a cool
head and close attention; and this necessity justifies the
remark that ringing requires a mental as well as a
bodily effort."†

To meet this new art of ringing, important changes in
the bells were necessitated. The old rings consisted, usually,
of few bells and heavy ones. To ring the changes, introduced by Stedman and his disciples, a larger number of
bells was required. This want could be met in two ways,
either by adding new trebles to the existing heavy rings,
which was the best, but the most expensive way, or by re-

---

* *Bells of the Church,* p. 32.    † *Bells of the Church,* p. 33.

E

casting say four heavy ancient bells into six or eight light ones, and so increasing the number without buying more metal. This was the least expensive, and, therefore the most popular plan, and was the course pursued in many of our churches in Leicestershire. By this means a great number of our ancient bells disappeared from our larger town churches. It ceases, therefore to be a matter of surprise that it is chiefly in small rural churches, with few bells, where the temptation to change ringing could not exist, that we chiefly expect, and usually find, ancient bells.

Not understanding the art of change ringing, my readers will not expect or desire me to attempt to explain its subtleties. I, with pleasure, turn to the genial pages of Mr. Gatty and say:—"When we regard the discovery of this gentleman (Fabian Stedman) 'great' may all say with Dr. Southey 'are the mysteries of bell ringing!' The very terms of the art are enough to frighten an amateur from any attempt at explanation—*Hunting, dodging, snapping*, and *place-making : plain bobs, bobs-triples, bob-majors, bob-majors reversed, double bob-majors*, and even up to *grand-sire-bob-cators*. Heigho! who can hope to translate all this gibberish to the uninitiated?"

"Nothing, therefore, is to be done, but to convey the reader up the dark, narrow, winding and worn stairs of the church-tower, into the bell-chamber itself, where eight stout young men, stripped of coats and waistcoats, are standing in a circle, rope in hand, ready for a merry peal. What a neat and nervous effort is that, by which each straight stripling in his place handles his rope, like a well-accustomed plaything, and shows by a stroke or two that he is master of his bell! The ropes hang through holes in the bell-chamber ceiling; and when touched by the ringer's practised hand, the brazen monsters groan in their airy loft above, as they begin to swing on their gudgeons. It is like the first growl of the lion, when the keeper stirs him in his den—but there is no use in their resisting. One moment more, and the ringer has dropped his bell one-half full, and set her the next—all eight are now fairly raised—hand, ear, eye, and heart of every ringer are intensely strained, and engaged in the work: yet, cool withal, no flurry or disorder appearing— and through the whole tower there begins to ring a glorious din, which, with the creaking of the wooden bell-frames, and the shaking of the very building itself, much reminds one of the noise and recoil of a battle-ship, when she opens her broadside fire."

"Now is the moment for the spectator to hurry up the broad ladder into the belfry, to watch the wild summersets, performed at intervals, by every bell in the peal. For a moment the bell rests against the slur-bar, turned completely upwards; and the next it swings down, and is immediately turned up again on the other side,—the clapper striking as it ascends. Poor fellows! see how they whirl upon their axles. The gazer almost sickens as he watches their extraordinary revolutions and tossings: but the ringer's heart is merciless—and when you look at the wretched bell, as at 'a thing of life,' and almost expect it to drop motionless and dead on the stocks, a 'cannon' is suddenly struck on all eight at once, as if to rouse them afresh for the course of seemingly interminable changes which immediately follow. Henceforth the bells appear to roll about in frantic disorder; and, stunned by the noise, chilled by the draughts of cold wind, and shaken in nerve by the reverberation, the spectator descends with careful steps from his tyro-visit to the belfry."

"Eight bells, which form the octave, or diatonic scale, make the most perfect peal. Ten and twelve bells are very often hung, and of course increase to an almost incalculable extent the variety of *changes*. This term is used because every time the peal is rung round a change can be made in the stroke of some one bell, thereby causing a change in the succession of notes. The following numbers are placed to show how three bells can ring six changes:—

| | | |
|---|---|---|
| 1 | 2 | 3 |
| 1 | 3 | 2 |
| 2 | 1 | 3 |
| 2 | 3 | 1 |
| 3 | 1 | 2 |
| 3 | 2 | 1 |

"Four bells can in the same manner be shown to ring four times as many changes as three, viz., 24. Five bells five times as many as four, viz., 120. Six bells six times as many as five, viz., 720, and so on. And in this way it has been calculated that it would take 91 years to ring the changes upon twelve bells, at the rate of two strokes to a second; and the full changes upon 24 bells would occupy more than 117,000 billions of years."*

---

* *The Bell*, p. 59—62.

The English have been for many generations enthusiastic admirers of the melody produced by a ring of bells. Whilst other nations—the Russians and Chinese for example— possess far heavier bells, and make much more noise by a rude irregular clanging, we have long been accomplished ringers, and our joyous peals—our "rounds" and number- less "changes" have in no slight degree added to the cheerful temperament of "merrie England." Indeed so popular did the art of ringing become after the invention of "changes" that England became known as the "ringing Island."

This love of the English for bell-ringing is amusingly referred to by P. S. in *"A Theory of Compensation":*—"And even to this day next to the Mother Tongue, the one mostly used (in Britain) is in a Mouth of Mettal and withal so loosely hung that it must needs wag at all Times and on all Topicks. For your English man is a mighty Ringer, and besides furnishing Bells to a Belfry doth hang them at the Head of the Horse, and at the Neck of his Sheep—on the Cap of his Fool, and on the Heels of his Hawk: And truly, I have known more than one of my Country men who would undertake more Travel and Cost besides, to hear a Peal of Grandsires than they would bestow upon a Generation of Grand children." *

Leicestershire was not behind in this national taste. The rings of bells in many of our churches were soon increased in number. S. Martin's, Leicester, has been gradually

---

* See *Hood's Poems of Wit and Humour*, p. 42.

raised from five to ten, and S. Margaret's from six to ten.
Hugh Watts, as a first rate founder and an enthusiast in
his art, no doubt did much to encourage the growing taste.
The married men, and the bachelors of Wigston Magna,
emulated each other in buying new bells in 1682.    The
youths of Aylestone, wishing to increase their ring of bells,
went to the ruined church of Knaptoft to fetch its single
bell, but, unfortunately, for their scheme, they stopped at
Shearsby on their way home with their booty to drink :
the inhabitants of that place supplied them with beer, but
claimed the bell, and added it to their own ring.   When
Dr. Ford added two new bells to the ring at Melton he no
doubt expressed the sentiments of his parishioners as well
as his own by placing upon one of them :

> " Eight Bells we hear in the sacred Tower sound soft and
> loud.   O joyful joyful ! "

Mr. Wm. Fortrey, of King's Norton, in this county, was
an enthusiastic admirer of church bells, and did much
towards encouraging improvements in the rings in different
parishes in Leicestershire.   He rebuilt the church at Galby,
and placed in it in the year 1741, a ring of six bells.    He
did the same at King's Norton hanging a ring of ten bells—
preserving one of the old ones—since reduced to eight to
lessen the weight and consequent strain upon the steeple.
He gave two new bells to S. Margaret's Leicester in 1738,
a treble to Houghton on the Hill in 1771, and his name is
mentioned in connection with other bells in the county.
His memory is still cherished by the old change ringers of

Leicester who speak of him as "Squire Fortrey." Nichols says: "William Fortrey Esq. of Norton by Galby made it his business all his life to enquire into these matters (*i.e.* Bells and ringing). He is possessed of all the anecdotes that remain relating to the founder of the old bells in that steeple (S. Margaret's Leicester) Hugh Watts, once Mayor of Leicester, and was himself the patron and director of Thomas Eayre, late of Kettering." *

Leicestershire men not only supplied themselves with bells, but knew how to ring them, as is testified by many a "peal board" nailed up in the ringing chambers of our churches. Nichols, describing Sileby, says :—the bells "are allowed by judges to be an excellent ring, and are rung by the inhabitants to astonishment." That might be said with equal truth of many other places in the county. The ringers were formerly frequently the young gentlemen, and the farmers' sons, of the parish. That was the case at Wymond-ham, and decency and order were kept by the enforcing of a set of rules—usually written in verse—placed upon the walls of the belfry. A specimen copy of these rules will be found under the description of Bowden Magna bells.

This love of bells is still so universal in this country that if after admiring a church tower of goodly proportions, fair design, and which carries its glorious spire tapering heaven-wards, we are told it contains no bells, a feeling of dis-appointment is mixed with our admiration, and we are tempted to exclaim, "how sad that a case so magnificent

---

† *Nichols' Leics., Gartree Hundred,* under King's Norton.

is without its music!—that a structure so pleasing to the eye, is without the usual means of proclaiming the passing events of human life by means of its iron-tongued melody!"

We need not be surprised at this affection for bells and their music, for not only do they summon all—as well the denizens of the crowded city, as the scattered inhabitants of the rural hamlet—to the House of Prayer; not only are they heralds of the Festivals of the church's year with their joyous and heart stirring music, but they are also connected with every marked epoch of human life; the birth in some instances, the marriage in more, the death in almost all, are marked by the joyous peal or the solemn toll of our church bells.

So again not only has the fancy of the poet revelled in the sweet sounds of the church bells, but the hearts of the stern and the impassable have been touched by their familiar tones. When William the Conqueror was dying, a prayer was called from his lips, by the sound of the early morning bell of the Cathedral of Rouen;* and when Napoleon, riding over a battle-field, and gazing, stern and unmoved on the dying and the dead, heard a ring of bells suddenly burst into a merry peal, he was softened, and dismounting from his horse, burst into tears.†

---

* *Ordericus Vitalis*, Bohn's Ed., vol. ii. pp. 417—18.    † *Bells of the Church*, p. 230.

# CHURCH
# BELLS OF LEICESTERSHIRE.

———————

THERE are in Leicestershire 998 Church Bells. Of these only 147 can be said, with any certainty, to have been cast before the year 1600.

Exclusive of churches with only one bell, Caldwell (3 bells), Sproxton (3 bells), Wanlip (3 bells), Brentingby (2 bells), Cranoe (2 bells), Walton Isley (2 bells), and Wyfordby (2 bells), are the only places in the county where complete rings of ancient bells still exist.

The Dedications and Legends of these 146 ancient bells may be thus summarised :—

Two are dedicated to the Ever Blessed Trinity (Cottesbach 2nd and Long Clawson 4th).

One bears simply the Holy Name

+ JHESVS (Wistow 3rd).

Ten have "the superscription of His accusation :"—

+ JHESUS NAZARENUS REX JUDEORUM

F

in various forms (Ashby-de-la-Zouch 6th ; Birstall 3rd ;
Caldwell 1st ; Kegworth 3rd and 4th ; the single bell at
Newton Harcourt ; Ratby 4th ; Sproxton 2nd ; Thorpe
Arnold 2nd ; and Witherley 5th).

Six carry the short invocation or prayer :—

+ JESVS BE OVR SPEED

(Church Langton 6th ; Croxton Kerrial 2nd ; Knipton 1st ;
Stoke Golding 3rd ; Swinford 1st ; and (slightly altered)
Thurcaston 3rd).

Thirty-two are dedicated to, or bear inscriptions relating
to, the B. V. Mary in these forms :—

1. + Maria.
1. J. H. S. Maria.
1. + Beata Maria.
2. Sancta Maria.
1. Libjbs Sancte Maria.
6. + Abe Maria.
3. + Abe Maria gracia plena.
11. + Abe Maria gracia plena Dominus tecum.
3. + In honore Bente Marie.
1. + Stella Maria Maris Succurre Piissima Nobis.
1. Clemens Atque Pia Miseris Succurre.
1. + Sum Rosa Pulsata Mundi Maria Vocata.

One bell is dedicated to the Archangel Gabriel, and three
to the Archangel Michael ; three are dedicated to S. Anne,
the mother of the B. V. Mary ; one to S. Botolph ; four to
S. Catherine ; one to S. Cornelius (Pope A.D. 252—a rare
dedication) ; one to S. Cuthbert ; one to S. Helen ; one to
S. James ; two to S. John ; one to S. John Baptist ; one to

S. Lawrence; two to S. Leonard; one to S. Mark; two to S. Mary Magdalene; one to S. Nicolas; one to S. Paul; eight to S. Peter; one to S. Richard (Bishop of Chichester A.D. 1253, an unusual dedication); one to S. Stephen the Proto-martyr; and one to All Saints.

There are two bells from the same foundry (Cossington 3rd and Welham 2nd) inscribed :—

Celorum xit placeat tibi Rex sonus iste.

One bell (Little Peatling 1st) bears a series of crosses; and two (East Norton 3rd and Cossington 1st) the letter S repeated.

Ten have a number, more or less, of the letters of the alphabet (Bruntingthorpe 1st; Edmonthorpe 1st; Hoby 1st; Illston 2nd; Peatling Magna 4th; Shearsby 2nd; Shepey 3rd; Swinford 4th; Thurlaston 3rd; and the single bell at Welby).

Four are inscribed :—

Vox . dni . ihu . xpi . vox . exultacionis.

Eleven have imperfect or unintelligible inscriptions, viz. : Barkeston 2nd; Beeby 1st; Croft 3rd; Houghton 2nd; Hungarton 3rd; Kegworth 2nd; Leicester, All Saints, 2nd; Long Whatton 1st; Narborough 4th; Newtown Linford 4th; Queniborough 1st.

Eighteen are dated; and the remainder of the 147 ancient bells are, Aylestone 2nd; Catthorpe 1st; Hoby 3rd; Illston 3rd; Pickwell 2nd; Scraptoft 1st; Sproxton 1st; Stoughton 1st; Thorpe Langton 1st, and Wanlip 3rd.

The earliest dated bell in Leicestershire is the 3rd of Old Dalby ring, dated 1584.

On the 3rd bell at Thurcaston are figures of the Virgin and Child (fig. 73) ; upon the 2nd at Welham appears the patron saint of the church, S. Andrew, (fig. 75), and upon the 2nd bell at Wanlip is the figure of an angel (fig. 80) on either side of the initial cross.

73

80

75

# THE
# LEICESTER BELLFOUNDERS.

JOHANNES DE STAFFORD. There are good reasons for believing that a Bell-foundry was established in Leicester at least as early as the middle of the fourteenth century.

The tenor bell of the ring at All Saints, Leicester, is inscribed :—

+ IHOHANNES : DE : STAFFORD : FECIT : ME : IN : HONORE : DE : MARIE.

That John of Stafford was the founder, and not the donor, of the bell is shown by there being a similar inscription in the same form of letter, &c., on the 3rd bell of S. Hibbald, Scawby, near Brigg, Lincolnshire :—

> I. H. C. Ihohannes de Stafforde fecit me.*
> +
> Maria.

---

* For a copy of this I am indebted to the Rev. J. T. Fowler, F.S.A.

We learn from the Fabric Roll of York Minster,* that a founder of this name was living in A.D. 1371 : under that date occurs the following entry, amongst many relating to the cost of the bells :—

> " Et in una Magna Campanâ, per Johannem de Stafford ex convencione operanda £6 ·13 4."

The initial cross and stop upon the Leicester bell are here given (fig. 45 and 48). Bells with the same cross and stop, and with inscriptions in letters of the same form, are found in this county at Ayleston (1st), Beeby (3rd), Dalby Parva (3rd), Glen Magna (5th),

45      48

Loddington (1st), Ratby (4th), Shenton (2nd), and Thrussington (1st); showing by their number that in all probability they were the work of a local founder. At the first of these places—Aylestone—the name of the donor is given on the bell; he lived, as will be shown when the Aylestone bells are described, early in the fifteenth century, at a time when John of Stafford, or his immediate successor, would be carrying on his business.

From these facts we may safely infer that John of Stafford was a bellfounder, that he lived in the middle, or later half, of the fourteenth century, and that from the

---

* Surtee's Society xxxv. (1858) quoted in *Bells of the Church*, p. 244.

number of his bells still found in Leicestershire, his foundry
was in Leicester. This last inference is strengthened, if it
cannot be accepted as a fact, by finding from the ancient
Rolls of the Mayors of Leicester, still extant, that "John of
Stafford" was mayor of Leicester in 1366, and again 1370.
He, and the founder of the same name then actively
employed in the art of Bellfounding, were, it is thought,
identical. If so, John of Stafford is the first Bellfounder,
having his foundry in Leicester,—and so not merely an
itinerant,—whose name we have to place on record.

Figs. 84 and 85 here given show the form and size of the

84                              85

letters used by John de Stafford in the inscriptions upon
his bells in Leicestershire. In all these inscriptions the
letter S is reversed.

WILLIAM MILLERS. The next Leicester Bellfounder to
be noticed is William Millers. He was admitted a member
of the Merchants' Guild, Leicester, "in tempore Will.
Wygston Junior quinto decimo Henry VII.;"* that is,

---

* *Hall Book* 1477—1553 p. 67.

during the mayoralty of Wm. Wigston the younger, 1499—1500. He is described as "Bell Heytaū."* He died soon afterwards (in 1506), for his will, dated the 29th of Nov. 1506, was proved on the 12th of the following January. The following is a translated copy :—

In the name of God, Amen. The 29th day of the month of November in the year of our Lord 1506, I, William Millers, of the parish of All Saints' of Leicester bell founder, of sound mind and of good memory, make my will in this manner. First, I bequeath my soul to Almighty God, to the Blessed Mary and to all the saints, and my body to be buried in the church of All Saints aforesaid. Also I bequeath for my principal my best garment.† *(Itm lego p meo principali meum optimum indumentu').* Also I bequeath one trental‡ to be celebrated on the day of my death. Also I bequeath to the high altar of the church aforesaid 3s. 4d. Also I bequeath for the repair of the church aforesaid 20s. Also I bequeath to William my son £10. Also I bequeath to John my son £10. Also I bequeath to Agnes my daughter £10. Also I bequeath to the Cathedral church of Lincoln 8d. Also I will that Margery my wife shall have my house in which I dwell with all its appurtenances for the term of her life, and after the decease of the said Margery I will that William my son shall have the said house with all its appurtenances to him his heirs and assigns for ever. And if it shall happen that the said William die before his mother, then I will that John my son shall have the said house with all its appurtenances to him his heirs and assigns. And if it shall happen that the said John die before Margery his mother, then I will that Agnes my daughter shall have the house aforesaid with all its

---

* "Heytaur" or Yeytaur, that is Bellyetter, Bellzetter, or Bell-founder.

† This by way of mortuary; see the will of Thomas Newcombe to be presently quoted.

‡ Trental (*unum trigentale*) an office for the dead that continued thirty days, or consisted of thirty masses.

appurtenances for ever. And if it shall happen that the said Agnes die before Margery her mother, then I will that the aforesaid house be sold and [the money] be distributed to the priests, the poor, and the repairs of the ways, for the safety of our souls and of all those faithful deceased. But the residue of all my goods not bequeathed I give and bequeath to Margery my wife whom I ordain make and appoint my true and lawful executrix so that she may dispose for the safety of my soul and of all those faithful deceased as she shall think best. These being witnesses Roger Agard, Notary public, William Browne, William Burgeas with many others.*

It will be seen that William Millers left by his wife Margery three children, William, John, and Agnes: none of whom, however, appear to have been associated with their mother in carrying on the business. Margery Millers, the widow, married for her second husband

THOMAS NEWCOMBE who describes himself in his will as of Leicester "*fusor campanarius.*" He carried on the business of the Leicester foundry until his death, which took place in the year 1520. He was buried in All Saints' Church, Leicester, where his tombstone, was, it is said, to be seen a few years ago, stript of its brasses and of the emblems (three bells) of his calling. Little is known of him beyond what he himself tells in his will, which is dated the 20th of March, and which was proved on the 25th of August 1520. It is (translated) as follows :—

---

* Proved at Lambeth 12 Jany. 1506. *Regr. Adeane* fo. 17. Richard Mellour or Mellor was a Bellfounder at Nottingham in the fifteenth century. He was a party to a Deed dated 1488 in which he is de- scribed as "Rico Mellour de Notyngham Belyetter" (*Reliquary* xiii. p. 81). Possibly the above William Millers may have been one of the same family.

G

In the name of God Amen the 20th day of March in the year of
the incarnation of our Lord 1520 I Thomas Newcome of Leicester
bellfounder of right mind and sound memory do make my testament
or last will after this manner and form.   First I give and bequeath
my soul to Almighty God the Blessed Mary and all Saints and my
body to be buried in the church of All Saints of Leicester aforesaid.
Item I bequeath my best cloak (as the custom is) in the name of my
mortuary.   Item I bequeath to the cathedral church of Lincoln
xij*d*.   Item I bequeath to the high altar in the said church of All
Saints iijs. iiij*d*.   Item to the reparation of the said church iijs. iiij*d*.
Item I give and bequeath to every one of the places of friars in the
said [town of] Leicester iijs. iiij*d*.   Item I give and bequeath to
the reparation of the parish church of Podington iijs. iiij*d*.   Item
to the reparation of the parish church of Bosworth xx*d*.   Item I
give and bequeath to the use or towards the hiring of one chaplain
for a part of his stipend or salary for one year xxvj*s*. and two
torches* to the use of the church of All Saints aforesaid.   Item I
give and bequeath to Robert Newcome my son vj$^{li}$.   Item to
Edward my son vj$^{li}$.   Item to Joan my daughter vj$^{li}$.   Item
to Agnes my daughter vj$^{li.}$   Item I give and bequeath to Margaret
my daughter vj$^{li}$. and if it fortune that any one of my before named
sons or daughters die before their years of marriage then I will that
his or their portion or portions do remain to the survivor or survivors
and if it chance that all my aforesaid children depart this life before
their years of marriage then I will that Margery my wife may
ordain and dispose of their portions for the salvation of our souls.
Item I give and bequeath to William Mellers my stepson vjs. viij*d*.
Item to John Mellers brother of the same vjs. viij*d*.   Item I give
and bequeath to Robert Newcome my brother and servant xls. and
my best jerkin which I was wont to use in riding and my violet
gown trimmed with black lambskin, a little coat of frieze with
sleeves (*mancis*) of fustian a night shirt a pair of hose and my hanger.

---

* That is, two large altar tapers or candles.

Item I give and bequeath to Katherine my sister vj*s*. vuj*d*. and to her husband iij*s*. iiij*d*. Item I give and bequeath to Petronilla my sister vj*s*. viij*d*. Item I give and bequeath to John Bayly my servant my old violet Jerkin. Item I give and bequeath to John Dickson vj*s*. viij*d*. Item to John Tady iij*s*. iiij*d*. Item I will that a trental be celebrated in the said church of All Saints on the day of my obit. Item I will that on the same day there be distributed to the poor thirty shillings worth of bread. Item I will that nine masses be celebrated for the salvation of my soul and those of my relatives and benefactors at the altar which is called *scala celi* within the [monastery] of Augustine Friars in Leicester aforesaid. Item I give and bequeath to the three children of William Ireland of Bosworth vj*s*. viij*d*. conjointly. Item I give and bequeath to the vicar of the parish church of All Saints in Leicester aforesaid iij*s*. iiij*d*. Item I give and bequeath to John' Hardy chaplain vj*s*. viij*d*. and my camlet doublet (*deploidem*). Item I give and bequeath to Edward Alsopp vj*s*. viij*d*. my camlet jerkin and my bay coloured horse whom, that is to say, John and Edward I ordain and appoint supervisors of this my present last will. But the residue of my goods moveable and immoveable not bequeathed I give and bequeath to Margery my wife whom I ordain and constitute my sole executrix that she may dispose of and ordain the same for the salvation of my soul as shall seem to her best. Dated at Leicester on the said day and year these being witnesses Thomas Walshe Vicar of All Saints in Leicester aforesaid William Burges Thomas Hewit Jr. Thomas Wymod Thomas Braseld and many others.*

Thomas Newcombe left by his wife, Margery the widow of Wm. Millers, two sons and three daughters, namely Robert, Edward, Joan, Agnes, and Margaret. His widow (now

---

* Proved at Lambeth 25 August 1520. For this transcript I am indebted to John L'Estrange Esq.

twice a widow) having succeeded, apparently, to the bulk of her second deceased husband's property, and to the foundry, married a third husband, viz.:

THOMAS BETT. He was Mayor of Leicester in 1529, and is styled in a Roll of the Mayors of Leicester "Bell-founder of All Saints" and "ancestor of the Newcombs," a descriptive expression which will be referred to presently. There is little to relate of him. The Town Records preserve a curious incident which occurred in the spring of the year during which he filled the chair as Mayor:—

> "Mem: the 27th day of March there was brought to Thomas Bett then Mayor of Leicester hawthorn bud'ytt furth, beane flowres, and a cullumbell flour."*

Although not mentioned by name, Thomas Bett is clearly the bellfounder referred to in the following entries in the accounts of the wardens of the Parish Church of Peterborough (S. John the Baptist) for the year 1537-8.

xxviij Hen. viij      s.    d.

Itm̄ Gyven to the Founder of Lester in ernest for
  mendyng of the grett bell ................................ vij. ij.
Itm̄ Payd to the Workemen for mendyng of the grett bell xxj.
Itm̄ To Thomas Pyx for his labor going to Leyster to
  bydd the bellfounder he should not come.............. ij.†

Thomas Bett outlived Margery and afterwards married Anne . . . . for whom (judging from the wording of his last will) he had no great affection. This will was dated

---

* *Nichols' Leics.* vol. i. p. 391.

† Kindly extracted for me by James about this bell under *Leicester Abbey* Cattel Esq. of Peterborough. See more further on.

19th December 1538, and was proved on the 6th of February following.   A copy is here given :—

In the name of God Amen the xix<sup>th</sup> day of Decembre in the yeare of Our Lord God thousand fyve hundreth xxxviij I Thomas Bett of Leicestre Belfounder being of good and parfyte mynde and remembraunce thanked be God by deliberacion and advisement make my last wille and testament concernyng the disposicion of my londes and goodes in maner and fourme folowyng First and principally I geve and bequeth my soule to the Holy Trinitie humbly besechinge him that I may be parte taker of the possession of Jhū Crist and one of the number of theym that shalbe saved besechyng our Lady Saint Mary mother of mercy and all the holy company of hevyn to pray for me.   Secundary my bodie to be buried within the parishe churche of All Saintes in Leicestre.   Also I bequeath to the reparacions of the same church vj*s*. viij*d*.   Item to the high awter within the same churche ij*s*.   Item I bequeth to our mother church of Lincoln xij*d*.   Also my will is that Anne my wife shall have all such goodes as she brought with hir to Leycestre when I maryed her and over this I will that she shall have in recompense for weryng of the same goodes tenne poundes sterling.   And also I give and bequeth unto the same Anne my wife other tenne poundes sterling willing that she shall not medle no further with any parte or parcell of my landes goodes or testament.   And yf she do make clayme further then my will is that the premisses be voide and in noon effect which I willed and bequethed to her.   Item I geve and bequeth to Robert Newcome my sonne in lawe and to Kateryn his wife my doughter all my landes and tenementes with the appurtenances in Leicestre in the Countie of Leicestre and in every other place and to the heires of their bodyes lawfully begotten for ever. And if the said Robert Newcome and Kateryn departe without yssue of their bodyes lawfully begotten then I will that the howse wherin I now dwell remayne to Joan Gaddesby and to the heires of hir body lawfully begotten for ever.   And if the said Joane departe without yssue of her body lawfully begotten then I will that the said howse be solde and the money thereof distribute amonge poure people for my soule health and for the soules of William Mellers and Margery late my wife. Item I bequeth to my sister Alice Langham xxs. and she to have it paid to hir by myn executours as she therunto shall have nede. Item I bequeth to Anne Newcome my doughter childe fyvetene powndes sterling and her father to have the keping therof till she be at full age. Item I will that Robert Newcome my sonne in law have my leasse or indenture of the tenement in Warwickshire with all my goodes and catall there so that the tenauntes there have it in maner as I have promysed them towardes theyr lyvinges. Item I will that myn executour shall distribute in almes to poure people for the soules of William Mellers and Margery late my wife xls. sterlyng. The residue of all my goodes not bequethed my dettes being fully paid and my bequestes truely perfourmed and also my body brought home I geve and bequeth to Robert Newcome my sonne in lawe and to Kateryn his wyfe whom I make my faithfull and lawfull executours. And also I make supervisours of this my last will and testament Maister John Burton of Leicestre Adam Eyre and John Burton of Newton in the countie of Darby desiring them and everie of them to see this my last wille and testament trulie perfourmed as my trust is in theym. And I will that everie of theym shall have for there labours xxs. These witnesse Sir Thomas Walshe Vicar of Alhalowes of Leicestre John Norres Richard Baker John Pare Thomas Bradfelde Richard Darker with other moo.*

It will be seen that Thomas Bett left nearly the whole of his property to Robert Newcombe, who had married his daughter Katherine: he by this means enriched his son-in-law, who also succeeded to the foundry, and so in this way

---

* Proved at London 6 Feb. 1538-9 *Regr. Dingley* 25.

Thomas Bett became, in a sense, according to the Mayor's Roll "ancestor of the Newcombs."

ROBERT NEWCOMBE thus became a prosperous man. In the year 1540 a messuage in All Saints' parish was conveyed to him by George Belgrave, Esq.; the consideration money of which was £18. It was described as being situate between Robert Newcombe's tenement on the south, and Thomas Bridge's on the north, and as abutting on the east part upon the church of All Saints, and on Clement's Lane on the west part.* The residence of the Newcombes, and the site of their foundry are thus shown. He purchased the great bell of Leicester Abbey (and so most probably the other bells also) at the Dissolution, and exchanged it, in the year 1542-3, with the churchwardens of Peterborough (S. John Baptist) for their cracked bell, receiving the difference of value in money.† In the year 1547 Robert Newcombe purchased from the churchwardens of S. Martin's, Leicester, "iiij hundrith and a qr of bras at xixs. the hundrith,"‡ being probably, in part, effigies torn from the recumbent gravestones on the floor of the church. He was elected Mayor in 1550. This Robert Newcombe left four children, Thomas, Edward, Anne, and Robert. The three sons being all associated in the foundry, it may be well to speak of them separately :—

1. THOMAS NEWCOMBE "primus filius Robti Newcombe"

---

* *Nichols' Leics.* vol. i. p. 549.

† See a full account of this transaction further on in the description of Bells under Leicester Abbey.

‡ *North's Chron. S. Martin's Ch. Leicester,* p. 98.

was admitted a member of the Merchants' Guild in the mayoralty of William Norris (the 10th year of Elizabeth).*

In the year 1562 the townsmen of Melton Mowbray employed "Mayster Newkom" of Leicester to recast "o' Ladye bell" there. Some curious entries in the Church and Town wardens' accounts referring to this transaction will be found quoted in the description of the bells of that parish further on in this volume. That bell—the 5th of the present ring—still hangs in the fine tower of Melton Church, and it enables us to shew the founder's mark, bearing his initials, used by this Thomas Newcombe, if not by his predecessor of the same name in the craft in Leicester, it is

fig. 6 here given. The same shield is found upon bells at Ab-Kettleby (2nd), Cosby (3rd), Croft (3rd), East Norton (3rd), Garthorpe (1st), Gaddesby (2nd), Higham (3rd), Lockington (1st), Nailstone (2nd), Peatling Parva (1st and 2nd), Saxelby (2nd), Shawell (3rd), Theddingworth (3rd), Thorpe Arnold (3rd), and Wistow (3rd).

6

On the Melton bell this shield is accompanied by figs. 49 and 53, one or other of which are found (in addition to some already mentioned) upon bells at Edmonthorpe (1st), Houghton (2nd), Illston (1st), Kegworth (2nd), Market Bosworth (2nd and 5th), Narborough (4th), Scraptoft (1st), and Whatton (1st).

---

* *Hall Book.*

49                                    53

Thomas Newcombe's shield is frequently associated with the initial cross fig. 3 which is thus shown to have

been used by the Newcombes, and probably by their connections the other early founders of Leicester.

This cross, without the shield, appears upon bells at Aylestone (2nd), Bruntingthorpe (1st), Edmonthorpe (1st), Illston (1st) Kirkby Mallory (1st),

3

Lutterworth (Sanctus), Market Bosworth (2nd), Sapcote (1st), Scraptoft (1st), Wanlip (3rd) and Welby. This cross is also found in company with fig. 62 upon the 2nd bell at Aylestone and the 1st bell at Edmonthorpe, which figure is also upon bells at

62

Pickwell (2nd), Thurlaston (2nd), and Wanlip (1st).

H

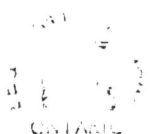

The cross fig. 71 accompanying fig. 62 upon the 2nd bell at Thurlaston is also found upon Beeby 1st bell and upon Queniborough 2nd bell.

71                                    70

The handsome cross fig. 70 is found upon Kegworth 2nd, Whatton 1st, and Peatling Parva 1st—at the latter place in

  union with New-combe's shield, fig. 6. Again, Thomas New-combe's shield is found in com-pany with a most beautiful cross and intervening stop, figs. 42 and 43, upon bells at

42                    43    Higham-on-the-

Hill (4th), and Theddingworth (3rd). The same cross and

stop are used on bells at Ashby-de-la-Zouch (6th), Cranoe (1st and 2nd), Fenny Drayton (1st), and Syston (4th). The cross is upon Lockington 1st bell and the stop upon Market Bosworth 5th.

64

The cross fig. 64 is found upon the 3rd bell at Barkby, and upon the 2nd bell at Peatling Parva—at the latter place in company with Newcombe's shield fig. 6 on plate 1. All these bells bearing figs. 3, 6, 42, 43, 49, 53, 62, 64, 70, 71, 81, may therefore be ascribed to the early Leicester founders—this Thomas Newcombe and his predecessors: among· them are included four bells (Lockington 1st, Market Bosworth 2nd and 5th, and Peatling Magna 3rd, all bearing the inscription "Vox dn̄i ihū xp̄i wox exultacionis," and having fig. 81 for the initial letter.

81

Thomas Newcombe purchased the ancient bells of S. Peter's Church, Leicester, when that edifice was taken down in the year 1563-4.

In 1570 he bought the brass eagle then belonging to S. Margaret's Church, Leicester, for which he gave £5.*

He died in 1580, being buried (as we learn from the Register) in All Saints' Church on the 7th of February in that year. His will was proved in the Archdeaconry Court of Leicester in the following year (1581). By it he directs his body to be buried in All Saints, Leicester: gives his goods, &c., to his executors to be sold for the payment of his debts, and directs his real property to be held by his executors for a space of . . . years for the like purpose, with a provision that the surplus of the proceeds shall be divided amongst his children. At the expiration of that term he devised to his eldest son, Robert Newcombe, the reversion of the whole Mansion house and tenement wherein he (the testator) dwelt,† of the old and new orchards, the dovehouse and close with the house next adjoining, and of a close called Sheppard's close over against "St. Jones" in Leicester. He devised to his middle son, Thomas, the reversion of a house in High Street [now High Cross Street] over against "Allhallowes " . . . . of a tenement in "Senvy Gate" . . . and of a little house in St. Nicholas Parish, with a garden, &c. He devised to his youngest son, Edward, the reversion of a little house in the Abbey Gate . . . and of a close adjoining: Finally he bequeathed to his daughter Anne £10 on her marriage, beyond the £30 due to her by the bequest of her uncle Thomas, late of

---

* *Nichols* vol. i. p. 561.

† This was in "High Street" now High Cross Street.

London Tower, deceased.* None of Thomas Newcombe's sons appear to have been afterwards connected with the foundry.†

2. ROBERT NEWCOMBE was another son of Robert the son-in-law of Thomas Bett. He was connected with the Leicester foundry, and placed his name upon the 4th bell of All Saints, Leicester, which was cast in 1586. Upon this

44

bell appears the cross fig. 44 which is also found upon bells at Peatling Magna (4th), Skeffington (5th), and Wymondham (3rd), and again in company with the mark of Watts (to be referred to hereafter) upon bells at Fenny Drayton (2nd), Illston (2nd), and Swinford (1st).

All these bells may therefore be assigned to the Newcombes, or to them in union with Francis or Hugh Watts of Leicester, with both of whom, as in the cases of Loughborough and Wymondham bells, we know them to have been occasionally in partnership. This cross is found upon earlier bells in Norfolk and elsewhere bearing the mark of Richard Brasyer of Norwich;‡ it may have

---

* This will preserved in the Probate Office of the Archdeaconry of Leicester is in an imperfect state.

† In 1582-3 Bartholomew Atton Tann' and Bellfounder the apprentice of Thomas Newcome Tann' and Bellfounder then deceased was admitted to the Merchants' Guild, or made free of the town: of him nothing more is known as a founder.

‡ *Church Bells of Norfolk*, p. 32.

fallen into the hands of the Leicester founders when the Norwich foundry was closed for a short time after the year 1513. This Robert Newcombe also placed his name upon the 1st bell of Gloucester Cathedral which was cast by the Leicester founders in 1598.*

3. EDWARD NEWCOMBE was the·third son of Robert Newcombe, the son-in-law of Thomas Bett. He married Elizabeth Martin in All Saints' Church on the 12th January 1573. He lived in S. Martin's parish, was one of the "Stewards of the Fairs" in 1574-5,† was "appoynted of the Company of the forty-eight," that is, became a member of the Town Council on the 10th May 1577,‡ and was put in nomination for the Mayoralty in 1598. Apparently wishing to avoid the office he signed a bond either to be mayor the next year, if elected, or to forfeit £20.§ He was elected, and filled the office, thus becoming the fourth Leicester Bellfounder who had been chief magistrate of the Borough. He is, I presume, the "Edward Newcwm" whose name appears on the 1st bell at Illston-on-the-Hill, and whose initials are upon the 2nd bell of the same ring, in both cases in union with the shield used as a mark by Francis Watts. Edward Newcombe had a numerous family—five sons and two daughters. Three, at least, of his sons were associated with him in the business of the foundry.

ROBERT NEWCOMBE his eldest son baptized 20 January 1576 was admitted to the Merchants' Guild in 1600—1601

---

* Lukis' *Church Bells* p. 73.  ‡ *Hall Book.*
† *Chamberlains' Accounts.*  § *Ibid.*

as appears from the following entry in the "*Hall Book*" of that year :—

> "Robertt Newcome Bellfounder and Tann' the first son and apprentice of Edwarde Newcome Bellfounder and Tann' made free his fyne ..................................... a pottell of wyne."

Thus Robert is mentioned with his father as casting the 2nd bell of S. Martin's, Leicester, in 1611.

THOMAS NEWCOMBE, the third son of Edward, placed his name upon the 1st bell at Hoby, in 1604, and the 4th bell at Sapcote in 1611.

WILLIAM NEWCOMBE, the fifth son of Edward, in partnership with Henry Oldfield of Nottingham, cast "Great Tom" of Lincoln in the Minster yard in the year 1610.*

At the commencement of the seventeenth century the Newcombes appear to have cast aside their old initial crosses and other marks as well as their old sets of letters and forms of inscription. There are one or two examples of a later use of the cross, fig. 44 (on plate ix.), but in 1602, (as at Sharnford) they began to use the form (in plain Roman capitals) which they subsequently as a rule adhered to :—

> + Be . yt . knowne . to . all . that . doth . me . see .
> that . Newcombe . of . Leicester . made . mee.

with the cross fig. 22 on next page prefixed.

---

* "This partnership, which extended to this one transaction only, arose from Holdfield being a man of the first eminence in his profession, and from William Newcomb living within the diocese: for the honour of which it was deemed necessary he should have some share in the business."—*History of Lincoln*, (1816) p. 75.

Early in this century we find the Newcombes were employed in various parts of the country to cast church bells.   At Stowe in Northampton-shire there is one of their bells dated 1607 ; at Elford in Staffordshire one dated 1604, and at      22
Eltisly in Cambridgeshire another dated 1608.    But the most noteworthy bell of this date from the Newcombes' foundry is one which is—so far as at present known—quite unique in the form of its inscription.    It is the fourth bell at S. Mary's Oxford.    Round the crown of the bell is the familiar inscription of the Leicester founders preceded by their initial cross fig. 22 :—

+ Be . yt . knowne . to . all . that . doth . me . see .
   that . Newcombe . of . Leicester . made . mee . 1612.

The band ornament (fig. 12, plate III.) used so generally by the Nottingham founders is introduced showing, I think, that Oldfield of Nottingham was in partnership with New-combe in this transaction.    Below this are two lines of music, the upper one going all round the bell, and the lower one only part of the way.    The music comprises four detached pieces.    They are written on the five line staff, in the square or rather lozenge shaped notes usually seen in prick-song of the period.    There are no bars except a double one at the end of each strain.    Each strain is headed by a distinct cleff (three parts having the C cleff and the fourth the F) and all the parts have the signature of B flat. Each strain or division is preceded by a roundel containing a man's profile and bust in relief, in the dress of the period, and encircled by a legend as follows :—

1. + KEEPE . TYME . IN . ANYE . CASE
2. THE . LAST . STRAYNE . WAS . GOOD
3. THEN . LETT . VS . SINGE . IT . AGAINE
4. EXCELLENT . WELL . SONGE . MY . HARTS.

The music has been scored by Dr. Rimbault, and is said to be very quaint and beautiful, in the style of the well known Madrigal "In going to my lonesome bed." Nothing what-ever is known as to the origin of the music—which has not been found elsewhere upon any other of Newcombe's numer-ous bells, nor in print or manuscript. The object of placing it here is also a mystery. The parish archives give no information.*

About this time (that is in 1611) when Edward New-combe and his sons recast the second bell at S. Martin's, Leicester, he was styled by the churchwardens there "old Mr. Newcome." Although I find no record of his death in the Registers of All Saints' parish, he probably died soon after this date, after which the foundry appears to have been merged into, or to have been eclipsed by, that of Hugh Watts (the son and successor of his father Francis

---

* The Rev. J. T. Fowler F.S.A. com-municated a full account of this Bell to the Society of Antiquaries in the year 1868. This account illustrated with a sheet of facsimiles from the bell, a lithograph of the music in the old notation, and Dr. Rimbault's version set in modern "short score" will be found in the *Archæologia*, vol. xlii. pp. 491-493. From this account (with Mr. Fowler's permission) and from *The Bells of the Church* by The Rev. H. T. Ellacombe F.S.A. who also gives an in-teresting description I have compiled the above notes upon this singular bell.

I

Watts) who about that time began to acquire a great reputation as a Bellfounder. The last dated bells of the Newcombes in Leicestershire are in the year 1612.

Before giving a few particulars about the contemporaneous foundry in Leicester belonging to the family of Watts, extracts from the Registers of All Saints', Leicester, relating to the Newcombes are added, and a rough pedigree appended. These may tend to make the relative positions of the different members of that family to each other, as Bellfounders, rather more clear than hitherto, to those who are wishing to properly assign bells found in other counties, which were cast in the Leicester foundries.

### Extracts from the Registers of All Saints' Church Leicester.*

Baptisms :

1576. Robert Nucom son of Edward Nucom Jany. 20.

1578. July 5. Katherin Nucom filia Edward Nucom.

1580. Sep. 3. Edward Nucom son of Edward Nucom.

1584. March 26. Thomas Nucom son of Edward Nucom.

1585. Oct. 2. Edward Nucom son of Edward Nucom.

1587. Sep. 29. Anna Nucom daughter of Edward Nucom.

1590. Jany. 24. William Nucom son of Edward Nucom.

1600. Oct. 5. Elizabeth Nucom filia Robert Nucom.

---

* Very kindly made for me, with the permission of the Vicar, by Mr. S. Bull.

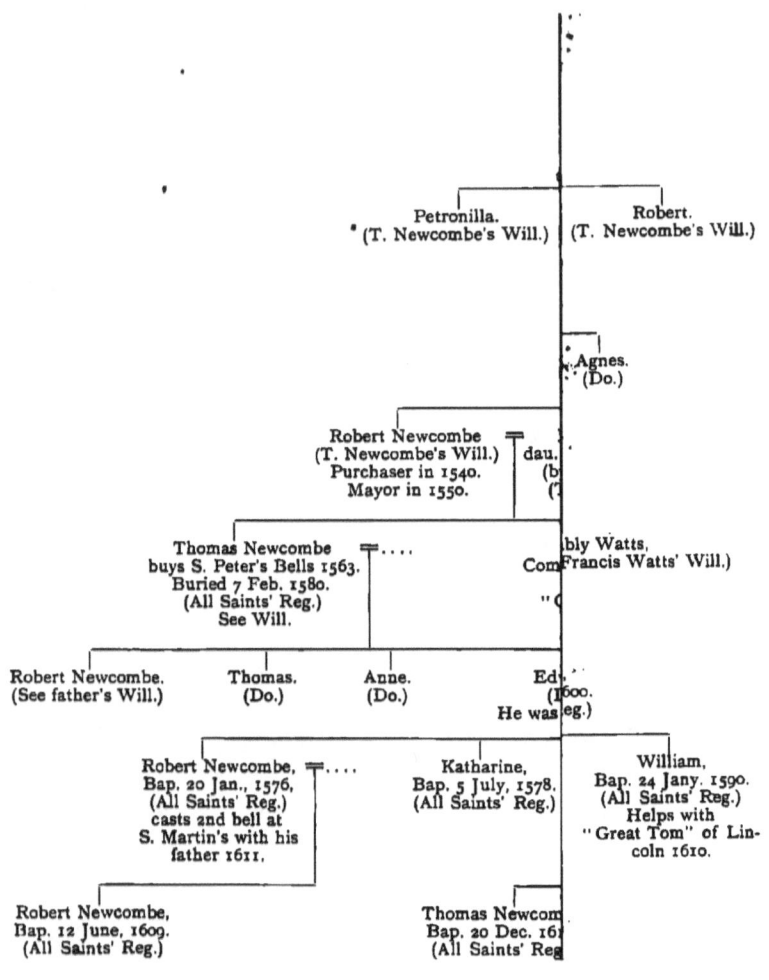

Petronilla.
* (T. Newcombe's Will.)

Robert.
(T. Newcombe's Will.)

Agnes.
(Do.)

Robert Newcombe
(T. Newcombe's Will.)
Purchaser in 1540.
Mayor in 1550.

dau.
(b
(

Thomas Newcombe
buys S. Peter's Bells 1563.
Buried 7 Feb. 1580.
(All Saints' Reg.)
See Will.

bly Watts,
ComFrancis Watts' Will.)

" (

Robert Newcombe.
(See father's Will.)

Thomas.
(Do.)

Anne.
(Do.)

Ed
(1600.
He was eg.)

Robert Newcombe,
Bap. 20 Jan., 1576,
(All Saints' Reg.)
casts 2nd bell at
S. Martin's with his
father 1611.

Katharine,
Bap. 5 July, 1578,
(All Saints' Reg.)

William,
Bap. 24 Jany. 1590.
(All Saints' Reg.)
Helps with
" Great Tom" of Lin-
coln 1610.

Robert Newcombe,
Bap. 12 June, 1609.
(All Saints' Reg.)

Thomas Newcom
Bap. 20 Dec. 16
(All Saints' Reg

1604. June 24. Elizabeth Newkom daughter of Thomas Newkom.

1609. June 12. Robert Newkom son of Robert Newkom.

1610. Dec. 20. Thomas Newkom son of Thomas.

Marriages:

    1573. Jany. 12. Edward Nucom and Elizabeth Martin.

    1605. Jany. 21. James Fewkes to Elizabeth Newkom.

Burials:

    1576. Sep. 17th. Margaret Nucom.

    1579. Feb. 7. Thomas Nucom.

    1582. Feb. 16. Edward Nucom son of Edward Nucom.

    1590. Sep. 1. Elizabeth Nucom.

    1606. May.22. Ellen Newcom wife of Robert Newcom.

    1611. July 9. Elizabeth Newcome wife of Edward Newcome.

    1616. July 13. Alice wife of Edward Newcombe.

    1645. Jany. 12. Mary the wife of Edward Newcome.

FRANCIS WATTS. The first member of the family of Watts, Bellfounders of Leicester, I find. mentioned, is Francis Watts, who, in the year 1564-5 bought the bell-wheels belonging to S. Peter's Church, Leicester, then being taken down.*

---

* Since writing the above I have obtained a rubbing of an inscription on a bell at South Luffenham, Rutland. It is very roughly put together, half the letters being upside down. I believe it reads HEW WAT MADE ME 1563. If so the founder is probably an earlier member of this family. This may be verified hereafter.

He resided, and probably had his foundry, in the Gallow-tree Gate.

In 1585 he, in partnership with the Newcombes, cast the tenor bell at Loughborough.

In 1596-7 his existence is pointed out in the Accounts of the Chamberlains of the Borough of Leicester:

> " It. pᵈ for the carryinge of a greate pott from the Towne-
>     Hall to Mr. Watts the Bellfownder to be wayed ...      iiijd."

Francis Watts died in the year 1600; his Will which is dated on the 8th of February 1599-1600, was proved on the 2nd of September in that year. From it we learn some particulars respecting his family :

> " In the name of God Amen the eight daye of Februarye in the yeare of oure Lord God one thousand five hundred nyentye and nyene and in the twoe and fortithe yeare of the raigne of oure Soveraigne Ladye Elizabeth &c. I Frauncis Watts of Galtrye gate of the burroughe of Leicester in the Countye of Leicester Bell fownder being sick in bodie but of good and perfect memorye I praise God therefore doe ordeyne and make this my last Will and Testament in manner and forme following That is to saye First and principallye I give and bequeath my sowle to Allmightie God whoe created me and to Jesus Christ whoe redeemed me trusting by his precious-bloudshedding for my synnes and by noe other meanes to be saved, and my bodie to the earth from whence it came to be buryed at the discrecōn of my executoʳ. As for the earthlie substance which the Lord hath lent me in this earthlie tabernacle I give and dispose in manner and forme following. First I give and bequeath unto my yongest sonne Jerrome Watts Fortie pounds to be paid to him when he shall accomplishe the age of xxjᵘ years. Item I give to my daughter Joane tenne shillings. Item I give to my daughter Elizabeth Allsoppe Twentie shillings and to her twoe

children eyther of them Fortye shillings. Item to my Daughter
Marye Paer Five pounds. Item to my Daughter Hellen Newcombe
three powndes sixe shillings eight pence. All the rest of my goods
and chattells whatsoever (my debts payed and funeralls discharged)
I give and bequeath unto Marye Watts my wief and Hugh Watts
my sonne whome I make my full executours of this my last Will
and Testament. In witnes whereof I have hereunto putt my hand
and seale the daye and yeare above written. Witnesses Hughe
Hunter and to this Will Henry Benington.*

Hugh Watts (who was born, as we gather from his
epitaph, about the year 1582) was about eighteen years of
age at his father's death. He placed his name, as founder,
in the same year, upon a bell at Burrow-on-the-Hill, in this
county, since recast :

"Hugh Wattes made me 1600,"

and upon the present second bell at Evington is a similar
inscription, dated 1605. These are the only instances that

have been found in which he followed
the custom so soon prevalent with
all founders of putting their names
on the bells they cast. Upon this
Evington bell is the shield (fig. 1)
here given. The presence of this
shield enables us to assign several
older bells, bearing the same mark,
to his father, Francis Watts, then
lately deceased.

I.

---

* Prerogative Court. *Wallopp*, folio 56.

Francis Watts had an elder son,* not named in his Will, who therefore probably died young, for in 1611-12 when Hugh Watts was admitted into the Chapman's or Merchants' Guild he was described as the *second* son of his father :†

> "Hugh Wattes second sonne of ffrancis Wattes Bell-
>    founder deceased made free his fyne .................   vs."

Hugh Watts soon obtained a high reputation as a founder; his bells are still extremely numerous in Leicestershire—there are nearly two hundred of them—where they are noted for the beauty and fulness of their tone.   Several complete rings are to be found ; as at Asfordby, South Croxton, Whitwick, Arnesby and Thorpe Langton.

Francis and Hugh Watts appear to have used no other mark (excepting perhaps in one or two uncertain instances as at Houghton-on-the-Hill (2nd) and Narborough (4th) ) in addition to the shield already mentioned (fig. 1) unless they were, in special cases, in partnership with their neighbours and relations the Newcombes.‡   It is therefore unnecessary to enumerate in detail their numerous bells still existing in Leicestershire.   The presence of this shield upon them, which will always be pointed out in connection with the inscriptions, will sufficiently identify them.   It is

---

worthy of note that this mark was used for a short time by the Norwich founder, Richard Brasyer (*circa* 1450), who, however, afterwards exchanged it for a more heraldic one with an ermine field, in place of the diapered one. At the death of Richard Brasyer, in 1513, the foundry at Norwich was closed for a short time.* It is not improbable that the father of Francis Watts had been employed there, and leaving at the closing of the foundry, found his way to Leicester, opened a foundry there on his own account, and used as a mark the shield with which he had been familiar at Norwich.

For many of their inscriptions both Francis and Hugh Watts used handsome Gothic Capitals (see figs. 86 and 87—the latter from S. Margaret's, Leicester), but Hugh Watts more generally used a rather clumsy Roman capital letter. His favourite inscriptions were "God save the King," of which there are over twenty examples still existing in Leicestershire; "Celorum Chrste platiat tibi Rex sonvs iste," (the letter I being always wanting in the second word) of which there are about twenty-five examples; "Cvm sono si non vis venire, nvnqvam ad preces cvpies ire," of which there are ten examples; "Cvm Cvm

86

---

* L'Estrange. *Church Bells of Norfolk,* pp. 28-33.

87

and pray" and "Praise the Lord" of each of which there
are six or seven examples; and portions of the alphabet
which appear upon many of his bells.  His most frequent
inscription however was the well known one:—"IH'Ƨ:
Nazarenvs : rex : Ivdeorvm : Fili : Dei : miserere : mei" (the
first S being in all cases reversed) ; of this inscription there
are still nearly ninety examples to be found in Leicestershire ; indeed so frequently did Watts use this form that
his bells became known as "Watts' Nazarenes."  A pecu-
liarity in his Gothic lettered inscriptions may be noted:  he
possessed no capital letters W and Y (those letters being
seldom required in Latin inscriptions) they always appear
in small black letters.  Hugh Watts' inscriptions are usually
carried all round the bell, the space between the words

being filled up in the majority of cases with the ornamental band fig. 9 :—

9

Hugh Watts was elected one of the Chamberlains of the Borough in 1620-1, and in the year 1633-4 he was chosen Mayor. The Chamberlains in their Accounts under that date say :

" Mr. Hugh Wattes Maior.
" Imprimis payed to Mr. Hugh Wattes Maior for his yearly
allowance according to the ancient order ... xiij*li*. vjs. viij*d*."

That he was an enthusiast in his art, and had a son equally ambitious to produce the very best specimens possible of a founder's skill, may be gathered from the following anecdote respecting the casting of the fine tenor of the ring at S. Margaret's Leicester, supplied by the Rev. Philip Hackett to Nichols the historian of Leicestershire :

" When the metal and moulds were preparing, and almost finished for casting, the son would have the father go to London to hear the best toned tenor he could, before they put to the final hand. The father went up accordingly,

K

at the son's request; who set to work without loss of time, immediately after his father's departure. He cast the great bell which did not exactly please him; he recast it; and finding it had every qualification he wished for, he wrote to his father in town, to come upon a certain day in the following week; nay, even a certain hour. The father could not make out what his son meant by being so particular; however, he obeyed him. The son, upon casting a second tenor which so fully answered all his expectations, set to work to hang it: and at the critical minute the father was to approach the town of Leicester on his return, this inimitable great bell was ringing, to the no small joy of the father, who cried also, for he guessed and knew what the younger Watts had been at and contrived, as there could be no such bell in existence at the time he left his foundry.*

This son, whose skill was so highly appreciated by his father, was probably Francis Watts, a younger son (for there is no mention of his eldest son, Hugh, in connection with the foundry), who was shortly afterwards admitted to the Chapman's Guild, or made free of the town :—

"1635-6
"ffranc Watts apprentice of Mr. Hugh Watts Bellfounder
made free the 11th of Maye 1636 his fine  ............     xs."†

It was during the Mayoralty of Mr. Hugh Watts that Charles the First paid his first visit (as King) to Leicester. On the 9th of May 1634 the mayor received from the

---

* Vol. i, part 2, p. 558.          † Chamberlains' Accounts.

Yeomen Ushers of his Majesty's Chamber the "Gests" of the King's Progress. He, at once, as required, forwarded a certificate to the Lord Chamberlain that the town was "clear and free from all infectious and contagious diseases." Immediate preparations were made to receive Charles and his Queen in a proper and loyal manner. Saturday, the 9th of August, being the day fixed for their arrival in Leicester, "it was agreed that all the members of the Corporation, under a penalty of £5 and £10 according to rank, should attend at the Guild Hall, at one o'clock in the afternoon, of the 9th of August, to accompany the mayor to such place as should be appointed, to receive their majesties at their coming into Leicester. Such of the 'Four and Twenty' as had been mayor were required to appear in their scarlet gowns and tippets, and the rest of that body 'with fair decent gowns and suits' and the 'Eight and Forty' in black suits, black gown and ruff bands." The royal visitors entered Leicester by S. Sunday's, or the North, Bridge, and were received by Hugh Watts and his brethren between that bridge and "Frogmore bridge," where the Recorder, Mr. Thomas Chapman, delivered an address. Handsome presents of plate were made to their majesties, and all their servants received their customary fees.* On the following day—Sunday—the King attended Divine Service in S. Martin's Church, where also Hugh

---

* See "*Royal Progresses to Leicester*," an admirable series of Papers by Mr. Wm. Kelly. The Chamberlains of the Borough give, under the head of "Extraordinary Payments," a long list of payments connected with this visit.

Watts and the members of the Corporation in their robes of office, and attended by the mace-bearers, would be present. This event is thus noticed in the accounts of the churchwardens :—

> Paid Rich. Beresford and Harrison for paynting the
>     Kings Armes &c. ..................................... iij*li*. vij*s*. ij*d*.
> Pd Moses Andrew and his man for takeing awaye the two
>     rowes of Seats in the church against the King's
>     comeing .......................................................... iiij*s*.
> Pd Willm Read for helping to cleanse the church ......... viij*d*.
> Pd for ij lodes of Rushes and moweing of them against
>     the King's Ma^tie^ comeinge ............................ xx*d*.
> Paid more for bowes and rushes vsed about the church ... xix*d*.
> Pd for a Comon prayer booke to goody Langford ......... xv*s*.
> Paid Tho. Sheene and Moses Andrew for takeing awaye
>     the maior brethrns seates against the King's ma^tie^
>     comeinge ...................................................... ij*s*. vj*d*.
> Pd the Kings offycer for fees for the ffloare where his
>     maiestie sat ................................................. iiij*s*.
> Pd the ringers beeing viij for the tyme that his maiestie
>     stayed in Leic. ............................................... xv*s*.
> Pd for flowers for the Kings Cushion ......................... iiij*d*.

The King left Leicester on the following day—Monday the 11th of August.

There are several entries in the Chamberlains' Accounts relating to Hugh Watts, such as :—

> 1623-4 Item recd. of Mr. Hugh Watts for the halfe of his
>     fine for the Goslinge close ........................ xij*li*. x*s*.

and a similar entry the next year. He upon more than one

occasion lent money to the Corporation of Leicester to help them in the difficulties, which the exigencies of the stirring times in which he lived placed them :—

> 1637-8 Itm. pd for a bond for Mr. Watts his 100*li.* and
> the seale ............................................... 0 . ij*s.* . 0
> 1638-9 Item paid to Mr. Hugh Watts for the use of
> Three hundred pounds ......................... xxiiij*li.*

and several other similar entries.

After the conflict between Charles the First and his Parliament had reached an open rupture, and the king had set up his Royal Standard at Nottingham, the head quarters of Prince Rupert were, for a time, at, and around, Queniborough in this county. From that place the fiery and impetuous prince wrote his well-known letter to "His Friend the Maior of Leicester " demanding a sum of £2000, which was to be "repaied in convenient time." To this letter was added the postscript "If any disaffected persons with you shall refuse themselves, or perswade you to neglect this comand, I shall tomorrow appeare before your towne in such a posture with horse, foote, and cannon, as shall make you knowe tis more safe to obey than resist his majesties commands." After some difficulty £500 was borrowed, and handed over to the Prince's representatives. Hugh Watts lent part of this sum to the Corporation, as the next extract from the Chamberlains' Accounts shows :

> " 1641-2 Item pd Mr. Palmer [Town Clerk] for three
> bonds given to Mr. Watts Mr. Tompson and John
> Clarke for the 500<sup>li</sup>. sent to Prince Rupert............ iij*s.*"

In the year following (1643) Hugh Watts died, and was buried in S. Mary's Church, Leicester. Nichols preserves his epitaph :

"On a gravestone erected against the North corner of the East wall are the arms of *Watts*: three greyhounds erased ducally gorged or ;· crest, a greyhound sable ducally gorged or ; and this inscription :

Tempora mutantur, et nos mutamur.

Here lieth the body of Hugh Watts the Elder gent.—
sometime Mayor and Alderman of this Corporation
who deceased in the 61 yeare of his age ano D̄ni 1643."*

In his will dated 1 February 1642-3, and proved on the 23rd of the next month—March—he describes himself as " Hugh Watts of the Borough of Leicester the Elder Bell-founder," he says :

> " I give to my wife Mary Watts and to my said son Hugh Watts and to my said daughters Frances and Ellen Watts all my move-able goods within and about my said dwelling house (the Talbott) (except the bellmettle, tools, instruments, utensils, and implements, which are in and about my said house, yard and backside, used about the trade of a bellfounder) . . . I give all my tools and imple-ments belonging to the trade of a bellfounder to my son Hugh Watts."†

It is clear that the foundry was worked by Hugh Watts until his death, for there are two bells at Barrow-on-Soar,

---

* Vol. i., p. 316.      † Prerogative. *Crane folio* 25.

and one at Kimcote, dated 1642. These are the latest of his bells I find in Leicestershire.

As George Curtis has been more than once mentioned as a Leicester Bellfounder, I may say that I think he was never more than a foreman under Hugh Watts. He was admitted to the freedom of the Borough in the year 1627. This we learn from the " *Hall Book* " of that date :—

> " George Curtes apprentice of Mr. Hugh Watts Bell-
> fownder made free the ixth of May 1627 his fine ...    xs."

He occupied a tenement in the Southgate which Mr. Hugh Watts (his employer, as I think) held of the Corporation of Leicester,\* and the only other reference to him I have seen in connection with the foundry is the following entry in the Chamberlains' Accounts for the year 1644-5 :—

> " Itm paidd to George Curtice for exchangeinge of
> Thomas Hartshorne's bell ............................ ijs. vjd."

Hartshorne being the cryer.

This would be shortly after Hugh Watts' death, and when Curtis was probably winding up his business., His' name is not on any bell in Leicestershire. He died in 1650, as we are told in the following entry in the Register of S. Martin's Church, Leicester :—

> " Ano Dni 1650
> Septem. 5th George Curtis Bellfounder was burydd."†

---

\* Chamberlains' Accounts 1644-5.

† I am indebted to the Rev. A. Bunting for making this extract for me.

To show that the Leicester Foundry was closed about this time we find the following entry in the Chamberlains' Accounts for the year 1655-6 :—

"Itm payd for castinge the Cryer's Bell and for the carriage thereof *to Nottingham and backe againe*   oo . o7 . o4"

Portions of the foundry gear passed into the hands of the Nottingham founders. We find Watts' letters used by them upon bells cast in 1672, and afterwards, at Swepstone (3rd), Sutton Cheney (4th), Thorpe Arnold (2nd), Diseworth (2nd), Wigston Magna (2nd and 3rd), &c., &c., but Watts' mark (fig. 1) and his band ornaments never appear after his death.*

THOMAS CLAY. After the closing of Hugh Watts' foundry, and the dispersion of the gear, there seems to have been no attempt to revive the craft in Leicester for several years. At length, in the year 1711, the name of Thomas Clay of Leicester appears as a founder upon two bells yet existing —Dunton Bassett (2nd) and Earl's Shilton (2nd). Beyond these indications of his presence in Leicester, and the fact that he cast a ring of eight bells for Southwell Collegiate

---

* After the death of Hugh Watts there are many entries in the Chamberlains' Accounts of payments to his son Hugh on account of his late father. This Hugh Watts "son and heir of Hugh Watts the elder gent," married Jane, fourth daughter of Sir Tho. Burton, of Stockerston, in the County of Leicester, Bart. He died 26th Aug., 1656, leaving one son and four daugh- ters (see his epitaph in Nichols, vol. i. p. 316.) There are several tablets in Great Dunmow Church, Essex, to his descendants.

It may be inferred from several entries in the Chamberlains' Accounts that the Watts family, after the death of Hugh the Bellfounder, occupied as a residence a house in the Newarke, Leicester, "heretofore Dr. Chippendale's and Mr. Walker's."

Church, which were so much disliked that they were speedily recast by Rudhall of Gloucester,* I know nothing.

EDWARD ARNOLD. After another interval of several years a foundry was again opened in Leicester by Edward Arnold, who had worked with, and succeeded Joseph Eayre of S. Neots. This foundry is said to have been in Hangman's Lane—now called Newarke Street. The first ring of bells he cast in Leicester was that of Rothley, in the year 1784. There are many of his bells in the county, and his name is constantly mentioned in the Accounts of the Churchwardens of S. Martin's, Leicester, until the year 1798-9.†

MESSRS. TAYLOR. During some of the time Edward Arnold occupied premises in Hangman's Lane Leicester, he had also an establishment at S. Neots, into which he received, as an apprentice, Robert Taylor, who towards the close of the eighteenth century succeeded to the business there, which at that time was carried on in a lofty brick building situate in the Priory, and built in the form of a bell. The business was carried on there by Robert Taylor, and then by Robert Taylor and Sons, until the year 1821, when they removed to Oxford. In 1825 the late Mr. John Taylor, one of the above firm, went to Buckland Brewer, near Bideford, Devon, to cast the bells there, and after casting several rings, and odd bells, in Devon, Cornwall, &c., returned to Oxford in 1835. In 1840 he, and his son, came to Loughborough to recast the bells there, and finding the town well situated for business took up their residence

---

* *Midland Counties Hist. Col.*, vol. ii. p. 355.    † See further on pp. 94-5.

L

in that place.   Since that time Mr. John Taylor has died
leaving his son, the present Mr. John William Taylor, the
head of the Leicestershire Foundry.   The Oxford Foundry,
which had been chiefly under the superintendence of Mr.
William Taylor, brother of the above-mentioned Mr. John
Taylor, was closed upon his decease which occurred in 1854.*

---

* For this information respecting the Messrs. Taylor I am indebted to Mr. J. W. Taylor, of Loughborough, whose practical knowledge and successful prosecution of his business are well known.

*From an Illuminated MS. of the Psalms (fourteenth century) in the King's Library,*
*British Museum; marked 20. B. xi.*

# OTHER FOUNDERS

OF

# LEICESTERSHIRE BELLS.

---

IN addition to the Bells already enumerated as cast by the Leicester Founders, there are, of course, a goodly number in the County by other Founders, known and unknown.

The ancient bells first claim attention, and then notes upon the founders of those of a more recent date will follow. These notes—after the lengthy account already given of the Leicester Founders—will be as brief as possible, because, whilst the historian of the campanology of each county should give as full an account as possible of the Foundries therein, he may well leave those of neighbouring counties to be described in detail by those campanists who may in the future describe their bells.

JOHANNES DE YORKE. There is a very interesting bell hanging at Sproxton (the 2nd of the ring), bearing round its upper part the inscription in small Gothic capitals:

+ JHOHANNES ▫ DE ▫ YORKE ▫
ME ▫ FECIT ▫ IN ▫ HONORE ▫
BEATA ▫ MARIE

The cross and intervening stop used are figs. 54 and 56 here given :

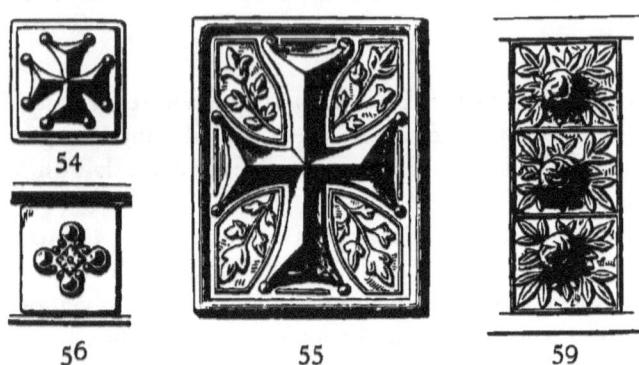

Round the lower part of the bell is the inscription in larger handsome Gothic capitals :

+ JHESVS ▢ NAZARENVS ▢ REX ▢
IVDEORVM

The initial cross and intervening stop of this second inscription are here engraved—figs. 55 and 59 above.    There is a cluster of bells in Leicestershire that can be traced to the same founder by the use of the same letters, cross and stop, but this is the only one upon which the name of the founder is given.    The other bells are Billesdon 4th, Birstall 3rd, Brentingby 1st, Cotesbach 2nd, Hungarton 3rd, Long Clawson 4th, Sproxton 1st and Witherley 5th.    At Wanlip the same cross with the figure of an angel (see fig. 80 on plate XVII.) on each side appears upon the 2nd bell, but the inscription is not in the usual capitals, but in small "black letter."

The form of the letters points to the latter part of the fourteenth century as the date of these bells. The number of his bells still remaining in Leicestershire, considering their antiquity, leads to the inference that Johannes de Yorke supplied many more in the county which have been since his time, from various causes, recast. If this be so, he was probably established in Leicester, or in its neighbourhood, at least for a time, even if he were not a permanent resident. But of this we know nothing. A foundry was in full work at York early in the fourteenth century by Richard Tunnoc a Bailiff of the city in 1320-1, and a representative of York in Parliament in 1327. The well-known Bellfounder's window in York Cathedral, in which the art of Bellfounding is represented, was either erected by him, or to his memory. It is not unlikely that Johannes de Yorke learned his art from that prominent founder.

40

AVSTEN BRACKER. Upon Catthorpe 1st bell appears this cross (fig. 40) which was used by Avsten Bracker, a London founder of the early part of the sixteenth century (?). His bells, with the same cross upon them are found in Norfolk.* The initial cross (fig. 39 over) precedes the inscription in small neat Gothic capitals upon these bells—Barleston (2nd), Foxton (3rd), Gumley

---

* *Church Bells of Norfolk,* p. 56.

(3rd), Hungarton (2nd), Rotherby (2nd), and Walton Isley (1st). Fig. 41 precedes inscriptions in letters of the same form, but a trifle larger, upon Brentingby 2nd bell, Caldwell 1st, and Walton Isley 1st. The early stamp fig. 63 is found upon the following bells: Caldwell 2nd and 3rd, Castle Donington 4th, Claybrooke 4th, Croxton Kerrial 3rd, Ibstock 4th, Saltby 3rd, Segrave 2nd, Sproxton 3rd, Wyfordby 2nd, and, with it fig. 61 on Claybrooke 4th and Saltby 3rd.

39

63

41

61

83

Figure 83 is the initial cross upon the 2nd bell at Cossington, the 3rd at Markfield, and the 3rd at Thrussington. Figure 2 is only found on two bells, viz.: Aston Flamville 1st and Ashby Parva 1st; upon the latter it is in company with fig. 4. Figure 5 appears only on the 2nd bell at Aston Flamville.

2

5

4

17

The very handsome cross fig. 17 with the legend " Ihu merci ladi help" is upon Bottesford 4th bell, Narborough 4th and Shawell 4th. This cross is found upon bells in all parts of England, and is supposed to have belonged originally to a London founder. Upon the bell at Shawell it is in com-

pany with figs. 30 and 31; upon that at Bottesford with
figs. 31 and 23.   Upon the one at Narborough it is found
with several other stamps, including that used by Watts of
Leicester (see fig. 1 on plate 1).

30

23

31

Figure 15 appears on the 1st
bell at Frisby.   Figure 16 is upon
the 3rd at Cosby and the 1st at
Lockington, both of which bells were

from the Leicester
foundry.   These
stamps appear to
have been used by
the Brasyers of Nor-
wich, and probably
passed from them in-
to the hands of the
Leicester founders.

15

16

The initial cross, fig. 18, is upon the 2nd bell at Nether Broughton. Figure 26, which is found in all parts of England, is upon Garthorpe 1st bell in company with Newcombe's initial cross (see fig. 3 on plate 1). Figure 20, here given, appears upon the single bells of Newton Harcourt and Sysonby.

18

26

20

32

52

The shield, fig. 32, the mark of an unknown founder, is upon the 2nd bell at Croxton Kerrial, the 3rd at Dalby on the Wolds, the 1st at Knipton, and the 2nd at Welham:

M

in all which places it is accompanied by fig. 52, which stamp further appears upon Cossington 3rd and Saltby 2nd bell. There are good reasons for thinking these stamps belonged

37

to the early Nottingham founders. Again in one or two instances the ornate initial letters (figs. 37 and 38) H. D. —the second letter being a C reversed and so made to do duty for a D—are found upon bells with the above marks (figs. 32 and 52). These initials of some unknown founder are upon Church Langton 6th bell, Croxton Kerrial 2nd, Knipton 1st, Oadby 4th and Stoke Golding 3rd.

38

The cross fig. 24 is upon the 3rd bell at Thurcaston, and the 3rd at Muston—at the latter place in company with the mark of H. Oldfield of Nottingham. A cross similar in character (fig.

25) is upon the 4th bell at Sutton Cheney also from the Nottingham foundry.

24                                    25

Certain crowned heads have been found upon ancient bells in various parts of the kingdom. They are supposed to have belonged originally to London founders. They are known to campanists as " Royal Heads," and have been assigned from peculiarities of treatment to Edward I. and Queen Eleanor, Edward III. and Queen Philippa, Henry VI., Margaret of Anjou, and her son Prince Edward.* Those assigned to Edward I. and Queen Eleanor (figs. 28 and 29)

28                                    29

* *Church Bells of Devon*, p. 253.

are found upon the 4th bell at Claybrooke and upon the 3rd at Thurcaston—at the latter place in company with a figure of the Blessed Virgin and Child (see fig. 73 on plate xv.) and a Fleur de lys (see fig. 19 on plate iv.). The same "Royal Heads" are also upon the 4th bell at Kegworth, and from the presence on the same bell of the mark of Henry Oldfield we know that in his time they were in the hands of the Nottingham founders. One "Royal Head" much corroded, but apparently that called Edward I., is upon the 1st bell at Garthorpe, the 1st at Lockington, and the 3rd at Peatling Magna—in all three instances in company with stamps used by the Newcombes of Leicester—and upon the 4th bell at Narborough in company with the shield of Watts of Leicester.

The cross fig. 50 I find on only one bell—the 3rd at Dalby on the Wolds. The shield fig. 51 appears in company

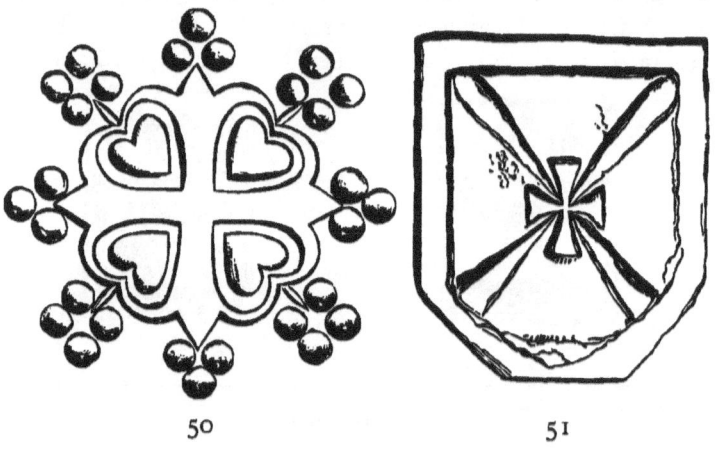

50                      51

with other stamps upon the 1st bell at Muston, and upon the 3rd at Thurcaston.

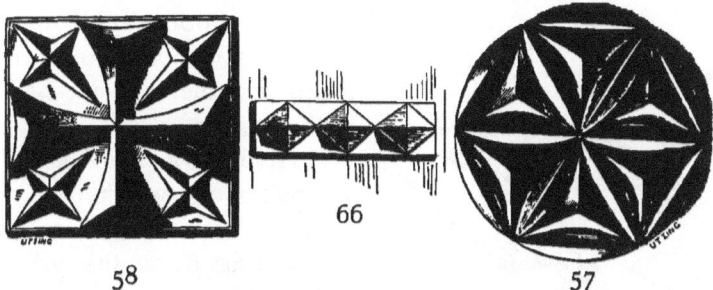

58         66         57

These handsome stamps—fig. 58 as initial cross, fig. 66 as a mark of contraction, and fig. 57 as an intervening stop —are only on the 2nd bell at Dalby Parva.

65         67         72

The cross fig. 65 appears on Catthorpe 2nd bell; the cross fig. 72* on Bringhurst 3rd, Burbage 4th, and on Welham 1st, and the intervening stop, fig. 67, is found on the 3rd bell at Bringhurst, the 3rd at Ibstock, and the 1st at Welham.

---

* Since writing the above I am able to assign this cross to the Stamford Foundry. Tobie Norris, Thomas Norris and Tobias Norris all use it upon their bells in Rutland churches.

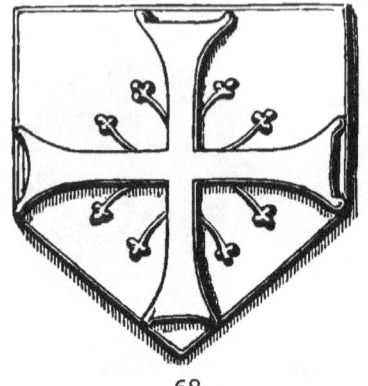

68

This shield is on the 4th bell at Melton only, but the handsome Gothic capitals used for the inscription thereon are found on other ancient bells in the county.

Fig. 60 is a cross on the 3rd bell at Kegworth; fig. 74 is on the 1st bell at Cossington, and fig. 69 on the 3rd at Willoughby Waterless.

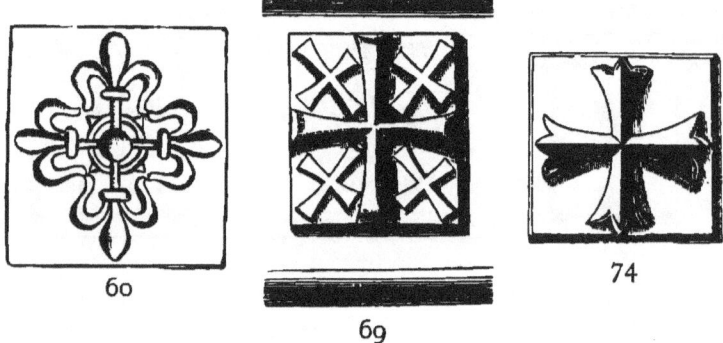

60                    69                    74

This large initial cross, fig. 76, on the next page, appears on one bell only—the 3rd at Frolesworth.

The other marks engraved on the next page are only found once in the county. Fig. 78 is the initial cross and fig. 77 the intervening stop on the 1st bell at Horninghold; and the pretty cross, fig. 82, is on the 1st bell at Wyfordby.

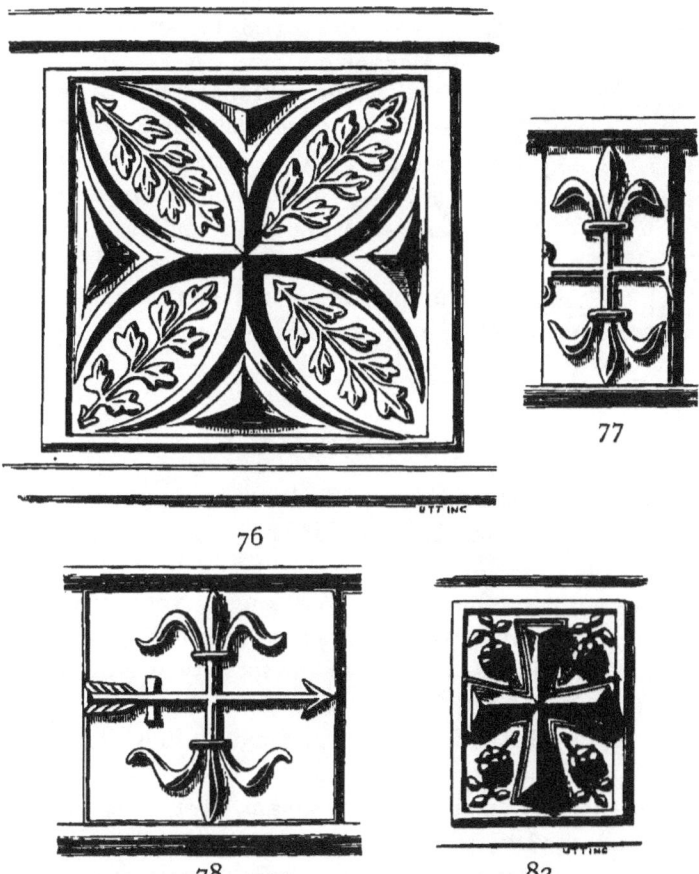

76

77

78         82

The slipped pomegranate, fig. 79 on the next page, is
on the 4th bell at Kegworth, and the same Tudor badge,
crowned, appears on the 3rd bell at Muston.

79

The cross fig. 51*a* is on the 1st bell at Ragdale.

It will be seen that many of the ancient bells in our Leicestershire churches cannot at present be assigned to any known founders.   A few 51*a*    notes are now added upon the founders of the more modern bells hanging in our steeples.

## NOTTINGHAM.

THERE are a large number of bells in Leicestershire from the Nottingham foundry, the history of which has yet to be written.

It is not improbable that William of Notyngham and William of Norwich, who were casting bells in the fourteenth century, were identical.*   If so the foundry at Nottingham was of ancient date.†

RICHARD MELLOUR, of Nottingham, "Belyetter," was alive in 1488.†

GEORGE OLDFIELD, of Nottingham, cast bells between 1537 and 1558.†

THOMAS "OWEFELD," of Nottingham, cast the sanctus bell at Melton Mowbray in this county in 1553.

---

* *Church Bells of Norfolk*, p. 84.        † *Reliquary*, vol. xiii. p. 81.

HENRY OLDFIELD, of Nottingham, cast bells now in Leicestershire churches from 1589 to 1620 inclusive.*

GEORGE OLDFIELD'S (the second's) mark appears in the same way from 1620 to 1673 inclusive.

WILLIAM NOONE, of Nottingham, cast the 5th bell of S. Martin's, Leicester, in 1700.

THOMAS HEDDERLY'S (of Nottingham) name appears in Leicestershire from 1749 to 1784. He was however casting bells eight years earlier. The name "Thomas Hedderly" on the Leicestershire bells probably represents father and' son : the father died about 1778, the son in 1785. The elder left four sons—Thomas (just mentioned), George, John, and Samuel ; the first of them—George Hedderly— has bells in Leicestershire dating from 1787 to 1791, a few years after which date he emigrated to America.

The mark of the Oldfields (who seldom placed their names upon their bells) was a cross calvary between their initials with a crescent and a star above (see figs. 7, 8, 10, 11, on plate II., and fig. 33 on plate VII.). The crosses, see figs. 21 on plate V., and 34, 36, on plate VII., are also found upon their bells in Leicestershire. The Nottingham founders used several band ornaments between the words of their inscriptions. Three of these are figures 12, 13, and 14, on plate III. Figure 35 on plate VII. is also found upon one of their bells at Sileby.

The presence of these, or any of them, upon Leicester-

---

* He is said to have died in 1615: if so his stamp was used by his successor for several years. This is not improbable.

N

shire bells, which will be pointed out hereafter, are sufficient to assign such bells to the Nottingham founders without enumerating them here. The figures will be found numbered on the plates hereafter given.

The Nottingham founders became possessed of a large number of ancient stamps, letters, &c., which they sometimes introduced upon comparatively modern bells: see pages 82, 83, and 84.

## BAWTRY.

DANIEL HEDDERLY, of Bawtry, in Yorkshire (the ancestor of the Hedderlys of Nottingham), cast the ring of five bells at Nether Seile in 1707, and that of six bells at Peckleton in 1714. Upon the 4th bell of the latter appears, before the founder's name, that of J. M. Halton.

J. M. HALTON was probably foreman to Daniel Hedderly, and may have closed the foundry at Bawtry upon the death of his master. His name will be seen, as founder of the whole ring, upon the 2nd bell at Ansty in 1723.

## CHERTSEY.

THOMAS ELDRIDGE had a foundry at Wokingham 1563-1577, where he was succeeded by

RICHARD ELDRIDGE. He subsequently removed to Chertsey, where under

BRYAN ELDRIDGE (or possibly two of that Christian name) and his brother

W<small>ILLIAM</small> E<small>LDRIDGE</small> the foundry continued to be the principal one in that part of England during the greater part of the seventeenth century.*   There are only two bells in Leicestershire from this foundry—Stoke Golding 1st, and Shawell 1st—upon both of which the inscription is in very bold, rudely formed, Roman capital letters.

## GLOUCESTER.

T<small>HIS</small> was a centre of the Bellfounder's art at an early period.   John of Gloucester flourished early in the fourteenth century ; Sandre of Gloucester, and others, followed.   The Rudhalls worked a foundry here with great success from the end of the seventeenth century till about the year 1830. There are only two bells in Leicestershire from this foundry. The 2nd at Bottesford, cast in 1713, bear the initials and mark (fig. 27) of

27

---

* *Notes and Queries,* 3rd s. vi. 443.   See also an account of the Eldridges in *Church Bells of Sussex.*

ABRAHAM RUDHALL, and the 4th at Stoke Golding was cast by

JOHN RUDHALL, the last of the Gloucester founders, in the year 1825, soon after which the foundry passed into the hands of Messrs. Mears of London.

## STAMFORD.

TOBIE NORRIS, Bellfounder, died on the 2nd of November 1626, and was buried in S. George's Church, Stamford.

THOMAS NORRIS (probably his son) supplied several bells to Leicestershire churches. His earliest bell is at Rolleston dated 1629, and his latest at Church Langton (4th) dated 1676. His son and successor

TOBIAS NORRIS was baptized 25th April 1634. There are two of his bells in this county, inscribed "Tobie Norris," viz.: Croxton Kerrial 4th, dated 1674, and Owston 2nd, dated 1699. Tobie Norris died in the latter year.* They all occasionally used the cross No. 72 plate xv. as I find from several bells in Rutland.

ALEXANDER RIGBY probably succeeded Tobie Norris. His bells in Leicestershire date from 1702 at Tugby, to 1706 at Houghton. He died at Stamford in the year 1708.†

On the treble bell at Badgworth, Gloucestershire, is:

> " Badgworth ringers they were mad,
>   Because Rigbe made me bad ;
>   But Abel Rudhall you may see,
>   Hath made me better than Rigbe."

---

* *Church Bells of Norfolk, p. 72.*    † *Church Bells of Cambridge, p. 34.*

## PETERBOROUGH.

HENRY PENN. There are only six bells in Leicestershire founded by Henry Penn of Peterborough, viz.: a complete ring of four at Bitteswell, dated 1706, one bell at Sileby, dated 1708, and one at Waltham, cast in 1726. He cast some good bells, but not pleasing the people of S. Ives, for whom he cast a ring, they instituted a law-suit against him. The case was tried at the Huntingdon Assizes held at S. Ives, in 1729, and the verdict given in favour of Penn. After the trial, as he was mounting his horse in the Inn-yard at S. Ives, to return to Peterborough, he fell down dead from over excitement.*

## CHACOMBE, NORTHANTS.

THERE was a foundry here worked by the Bagleys from 1664 to the end of the eighteenth, or beginning of the nineteenth century.† The only bells in Leicestershire from thence are two by

HENRY BAGLEY—one at Leire, and one at Misterton dated 1675, and the whole ring at Great Easton, cast by

HENRY BAGLEY and MATTHEW BAGLEY in 1684.

## KETTERING, S. NEOTS, AND DOWNHAM MARKET.

THOMAS AND JOSEPH EAYRE, both of whose bells are plentiful in Leicestershire, were in partnership in 1717, when

---

* *Nichols' Leicestershire, Framland Hundred*, under Waltham.    † Lukis' *Church Bells, p.* 14.

they cast a bell at Yelden, Bedfordshire.* Subsequently

THOMAS EAYRE established himself at Kettering. His bells in this county date from 1720, at Blaston, to 1762, at Saddington. Mr. Fortrey, of King's Norton—a great admirer of bells, and a liberal contributor to their improvement—was a patron, and a good customer of Thomas Eayre.

JOSEPH EAYRE had a foundry at S. Neots. He was casting bells in Cambridgeshire as early as 1735, but he appears to have found no employment in Leicestershire until the death of Thomas Eayre. Joseph Eayre's earliest bells in this county are dated 1763, at Church Langton, his latest 1770, at Catthorpe and Knighton. After his death the foundry at S. Neots was held jointly for a short time, by his late foreman, Thomas Osborn, and by his cousin, Edward Arnold. After they dissolved partnership

THOMAS OSBORN set up for himself at Downham Market,† from which place he supplied, in 1795, the ring of bells now in Wymeswold Church.

EDWARD ARNOLD continued the business at S. Neots, sending bells from thence into Leicestershire from 1773 (Quorndon and Countesthorpe) till 1778 (Ratcliffe Culey). In 1784 he opened his foundry at Leicester, and cast the Rothley ring, still, however, keeping on the S. Neots foundry, calling himself of S. Neots and Leicester, upon the Medbourne 4th bell, in 1784.‡ Arnold is said to have known little of the art of Bellfounding himself, but to have depended

---

* *Church Bells of Cambridgeshire*, p. 58.    † Ibid. p. 60, and *Church Bells of Norfolk*, p. 48.
‡ For more as to Arnold and his successors, see page 73.

upon the skill of one Islip Edmonds, his foreman. Upon the death of Arnold this Islip Edmonds transferred his services to John Briant of Hertford "a man of the Arnold stamp."*

## HERTFORD.

JOHN BRIANT, of Hertford, Bellfounder, who supplied many bells to Leicestershire churches, was born at Exning, in Suffolk. Though designed for Holy Orders, his love for mechanism was so strong that he was allowed to follow his natural bent. He died in 1829, aged 81 years, and was buried at Hertford.† His bells in this county date from 1802 to 1822. In one instance (Shepeshead) his son's name is associated with his own. Upon the 3rd bell at Walton J. Palmer's name appears as joint founder. He was probably a local ironmonger, as was B. Cort, whose name is given with John Briant as a founder of bells at Barkby and Diseworth.

## MODERN LONDON FOUNDERS.

THERE are many bells in Leicestershire from the White-chapel Foundry, London.‡

Thomas Lester held this foundry in 1738-1752,—Thomas Pack then became his partner.

---

* *Church Bells of Cambridgeshire, pp,* 60-61.

† *Notes and Queries,* 3rd s. vol. ix. p. 85.

‡ Interesting accounts of this foundry are given by Mr. A. Tyssen, Mr. L'Estrange, and Dr. Raven.

LESTER AND PACK supplied the 2nd bell to Normanton Church in 1769. In that year the firm was strengthened by the addition of William Chapman, and the new firm

LESTER PACK AND CHAPMAN cast five bells of the Appleby Magna ring in the same year. After Lester's death

PACK AND CHAPMAN held the foundry until 1781, sending bells into Leicestershire to Bringhurst in 1776, and to Shepey Magna in 1778. William Mears joined Chapman soon after the death of Pack in 1781, and in his family the foundry has continued to the present time.

THOMAS MEARS AND SON cast Blaby 3rd bell in 1807.

THOMAS MEARS' bells are plentiful in the county from 1809 (Tugby 2nd) till 1840 (Groby ring of five).

C. AND G. MEARS supplied the bell to Holwell in 1850.

MEARS AND STAINBANK cast, in 1873, two new bells for Buckminster.

MESSRS. JOHN WARNER AND SONS, of the Crescent Foundry, have supplied bells to S. John's Church, Leicester (1), and to Harston (3rd).

## BIRMINGHAM.

MR. JAMES BARWELL of Birmingham cast two bells for Higham on the Hill in 1872.

## ALPHABET BELLS.

UPON many of the Leicestershire Bells cast by the Leicester founders are portions of the Alphabet. It has been suggested that the founders being desirous not to offend by placing ancient, and therefore often unwelcome, inscriptions upon their bells, and yet being too illiterate to suggest new ones, adopted this plan to escape the difficulty. By it they ornamented their bells with a goodly show of Gothic capitals which could give offence to no one. This may have been the case with the later bells, but the use of the alphabet surely had another origin on the more ancient ones. We find the alphabet, or portions of it, on encaustic tiles on the floors of churches. It appeared on the top of a Norman Font discovered at Severn Stoke in Warwickshire. In the Pontificale Romanum the Bishop is directed in the dedication of a church to write in the form of a cross two alphabets, one in Greek and the other in Latin, first from the East to West, then from North to South. There was clearly some symbolic meaning in the alphabet. Some writers on the subject say the letters represented the beginning and rudiments of sound doctrine, and the simple and pure truths of the Gospel.

# PECULIAR USES.

T HE only direction as to the use of a Church Bell in the Rubrics of the Book of Common Prayer is in that relating to Daily Service:

> "And the Curate that ministereth in every Parish-Church or Chapel, being at home, and not being otherwise reasonably hindered, shall say the same in the Parish-Church or Chapel where he ministereth, and shall cause a Bell to be tolled thereunto a convenient time before he begin, that the people may come to hear God's Word, and to pray with him."

The Canons give a few more directions:

The 15th which directs "*Litany to be read on Wednesdays and Fridays*," orders, that warning be "given to the people by tolling of a bell."

The 67th Canon entitled "*Ministers to visit the Sick*" says:

> "And, when any is passing out of this life, a bell shall be tolled, and the Minister shall not then slack to do his last duty. And after the party's death, if it so fall out, there shall be rung no more than

one short peal, and one other before the burial, and one other after the burial."

So much for their use.

The 88th Canon directs churchwardens not to allow the superstitious use of bells upon "Holydays or Eves abrogated by the Book of Common Prayer, nor at any other times without good cause to be allowed by the Minister of the place, and by themselves." And the 111th Canon is directed against such as shall..."by untimely ringing of bells...hinder the Minister or Preacher."

RINGING FOR DIVINE SERVICE. Although one bell is all that is really essential for carrying out such of these directions as are now usually followed, it is generally only poverty or some other difficulty, which hinders the erection in our modern churches of a number of bells, with which to ring those peals, in which almost all English churchmen delight. And so it was in more ancient times. It will be seen that in Leicestershire some of the larger churches had five bells in the reign of Edward VI., and that whilst many had not more than three, scarcely any were satisfied with less than two. The chapel of S. John Baptist at Mountsorrell stood alone, so far as I can trace, in possessing "seven litell bells in the steple ther."

In churches where the Canonical Hours were kept the bells, or some of them, would be ringing very frequently; for "the ringing of these Canonical hours let the world know the time, by day and by night; and in those larger churches where such a custom was followed, the several bells, as well as the different ways in which they were rung for the purpose, told the precise service which was then about to be chanted."*   " Bishop Oldham (of Exeter) in his Statutes, 1511, directs how the *Annualarii* (or Chantry Priests) were to sound or toll a certain number of times with one bell, then a full tolling of all the bells, at the Canonical Hours, after the accustomed manner; at the close of which the service was to begin."†   In our smaller parish churches, too, those bells appropriated to the side altars in chantry chapels, or belonging to Guilds and Fraternities, would very frequently be sounding.   On Sundays and high-days all the bells appear to have been rung for Matins and Evensong—the two services which all were expected to attend : and so the custom has continued to the present time.   The Bell-master of Loughborough, in the time of Edward VI., was "to help to reng to sarvys if ned be."   Hooper, in his Injunctions, dated 1551, whilst forbidding ringing at unseasonable times, adds " but before services, as well morning as at even, to warn the people by as many peals or ringings as they think good."

In 1621 the Churchwardens of S. Martin's, Leicester, paid 3*s*. " ffor ringeinge to praiers every sabboth and holie daie." The mode of ringing or of chiming for Divine Service varies somewhat in different parishes.   The "uses" followed at the Leicester churches, and at a few others in the county,

---

* Dr. Rock's *Church of Our Fathers*, iii. part 2, p. 143.

† *The Cathedral Bells of Exeter*, p. 13. The Canonical Hours were Prime 6 a.m., Tierce, Mass, at 9 a.m., Sext at Noon, Nones at 3 p.m., Vespers at 6 p.m., Compline at 9 p.m., Matins and Lauds in the early hours between midnight and Prime.

are given under the different churches further on, when the bells are described.

With the introduction of the "new sarvis" (as the Book of Common Prayer was called) in the time of Edward VI., the singing of the Canonical Hours—with the exception of Matins and Evensong—was dropped. The only traces of them we now have in the use of our church bells, excepting the ringing or chiming for Morning and Evening Prayer, are in the ringing of the "first and second peals" on Sunday mornings, at seven and eight, or eight and nine o'clock, in many of our Leicestershire parishes. In Pre-Reformation times Matins were said in all parish churches before breakfast, as a preparation for mass. The "first peal" was the call to Matins, the "second peal" to tierce and mass.* It is a curious proof how tenacious custom is in having continued the ringing of these bells for over three hundred years after the purposes they served were abrogated, and when few even think of, or enquire as to, the meaning of their sound.†

With regard to the "Sermon-Bell" it may be remarked that the Royal Injunctions of 1547 order a bell in convenient time to be rung or knolled before the sermon. When Hugh Latimer visited Melton Mowbray, and preached in the

---

* Sir Thomas More said "Some of us laye men think it a payne ones a weeke to ryse so soon fro sleepe, and some to tarye so longe fasting, as on the Sonday to com and heare out theyr matins."—*Rock,* iii. part 2, pp. 5, 143, 146.

† See The Rev. H. T. Ellacombe's *Bells of the Cathedral Church of Exeter* for Bishop Grandisson's Statutes as to the ringing of the bells there in 1339, and for Bishop Oldham's Statutes relating to the same, in 1511.

church there, that custom was followed; for the church-wardens charge in their accounts :—

> "1553 October. Itm. payd to John Hynmane and to
> Robert Bagworth for rynginge of yᵉ great bell for
> master latimore sarmon ................................     ij*d*."

The Sermon bell was sometimes rung during the Litany to give notice to the people that the sermon was coming on;* and one of the duties of the Bell-ringer at Exeter Cathedral, in 1670, was "to toll yᵉ Sermon Bell every Sunday after the second lesson of the Quire Service in yᵉ morning when there is a sermon."† The Puritans were so often ready to go to Sermon, but not to Prayers, that the bishops tried to check the unseemly practice of going into church after Prayers were said, by directing attention to it in their Visitation Articles, and Wren (1640) directed with regard to the Sermon-bell " That the same ringing of bells should be observed at all times whether there was a Sermon or not."‡ The ringing of this bell before the service when a sermon is to be preached is now the general custom in Leicestershire.§

---

* See Lathbury's *Hist. of Book of Com. Prayer*, 2nd Ed. p. 83.

† *Bells of Exeter Cathedral*, p. 83.

‡ Lathbury, p. 175-6.

§ My friend Mr. Wm. Kelly very kindly calls my attention to the following regulation made in Leicester in the year 1625 when the Plague was there: "At a meeting of Mr. Maior, Mr. Recorder and the xxiiij^tie the xxvth day of July 1625—It is agreed that the Wednesday exercise of ffastinge, praying and preachinge be held at eu'ie seuerall parish church w^thin this Borough and that no bell shall be ru[n]ge for the sermon at any church in regarde of the heate of the wether and the daunger of the tyme."—*Borough of Leicester Hall Book*, p. 457.

The tenor bell at Banbury, dated 1667, referring to this custom, is inscribed :

> " I ring to sermon with a lusty boome
> That all may come and none may stay at home."

THE PASSING-BELL. Besides the use of bells for calling to Divine Service the Canons enjoin the tolling of the " Passing-bell." The custom of notifying, by this means, the passing of a soul out of this life, is almost, if not quite, as ancient, in this country, as the use of bells by the church. Bede mentions " the well known sound of the bell by which they [the Nuns of Hackness] were wont to be aroused or assembled to prayers when any one of them was called forth from this world," as being heard in the year 680.[*]

Durand, who wrote about the end of the twelfth century, says : " when any one is dying bells must be tolled that the people may put up their prayers, twice for a woman and thrice for a man ; if for a clergyman as many times as he had orders."[†] The Passing-bell was, of course, then rung at all hours of the night, as well as by day.

After the Reformation the custom of ringing the Passing-bell in the ancient way was continued.

Bishop Hooper in his Injunctions, issued in 1551, says :

> " Item. That from henceforth there be no knells or forthfares rung for the death of any man ; but in case they that be sick and in danger, or any of their friends will demand to have the bell toll whiles the sick is in extremes to admonish people of their danger, and by that means to solicitate the 'hearers to pray for the sick person, they may use it."

---

[*] Bede, Book iv. c. xxiii.    [†] *Brand's Pop. Ant.* ii. 129.

The Passing-bell is enjoined by the royal Injunctions of 1559, and the Advertisements, issued in the year 1564 show that it was still usual to ring or toll the Passing-bell whilst the person was believed to be dying, but not yet dead: "That where anye Christian bodie be passing that the bell be tolled, and that the curate be specially called for to comforte the sicke person." The bell was ordered to be used by Grindal in 1570, " to move the people to pray for the sick person."*

The Bishops, in after years, enquired in their Articles whether the Passing-bell was so tolled. In 1624 D'Ewes mentions the bell tolling for a person whom he visited, and who lived some hours afterwards. The Puritans used the Passing-bell, as Fuller shows in his account of John Rainolds, one of the Puritan advocates of the Hampton Court Conference: he says: " The morrow after, death seazing upon all parts of his body, he expressed by signes that he would have the passing-bell tole for him."†

Amongst the fees belonging to the Bell-ringer of Exeter Cathedral in 1670 were:

"For tolling the bell for every sick person...................... 1s.
For every childe .................................................. 6d."‡

The custom was continued to recent times. Nelson in his *Meditations for the Holy Time of Lent*, speaking of a good christian says: " If his sense hold out so long he can hear

---

* Lathbury, p. 86.    † Ibid. p. 151-2.    ‡ *Bells of Exeter Cathedral*, p. 32.

his passing-bell without disturbance."* At Melton Mowbray, in this county, the custom was first departed from in the case of Mr. Crane, who died about 1738. He "was the first person in Melton," says Nichols, "for whom the bell tolled after death, till when the custom was for it to pass before, agreeably to the primitive institution." The inscriptions on some of the tenor bells in the county refer to their use for the Passing-bell: *e.g.*: at Muston:

> " All men that heare my mornful sound
> Repent before you lye in grond."

At Stathern:

> " My roaring sounde doth warning geve
> That men cannot heare always lyve."

The bell now used for the Passing-bell, (or more properly the Death-knell) is usually the tenor, but this is sometimes changed in the case of children, as at Bowden Magna, Lutterworth, and Market Harborough, where smaller bells are used. At the close of the Passing-bell it has long been the custom to indicate the sex of the person departing, or departed, by certain strokes or tolls of the bell. These have generally been three for a male (in honour of the Holy

---

* *Bells of the Church*, p. 273, where the following instance is given from Brayley's *History of the Tower*, p. 460. " We have a remarkable mention of this custom in the narrative of the last moments of the Lady Catherine, sister of Lady Jane Grey, who died a prisoner in the Tower of London, in 1567; Sir Owen Opton, Constable of the Tower, perceiving her drawing towards her end, said to Mr. Bokeham, ' Were it not best to send to the church that the bell may be rung?' and she herself hearing him, said, ' Good, Sir Owen, be it so,' and immediately died."

P

Trinity) and two for a female (in honour of our Saviour born of a woman) on the tenor bell, as at Melton Mowbray, Wigston Magna, Bowden Magna, &c. Sometimes, as at Belgrave, the tolls are repeated on three bells, and sometimes, as at Syston, North and South Kilworth, Asfordby, Lutterworth, &c., the tolls are given on all the bells. Again, the tolls—three for a male and two for a female— are frequently repeated thrice on the tenor bell, as at Lutterworth, Skeffington, Billesdon, Claybrooke, Swinford, &c. At Kegworth, thrice three are tolled on three bells for a male, and thrice two on two bells for a female. Other peculiarities will probably be mentioned under the descriptions of the bells in some of the parishes.

At Frisby, and elsewhere, these tolls are called "tellers," and it has been suggested that the old saying:

> " Nine *tailors make* a man "

is a corruption of a saying arising from the thrice three tolls or " tellers " at the close of the passing-bell,

> " Nine *tellers mark* a man."

DEATH KNELL. In addition to the Passing-bell, the Canon enjoins that " after the party's death, if it so fall out, there shall be rung no more than one short peal." Durand mentions this custom, and after the Reformation it is referred to in some of the Articles of Enquiry issued by the bishops in such words as these…" or to ring a knell presently after the departure, that notice may be taken by all to give God thanks for that party's deliverance out of

this vale of misery."*   This custom has now fallen entirely
into disuse; but a trace of it may be found in some parishes,
as at Humberstone, where the bell is *tolled* for fifteen minutes,
and then *rung* for ten minutes.

In the Accounts of the Churchwardens of S. Martin's,
Leicester, are many entries of receipts for the ringing of
bells at the obits or anniversaries of the deaths of persons,
who left a provision for certain Offices to be said upon those
days for the benefit of their souls.†   This was sometimes
called a " soul-peal."

BURIAL PEALS.   The Canon mentions "and one other
(peal) before the burial, and one after the burial."

This sounding of bells at funerals was an ancient custom,
and had been carried to great excess ; indeed, so early as
1339 Bishop Grandisson, of Exeter, found it desirable to
check the long ringings on such occasions, on the grounds
that "they do no good to the departed, are an annoyance
to the living, and injurious to the fabrick and the bells."‡
We find traces of this custom constantly in Churchwardens'
Accounts.   For instance in those of S. Martin's, Leicester,
for the year 1546, under the head of burials, there is a long
list of such entries as these :

Itm̄ for yᵉ buryall of Mr. Clought v bells and lyenge in
    yᵉ churche ...................................................... xijs.
Itm̄ Agnys brown iiij belles ........................................ xxd.
Itm̄ Best Wyffe iij belles ........................................ viijd.

---

* *Vide* Walcott's Ed. of *Canons, &c.*, p. 94.   † North's *Chronicle of S. Martin's Church,
Leicester.*   ‡ *Bells of Exeter Cathedral*, p. 7.

Itm̄ ij chyldren of Wīllm Mābres thon iij bells and yᵉ
    thod' iiij bells ................................................. ijs. iiijd.
Itm̄ Mr. gyllotts dought' iiij belles ........................... xxd.*

The following regulations, made as to the ringing of bells
at funerals, in S. Martin's parish, are found in the same
Account Books, and throw some light upon the custom :

1570-1. An Acte made by Mr. Mayor and hys brethren
    yt yf anye of yᵉ xxiiij or theyr wyves do depte yᵘ
    Lyfe yf they have but yᵉ great bell they must pay
    for yt ................................................. vs.
    and for any one of yᵉ xlviij or theyr wyves do depte
    yᵘ Lyfe must pay for yᵉ same bell ................ iijs. iiijd.
    and for yᵉ best Com̄mners for yᵉ same bell ......... ijs.
    and yᵉ mydle Com̄mners for yᵉ same bell ........... xijd.

The next entry shows that the custom was not universal :

1584-5. It is agreed by this Pīsh that if any of the
    chyldren of the Mayors brethren or ther wyves
    departe thys lyf yf the have any bells the shall paye
    accordinge to the custome and if the have not the
    bells the shall pay for the buriall of every chyld...    xijd.
    and for every one of the xlviij for there chyldren...    vjd.
    and for every one of the best Commoners for there
    children ......................................................    iiijd.
    If the be buried in the churche yard.

1611-12. M̄. it is fully condiscended and agreed that if any bells
    be Ronge at any buryall hereafter and the Seckerston first
    not haveinge the churchwardens consent or one of them for
    the payment of the money for the saide buryall That then
    the Seckerston shall be dismissed of his office for the first

---

* See a long list in North's *Chronicle of S. Martin's Church,* pp. 82-4.

defaulte. And if the churchwardens have knowledge and take not sufficient securytie, that then they shall paye for the Ringinge themselves.

I find traces of the ringing at Funerals a few years later in this parish :—

1626-7. Item for the bells and buriall of Mr. Thomas
Erick's wife ................................................... xij*s*.

In 1649 the churchwardens of Loughborough say :—

It is agreed at this Assembly by the consent of all present that the great bell shall not be rung at any buriall except once for the passing peale and that there shall be no other ringinge but all ye belles or 2 or 3.

This custom of chiming or ringing all the bells lingered in several parishes in Leicestershire until recently. At Frisby it was used until the year 1842; at Oadby in the case of one family (see under Oadby further on) until 1844; and at Sapcote Mrs. Spencer, who died in the year 1847, expressed a wish that the bells should be chimed at her funeral, and her wish was granted. At Saxelby it is still the rule for the bells to be chimed on the arrival of the funeral procession at the church gates, and to continue to be chimed until all are within the church. I am not aware of any other instance of the retention of this custom in Leicestershire.

It is usual in most parishes for the great bell to toll during the procession from the house to the church, and in some cases again on the return of the mourners home. At

Hinckley the bell tolls during the recital of the Burial Office at the cemetery.

Nichols relates a custom as followed at Barwell, at the funeral of Mrs. Anne Power, who died 29 September 1785. She was he says a wealthy maiden lady, and at her funeral "agreeably to the custom of the country on the interment of a spinster, the corpse was welcomed to the church with a merry peal; and an elegant entertainment was distributed to a numerous circle of friends and neighbouring dependents." This custom was not peculiar to Leicestershire. In some places under similar circumstances a muffled peal was rung, and the giving of doles to the poor formed a large feature at funerals in mediæval times.

In addition to these uses of the church bell mentioned in the Rubric, and in the Canons, there are several others calling for brief notice.

THE SANCTUS BELL. In the Inventories of church goods taken in the reign of Edward VI. where the bells are enumerated, a "sanctus bell," a "sauntys bell," or a "lytyll bell in the stepull," is generally mentioned.* It was usually hung, in order that it might be heard by those outside, as well as by those within the church, in a little bellcote on the gable of the chancel roof between that portion of the church and the nave, or else in a convenient position in the belfry, so that the rope came down into the church within easy access to the server at the altar. When

---

* The Churchwardens of Melton Mowbray in their Accounts for 1553 call this bell "Sants bell"—"Sanctus bell" and "Saunce bell" indifferently.

the priest said the *Sanctus* in the Office of the Mass three
strokes were given on this bell (hence its name) so that all
—the sick man in his chamber, as well as the worshipper
in the church—could join in the holy song of adoration. A
few successors of the sanctus bell are in the bell-chambers
of our Leicestershire churches, in the "priest's bell" or
"ting-tang" usually rung immediately before the service
begins. These are, in almost all cases, modern, being
probably recasts of the ancient sanctus-bells. At Lutterworth, however, hangs a small bell 18 inches in diameter—
and so weighing about 1½ cwt.—which was used as a sanctus
bell in Pre-Reformation times. It was cast by the Leicester
founders, for it bears the initial cross used by the earlier
Newcombes (fig. 3) and the inscription or dedication :

+ PE + TER

It is a curious coincidence with its original use that this
(the only original sanctus-bell in Leicestershire) is now
called "The Sacrament-Bell," and is rung instead of the
sermon-bell, in the summons to Divine Service, whenever
there is to be a celebration of the Holy Communion.

THE SACRING-BELL. This was a small hand-bell also
used in the Office of the Mass to warn the people that the
Elevation was about to take place. The necessity for this
of course passed away when the Reformed Liturgy, or Order
of the Holy Communion, was commanded to be used in
English in 1547. In 6 Edward VI. these bells are mentioned ("hande belles") as belonging to several churches
in Leicestershire.

An interesting example of the ancient sacryng-bell was
found (in August 1870) in a putlog hole in the western wall
of the south aisle of Bottesford Church, Lincolnshire.  This
relic was exhibited by Mr. Edward Peacock F.S.A. at a
meeting of the Society of Antiquaries, London, and is fully
described by him in the *Proceedings* of the Society, No. xxiv.
1870, p. 24.

My best thanks are due to the Society of Antiquaries for
permission to use the annexed engraving of this bell.  The
engraving is two-thirds the size of the original.

THE CURFEW.  The origin of the Curfew is well-known.
It was heard in Normandy at an early date, and its use was

enforced throughout this country—where it appears to have been partially instituted by King Alfred—by William the Conqueror. When it sounded at eight o'clock every even⸱ ing, all persons were ordered to extinguish fire and candle, hence its name—*couvre feu.* Although its sound, and its use, were only enforced during the reigns of William the Conqueror and William Rufus—the law of Curfew was abolished by Henry I. in 1100—the custom of ringing the bell still prevails in many parishes in this country. Its continuance is to be attributed to a religious, and not to a civil, purpose. The evening " Hail Mary" was ordered by Pope John XXII., (1316-34,) to be said at the sound of a bell called the "*Angelus,*" and it is probable the Curfew was continued as a warning to all to say an " Ave " to the Blessed Virgin before retiring to rest. Dr. Rock says: " If this Curfew did not give pious individuals the earliest thought of saying an " Ave " at night-fall, the ringing of the bell was in itself so seasonable that it was looked upon, and employed, as a happy incident for calling upon the people, whether in town or country—throughout the land in fact—to say their greetings to the Virgin at sun- down."*

Previous to the Reformation (as we gather from Hooper's Injunctions in 1551) the ringing of the " Curfaye" in some places was accompanied by, or replaced by, the ringing of all the bells in the steeple.

---

* *Church of our Fathers,* iii. p. 337.

Q

Although since the Reformation the custom of ringing
the Curfew, or last Angelus, has gradually been waning,
still the practice lingers in many of our Leicestershire
parishes, where it has no doubt been continuously followed
since its first institution.   For instance, we know the
"Corfir" was rung at Loughborough in the reign of Edward
the Sixth, and it rings there still.   It is generally still rung
at eight o'clock, though in some instances this is varied.
At Waltham on the Wolds, and at Kegworth, it rings at
eight o'clock on all evenings, excepting Saturday, when it
rings at seven o'clock.

In several parishes in Leicestershire the continuance of
the Curfew was sought to be secured by an endowment,
provided by persons, who, in times when the roads were
badly defined, and crossed an open unenclosed country, lost
their way in the gloom of evening, or in the darkness of
winter early nights, but were enabled to find their village
home by its welcome sound.

At S. Martin's, Leicester, it is rung at nine o'clock, and
has been rung at that hour for a long period.   We learn
from the *Town Book of Acts* of the Borough of Leicester,
that on the 17th November, 1553, it was enacted at a
Common Hall—a man having been killed in the street—that
no person of what degree soever inhabiting in the town or
suburbs should go abroad in the street after nine o'clock at
night and after the Curfew bell had left ringing, excepting
officers and watch; and that the said bell should be rung
nightly from Michaelmas till Lady-day in Lent; for which
the twenty-four were to pay 2*d.* and the forty-eight 1*d.*

each.* The following stringent bye-law was also passed 22 February, 25th Elizabeth. "Item, that the keeper of any ale-house that suffers any townsman to remain in his house after the Curfew bell hath rung (without lawful cause) shall forfeit 12*d.* to be paid presently, or else to remain in ward that night."†

The Curfew at S. Martin's, Leicester, is called occasion-ally "Bow-bell," both in the Churchwardens' Accounts, and in the Borough Chamberlains' Accounts: *e.g.:* In 1640 Cockle, the parish clerk, being ill, and unable to ring the bell, the churchwardens finding a substitute, say:—

"Paid for Bow-bell when Cockle lay sick ..................... o o 6*d.*"

And in 1563-4 the Chamberlains credit their account with a fine received:

"Itm̄. of Anthony Gymson for walking in the streets
     after bobell ................................................. vj*d.*"

A correspondent informs me that, in 1469, Bow bell in London, was ordered to be rung at nine o'clock in the evening for the closing of shops, and so "Bow-bell" may have become a proverbial term.

After the ringing of the Curfew it is customary in some places, as at Melton Mowbray, to toll the day of the month.

---

* I am much indebted to Wm. Kelly Esq. for a verbatim copy of the curious *Acte for Nyght Walkers* in which the above regulation as to the Curfew is found. It is comprised in a Manuscript Book called the *Town Book of Acts*. This book was known to Nichols; was afterwards missing, and was supposed to be lost; but when the old Exchange, in the Market Place, was taken down it was discovered, with other local MSS., in a box within that building.

† Nichols.

A peculiar custom is followed at Sheepy Magna : the ringing of the Curfew is discontinued during the interval
between the death and the burial of any parishioner : at
Bottesford it is not rung during Whitsun week.

THE MORNING BELL. The origin of the ringing of the
Morning-bell arose from an extension of the practice of saying an "Ave" to the Virgin at nightfall. In 1399 Archbishop Arundel issued a mandate commanding that at early
dawn one "Our Father" and five "Hail Marys" should be
said.* As a reminder to all of this duty the Angelus was
rung. This bell was often called "Gabriel" after the Angel
of the Annunciation ; the second bell at Little Peatling is
so named, and was doubtless rung for this purpose. Again
it often bore an inscription indicative of its purpose, as at
Bottesford (5th bell) which is clearly a repetition from an
older bell :

> "I have the name of Gabriel sent from heaven."

This morning bell was continued to be rung at Melton
Mowbray, at four o'clock, until the year 1708 when it was
discontinued. It is still rung at Loughborough, Lutterworth, S. Martin's, Leicester, (where it was rung in 1549)
Wymeswold, Waltham and other places in the county. It
has long been used simply as a call to daily work. Henry
Penn, the bellfounder, had this in his mind, when he cast
the bell at S. Ives, which is rung there early in the morning ; for he placed upon it the pithy sentence :

> "Arise, and go about your business."

---

* Walcott's *Sac. Arch.* Rock's *Church of Our Fathers.*

A mid-day Angelus was rung in France in the fifteenth century, but the practice does not appear to have been introduced into England. In a few parishes in Leicestershire, as at Bottesford, and the two Kilworths, a mid-day bell is now rung, but—in the absence of all evidence to the contrary—the use may be attributed to a secular origin—the giving warning to agricultural labourers and others of the time—rather than to a religious one.*

THE PANCAKE-BELL. In addition to the occasional confession of sin to the priest, it was considered in mediæval times that the week preceding Lent was specially an appropriate time for all to perform that duty. It was hence called Shrove-tide, and the Tuesday in it called Shrove, Shrive,

---

* It may be worth noting that the "Hail Mary" as now used by Roman Catholics, consists of three portions: (1) the angelic greeting " Hail Mary full of grace, the Lord is with thee : " (2) the greeting of Elizabeth " Blessed art thou among women, and blessed is the fruit of thy womb, Jesus," and (3) " Holy Mary, mother of God, pray for us sinners now, and at the hour of death. Amen." The latter portion was unknown in the English Church, and also to English Roman Catholics three hundred years ago. The "Hail Mary" was unknown *in any form* to the Anglo-Saxons : they were taught the "Our Father" and the "Belief." Neither did the Anglo-Normans use it, the "Our Father" and the "Belief" were still to be taught; and down to the year 1212 "Our Father," but no "Hail Mary," was said before each of the Canonical Hours, according to Lincoln use. In 1237 the "Hail Mary" is first formally mentioned by Alexander de Stavenby bishop of Coventry. This salutation, however, only contained the first two portions of the modern "Ave" —the words of Scripture—and the only Salisbury book in which it appears in its present form is the folio edition of the Sarum Breviary, printed at Paris, in 1531. In this note I have epitomised the words of the learned Roman Catholic ecclesiologist the late Dr. Rock (*Church of our Fathers*, vol. III. pp 315-319) who also says : " In one of the last books of prayers printed in [Roman] Catholic England the "Ave Maria" is as follows: "Hail Mary ful of grace, our Lorde is with thee. Blessed art thou among women, and blessed is the fruyte of thy wombe. Amen." *The Primer in English and Latin after Salisburie use &c.*, A.D. 1556."

or Confession-Tuesday—shrive being an old Saxon word for confession.   The confession was made in the church, where the priest sat in an open chair, or stall, to hear the confessions of his people, to award them such penance as he thought good for them, or to give them absolution.   In order that all might be reminded of this duty, and be informed that the priest was ready to receive them, a bell was rung calling them to the church.   This was the origin of the ringing of the bell on Shrove-Tuesday.

But another custom was followed in those times when Lent was more strictly observed than now as a time of abstinence from flesh meat.   On Shrove-Tuesday, we are told by a writer in *Notes and Queries*, the housewives, in order to use up all the grease, lard, dripping, &c., made pancakes, and the apprentices, and others about the house were summoned to the meal by the ringing of a bell, which was naturally called "the Pancake-bell."*

The ringing of the Shrive-bell, now called the Pancake-bell, is still continued in a great number of Leicestershire parishes on Shrove-Tuesday.   At Belgrave it used to be rung by the oldest apprentice in the parish ;† at its close a peal on all the bells is still rung, after which, the rule is,

---

* *Notes and Queries*, 3rd s. vi, 404.

† The apprentices seem to have set up a claim to ring the Pancake-bell, for at Hedon all the apprentices in the town whose indentures terminate before the return of Shrove-Tuesday assemble in the belfry of the church at eleven o'clock, and in turn toll the tenor bell for an hour; at the sound of which all the housewives in the parish commence frying pancakes.— *Notes and Queries*, 2nd s. v. 391.

At Wolverhampton two bells are rung at twelve o'clock, the interpretation being "pan on."—*Church Bells'* Newspaper, vol. i. p. 154.

that the bells shall not be again rung (only chimed) until Easter Day, so avoiding all ringing during Lent. At Belton, Shrove-Tuesday is kept as a holiday by the children, so it was, to some extent, until recently, at Hinckley.

Shakespeare in *All's well that ends well* speaks of a pancake as fit for Shrove-Tuesday, and Taylor the Water Poet (1630) mentions the Pancake-bell as being then rung on Shrove-Tuesday.

WEDDING PEALS. We find traces of the wedding peal at Loughborough in 1588, when it was

> " Agreed at this accompt that every marridge haveing or reqring to have the bells rung shall paye vj*d*. to the poremens boxe and vj*d*. towards repairinge of the bells . . . . "

So also at S. Martin's, Leicester, it was agreed in 1612-13 that only three peals be rung at weddings for 2*s*. 6*d*. : sixpence to be paid for every peal beyond.

At Humberstone, and at Owston, a peal is rung after Divine Service, on Sunday morning, when the Banns of an intended marriage are first " put up." At Barwell it was customary some years ago to ring, at the funeral of a spinster what was called her wedding peal as her dead body was being conveyed to the church. A muffled peal (as in some places not in this county) would have been more appropriate.

THE FIRE-BELL. At Barrow-on-Soar the bells are rung backwards to give notice of a fire. This is not unusual. On the 7th bell at St. Ives are the words :—

> " When backward rung we tell of fire
> Think how the world shall thus expire."

CALL BELLS. Parish and Church meetings are called in some parishes by ringing a bell. At Melton Mowbray notice is given of a parish meeting by the ringing of the sixth bell for fifteen minutes. The ringers are called for a wedding peal at Hinckley by the treble bell : it is tolled thrice three times, then "pulled up" and "down" again very quickly, after which thrice three tolls are again given. Something similar is probably the custom in other parishes.

THE GLEANING-BELL. In several country parishes, as at Waltham-on-the-Wolds, and Wymondham, a gleaning bell is rung during harvest, both morning and evening, giving warning when gleaning may commence, and when it must close, for the day. This is done in order that all—old and feeble, as well as young and active—may have a fair start.

S. HUGH'S DAY. The bells of Loughborough and Leicester were formerly regularly rung on S. Hugh's day. It need scarcely be said that he was Bishop of Lincoln, and that Leicestershire was until lately in that diocese. He was consecrated in 1186. He rebuilt his cathedral church, carrying, it is said, many of the stones to the workmen employed with his own hands. His funeral was one of the grandest on record. He was carried to the cathedral, where he was buried, by "two kings, John of England and William of Scotland, assisted by some of their nobles, three archbishops, fourteen bishops, and more than a hundred abbots, and buried in a silver shrine."*

---

* *Cal. of Eng. Church, illustrated*, p. 136.

Godwyn, in his Catalogue of Bishops,* says:—" The anniversary of S. Hugh had used to be observed with great solemnity, particularly at Leicester."

The Loughborough Churchwardens charge, in 1584, and in subsequent years:—

"Item pd to the ringers on St. Hew Daiye ...................iiijs. iiijd."

and S. Martin's (Leicester) Churchwardens in 1588, and other years, say:

"Paid to the ringers on St. Hugh's day ......................... viijd."

CATCH-COPE BELLS. In the Accounts of the Church-wardens of S. Martin's, Leicester, are the following entries:

1549-50 Itm rec. of Willm Tayllor Srgant (?) in ernest of the iij Catche Coppe bells aftr xxvs. a hundryth ...    xijd.

Itm pd to Robt Sekerston and Rog. Johnson for takyn downe the iij Catche Coppe bells .....................    xijd.

1550-51. Itm rec. of Mr. Lambt and Mr. Herek for the leyst Catche Cope bell ................................ xxvijs. xjd.

Itm rec. of Willm Tayllor and Willm Syngylton for two of the same bells ...................................... iijli. xjs. viijd.

It will be seen that these bells were small: the first one sold weighed rather over a hundred weight: the others were somewhat larger. That they were rung by ropes is clear from the sale of a "Catche Cope rope" in the year 1547. It has been suggested that these bells were suspended, in a small belfry or campanile, on the gable end of the church, because *Cope* signifies an arch or hill on the top of a wall,

---

* Quoted by Nichols.

R

and that this belfry standing in that position might well be
called " Catch " *i.e.*, *cache cope* from its covering the top of
a wall.*   When the *Chronicle of S. Martin's Church* was
written I did not accept this explanation, but I am more inclined to do so now, because I find in addition to the sale
of the " Catche Cope" rope in 1547, the churchwardens
sold in 1560-1 a " Gable rope," and again in 1561-2 another " Gable rope."   When the chapel at the east end
of the small south aisle in S. Martin's Church was rebuilt
some years ago, a newell staircase was discovered in the
north east angle of the wall, which may have led to this
belfry.   The Rev. Mackenzie E. C. Walcott suggests that
these bells were used as a chime, warning for service, and
says, that at Winchester the bells are chimed after the peal,
and before the single bell.

MISCELLANEOUS RINGING.   In addition to these uses of
our Church Bells in Leicestershire may be mentioned
the "ringing of the old year out and the new year in"—an
old custom: the ringing on the great Festivals of the Church
—in Anglo-Saxon times "from Childermass all through the
holidays a full peal was rung for matins, mass, and evensong :"†—and now we welcome Christmas, Easter, and
Whitsuntide by our joyous peals.   Upon all loyal occasions
we still ring, though perhaps not so lustily as we did in more
exciting times, when we were unhappily frequently at war
with our neighbours.   Then, when our victories by land
and by sea called forth bursts of patriotic thankfulness and

---

* *Notes and Queries*, 3rd s. ii. p. 439.      † Rock, vol. iii. part 2, p. 56.

exultation from Englishmen, their feelings found expression in no way more strongly than in the joyous and jubilant ringing of our glorious and spirit-stirring rings of bells. The Accounts of the Churchwardens of S. Martin's, Leicester, teem with entries of payments to the ringers for their services on such occasions in the first fifteen years of the present century, winding up with the "capture of Bounaparte" in those for the year 1815-16.

No doubt Church Bells have been in past years rung upon most improper occasions. Happily they are now looked upon as part of the ornaments, or requisite furniture, of a church, and set apart with it to be used for holy and sacred purposes, and upon occasions, when by their exhilarating sounds, they can add to the joyous thankfulness and innocent pleasure of all within reach of their sound. Of their occasionally perverted use within the memory of many living, it will be well not to speak further, but rather to rejoice that a better feeling, and better customs, now prevail.

The few Traditions I have collected about the Leicestershire Church Bells will be found further on under the different parishes.

*Ancient Bell-tile found at Repton, Derbyshire.*

# LATIN INSCRIPTIONS

ON

# CHURCH BELLS IN LEICESTERSHIRE.

[ WITH TRANSLATIONS.* ]

———————◆———————

AD MAJOREM DEI GLORIAM.
[ *To the greater glory of God.* ]

AVE MARIA.
[ *Hail Mary.* ]

AVE MARIA GRACIA PLENA.
[ *Hail Mary, full of grace.* ]

AVE MARIA GRACIA PLENA DOMINVS TECVM.
[ *Hail Mary, full of grace, the Lord is with thee.* ]

AVE SANCTA MARIA.
[ *Hail Holy Mary.* ]

BEATA MARIA.
[ *Blessed Mary.* ]

CÆLORVM CHRISTE PLACEAT TIBI REX SONVS ISTE.
[ *Be Christ the King of Heaven*
*Pleased when this sound is given.* ]

———  —  ——————————————

* For these I am indebted to the kindness of a friend.

CLEMENS ATQVE PIA MISERIS SVCCVRRE MARIA.
[ *Mary, merciful and loving, succour the afflicted.* ]

CREDE RESIPECE MORI MEMENTO.
[ *Believe, Repent, Remember Death.* ]

CUM SONO SI NON VIS VENIRE
NUNQUAM AD PRECES CUPIES IRE.
[ *If you're unwilling to come when I call*
*To prayers you'll not wish to go at all.* ]

CUM VOCO VENITE.
[ *Come when I call.* ]

CYMBALA DULCITO QUO DEMULCENT CARMINE CAMPOS.
[ *Let the Bells sweetly sound*
*A strain to charm the fields around.* ]

DISSI MORE NOSTRI VIVERE DISSE SONO.
[ *To our people I cry*
*Learn to live, learn to die.* ]

ECCLESIAM CONSERVAT DEUS.
[ *God preserve the Church.* ]

EX DONO BELLAMONTIS DIXIE IN FELICISSIMUM
CAROLI REGIS SECUNDI REDITUM.
[ *The gift of Beaumont Dixie on the most auspicious return of King*
*Charles the Second.* ]

FILIO DEI UNIGENITO SACRUM.
[ *Sacred to the Only Begotten Son of God.* ]

GAVDETE IN DOMINO ET EXVLTATE IVSTI.
[ *Rejoice in the Lord ye righteous, and be glad.* ]

GERET NOMEN MAGDALENE CAMPANA.
[ *The bell shall bear the name of Magdalene.* ]

## GLORIA DEO SOLI.
[ *Glory to God alone.* ]

## GLORIA PATRI FILIO ET SPIRITUI SANCTO.
[ *Glory be to the Father, and to the Son, and to the Holy Ghost.* ]

## GLORIA DEO IN EXCELSIS.
[ *Glory to God in the highest.* ]

## GRATA SIT ARGUTA RESONANS CAMPANULA VOCE.
[ *Pleasant be the sound of this little bell's clear voice.* ]

## HEC CAMPANA CELIS RESONET SANCTI MICHAELIS.
[ *May this bell resound to the praise of S. Michael in heaven.* ]

## HEC CAMPANA BEATA SACRA TRINITATE FIAT.
[ *Be this bell sacred to the Holy Trinity.* ]

## HUIUS SCI PETRI.
[ *Saint Peter's Bell.* ]   There are several similar inscriptions to other Saints.

## IH'S NAZARENVS REX IVDEORVM FILI DEI MISERERE MEI.
[ *Jesus of Nazareth King of the Jews. O Son of God have mercy on me.* ]   There
are several bells bearing the first portion of this inscription only.

## IN HONOREM GULIELMI CUMBRIÆ DUCIS REBELLES SCOTOS VICTRICIBUS ARMIS DEBELLANTIS 1745.
[ *In honour of William Duke of Cumberland overcoming with victorious arms
the rebellious Scots.* ]

## IN HONORE SANCTI LEONARDI.
[ *In honour of S. Leonard.* ]·

## IN MULTIS ANNIS RESONAT CAMPANA IOHANNIS.
[ *For many years John's Bell resounds.* ]

## INTACTUM SILEO PERCUTE DULCE CANO.
[ *Untouched I am a silent thing
But strike me and I sweetly ring.* ]

ISTA CĀPANA EST CŌPOSITA IN HONORE B̄TE
MARIA VIR̄GIS.

[ *This bell has been founded in honour of the Blessed Virgin Mary.* ]

ISTA CAMPANA FACTA EST IN HONORE SANCTE
TRINITATE.

[ *This bell has been made in honour of the Holy Trinity.* ]   There are several
similar inscriptions.

LAVDATE DOMINVM CYMBALIS SONORIS.

[ *Praise the Lord on the loud cymbals.* ]

LAVDATE ILLVM CYMBALIS SONORIS.

[ *Praise Him on the loud cymbals.* ]

LAUS TIBI SIT TRIN'E TIBI GLORIA SIT SINE FINE.

[ *Praise be to Thee O Trinity, and to Thee be glory for ever.* ]

LAVS TIBI DOMINE.

[ *Praise to Thee O Lord.* ]

LAUS DOMINI NOSTRA MOBILITATE VIGET.

[ *The praise of the Lord flourishes through our motion.* ]

MEROREM MESTIS LETIS SIC LETA SONABO.

[ *Sadly to the sad, to the joyous joyful, will I sound.* ]

MISSI DE CELIS HABEO NOMEN GABRIELIS.

[ *I have the name of Gabriel sent from heaven.* ]   There are several similar
inscriptions.

MORABOR IN DOMO DOMINI IN LONGITVDINEM DIERVM.

[ *I will dwell in the house of the Lord all the days of my life.* ]

MORTE BEATA NIHIL BEATIUS.

[ *Nothing happier than a happy death.* ]

MORTEM REGINE DEFLEAT ANG: COLATUR PAX
FLOREAT ECCLESIA.

[ *Let England weep her Queen's death.   Let Peace be cherished, and the
Church flourish.* ]

MORS ADEST PARA.

[ *Death is here, prepare.* ]

MVLTI VOCATI PAVCI ELECTI.

[ *Many called few chosen.* ]

NOMEN MAGDALENE CAMPANA GERET MELODIE.

[ *This bell shall bear in its sound the name of Magdalene.* ]

NOMEN SANCTE IESU NOS SERVA MORTIS AB ESU.

[ *By Jesu's Holy Name be we
From the bite of death kept free.* ]

NON CLAMOR SED AMOR CANTAT IN AVRE.

[ *Love's voice not noise
Sings in the ear.* ]

NOS SVMVS CONSTRVCTI AD LAVDEM DOMINI.

[ *We are cast to the Glory of God.* ]

OMNE TULIT PUNCTUM QUI MISCUIT UTILE DULCI.

[ *Who hath blended the useful with the pleasing hath gained every point.* ]

OMNIA FIANT AD GLORIAM DEI.

[ *Do all to the glory of God.* ]

OMNIS CARNALIS VIS FORTIS CONGRUIT HERBIS.

[ *All the strength of flesh is as grass.* ]

OMNIVM SANCTORVM.

[ *(In honour of) All Saints.* ]

PATRI UNICO DEO SACRUM.

[ *Sacred to the Father the only God.* ]

QUOD A PLURIBUS COLLATUM HIC ME PONIT.
[ *A public subscription places me here.* ]

RESONABO LAUDES GENTIS BOOTHBEIANÆ.
[ *I will resound the praise of the Boothby family.* ]

SIT NOMEN DOMINI BENEDICTUM LAUDATE ILLUM
CYMBALIS SONORIS.
[ *Blessed be the Name of the Lord.   Praise Him on the loud cymbals.* ]

SOLI DEO GLORIA PAX HOMINIBVS.
[ *To God alone be glory, Peace to men.* ]

SOLI DEO O[PTIMO] M[AXIMO] GLORIA IN ÆTERNUM.
[ *To God alone most perfect and mighty be glory for ever.* ]

SOLI DEO IMMORTALE SIT GLORIA.
[ *To God alone immortal be glory.* ]

SONORO MEO SONO RESONO DEO.
[ *With my sonorous sound I sound to God.* ]

SPIRITUI SANCTO SACRUM.
[ *Sacred to the Holy Spirit.* ] .

STATUTUM EST OMNIBUS SEMEL MORI.
OCTO CAMPANAS SACRA EXAUDIMUS IN ARCE DULCES
ALTISONAS O HILARES HILARES.
[ *It is appointed unto all men once to die.   We hear eight bells in the sacred tower
sound soft and loud.   O joyful, joyful !* ]

STELLA MARIA MARIS SUCCURRE PIISSIMA NOBIS.
[ *Mary Star of the Sea most holy succour us.* ]

SUAVIUS IN NULLIS VOX CONCINIT ÆNEA CAMPIS IN
GYRUM GLOMERATA MELOS.
[ *No brazen voice, gathered into the circled bound,
In any other field is found
To sing a song of sweeter sound.* ]

S

SUM ROSA PULSATA MUNDI MARIA VOCATA.
[ *I being rung am called Mary, the Rose of the World.* ]

SURGE AGE.
[ *Arise and come.* ]

SUSCITO VOCE PIOS TU JESU DIRIGE MENTES.
[ *I arouse the pious with my voice. Thou, O Jesus, direct their minds.* ]

TEMPUS TRANIT DEUS VOCAT.
[ *Time passes, God calls.* ]

TEMPUS SED TACITUM SUBRUIT.
[ *Time though silent undermines.* ]

TINNITUS RAPIDOS SCINTILLANS SPARGO PER AURAS.
[ *Bright within, I spread around*
*Through the air rapid sound.* ]

VOX DÑI IHŪ X̄PI WOX EXULTACIONIS.
[ *The voice of the Lord Jesus Christ is the voice of exultation.* ]

VOX MEA EST DULCIS MEA SCINTILLANS VULTUS.
[ *Sweet is my voice and bright my face.* ]

LIST OF THE AVERAGE WEIGHT OF BELLS cast by Messrs. Taylor and Co., of Loughborough, Leicestershire. The diameter being known, a reference to this list will give the approximate weight of any bell.

| DIAMETER. | WEIGHT. | | | DIAMETER. | WEIGHT. | | |
|---|---|---|---|---|---|---|---|
| *Inches.* | *Cwts.* | *Qrs.* | *lbs.* | *Inches.* | *Cwts.* | *Qrs.* | *lbs.* |
| 12 | 0 | 1 | 20 | 37 | 9 | 0 | 0 |
| 13 | 0 | 2 | 6 | 38 | 10 | 0 | 0 |
| 14 | 0 | 2 | 20 | 39 | 11 | 0 | 0 |
| 15 | 0 | 3 | 16 | 40 | 12 | 0 | 0 |
| 16 | 1 | 0 | 0 | 41 | 13 | 0 | 0 |
| 17 | 1 | 1 | 0 | 42 | 14 | 0 | 0 |
| 18 | 1 | 2 | 0 | 43 | 15 | 0 | 0 |
| 19 | 1 | 3 | 0 | 44 | 16 | 0 | 0 |
| 20 | 2 | 0 | 0 | 45 | 17 | 0 | 0 |
| 21 | 2 | 1 | 0 | 46 | 18 | 0 | 0 |
| 22 | 2 | 2 | 0 | 47 | 19 | 0 | 0 |
| 23 | 2 | 3 | 0 | 48 | 20 | 0 | 0 |
| 24 | 3 | 0 | 0 | 49 | 21 | 1 | 0 |
| 25 | 3 | 2 | 0 | 50 | 22 | 2 | 0 |
| 26 | 4 | 0 | 0 | 51 | 24 | 0 | 0 |
| 27 | 4 | 2 | 0 | 52 | 25 | 2 | 0 |
| 28 | 4 | 3 | 0 | 53 | 27 | 0 | 0 |
| 29 | 5 | 0 | 0 | 54 | 28 | 2 | 0 |
| 30 | 5 | 2 | 0 | 55 | 30 | 0 | 0 |
| 31 | 6 | 0 | 0 | 56 | 31 | 2 | 0 |
| 32 | 6 | 1 | 0 | 57 | 33 | 2 | 0 |
| 33 | 6 | 2 | 0 | 58 | 36 | 0 | 0 |
| 34 | 7 | 0 | 0 | 59 | 39 | 0 | 0 |
| 35 | 7 | 2 | 0 | 60 | 42 | 0 | 0 |
| 36 | 8 | 1 | 0 | | | | |

# THE INSCRIPTIONS

ON THE

## CHURCH BELLS OF LEICESTERSHIRE,

With, in many cases, the Diameter at the mouth of the Bell from which its approximate weight may be ascertained (see page 131). To which are added Extracts, where procurable, from the Commissioners Returns *temp*. Edward VI., and from Parochial and other Records, together with Local Traditions, and Notes on the Uses of Church Bells peculiar to different parishes.

---

*Note.—The numbers between [ ] refer to the woodcuts on the Plates. It being impossible to reproduce here the various forms of mediæval Gothic letters used on the ancient bells, one form of letter is here used to indicate where Gothic capitals are used [ A B C ] and one form where small Gothic or " black letter " is used [a b c]. For the various forms of Roman letters found on modern bells one form [A B C] will suffice.*

*Errors of spelling, misplacement of letters, &c., &c., in the following inscriptions, are copied literally from the Bells. They are therefore Founders' blunders and not Printers' mistakes.*

# AB-KETTLEBY.

S. JAMES.                          3 BELLS.

1. GOD SAVE HIS CHVRCH 1653 [ ◻ 10.]
2. [ + 3 ] 𝕾 𝕬𝕹 𝖄𝕽 [ ▽ 6. ]
3. THOMAS CROSS C. W. THOMAS HEDDERLY FOUNDER
 NOTTᴍ 1765.

This bell was previously inscribed "Jhesus be our speede 1662."
In 6 Ed. VI. there were "iij bells and a sanctus bell."

# ALLEXTON.

S. PETER.                           4 BELLS.

1. 𝕰𝖉𝖜𝖆𝖗𝖉𝖊 𝕬𝖓𝖉𝖗𝖆𝖜𝖊𝖘 𝖆𝖓𝖓𝖔 𝖉𝖔𝖒𝖊𝖓𝖎 1597.
2. ROBERT BLACKWELL CHVRCHWARDEN 1715.
3. THOMAS   NORRIS   MADE   MEE   1662   T.H.
4. JOHES   BIDDLE   RECTOR   DE   ALASTON   1640   VIVAT
 CAROLVS   REX.

Edward Andrews was lord of the manor: he was a further benefactor
to the church, having given a Porch in the year 1594.
John Biddulph, the loyal rector, was buried 9 Jan. 1641-2.—*Nichols.*

# ANSTY.

S. MARY.                           5 BELLS.

1. GOD REWARD MY BENEFACTORS.
            ( Diam. 29 in. )
2. J. M. HALTON CAST US ALL ANNO MDCCXXᵀIII.
            ( Diam. 30 in. )
3. Blank.
            ( Diam. 32 in. )
4. Blank.
            ( Diam. 35 in. )

5. WILLIAM HARSTAFF JOSEPH LEWIN C. W.
(Diam. 38 in.)

In 6 Ed. VI. there were "Three bells."


## APPLEBY MAGNA.

S. Michael.         6 Bells.

1. THIS BELL RAISED BY SUBSCRIPTION 1774. THE SECOND GAVE BY MR. MOORE'S FAMILY 1769. THE 3rd AND 4th RECAST BY SUBSCRIPTION. THE 5th RECAST BY THE PARISH TO THE OLD TENNOR. LESTER PACK & CHAPMAN LONDON FECIT.
2. LESTER PACK & CHAPMAN OF LONDON
3. LESTER PACK & CHAPMAN FECIT 1769.
4. LESTER PACK & CHAPMAN OF LONDON FECIT 1769.
5. LESTER PACK & CHAPMAN LONDON FECIT 1769.
6. IH'2 : NAZARENVS [ 9 ] REX : IVDEORVM [ 9 ] FILI : DEI [ 9 ] MISERERE : MEI [ 9 ] 1619 [ ⛢ 1. ]


## ARNESBY.

S. Peter.         4 Bells.

1. GOD [ 9 ] SAVE [ 9 ] THE [ 9 ] kING [ 9 ] 1624 [ ⛢ 1. ]
2. CELORVM [ 9 ] CHRSTE [ 9 ] PLATIAT TIBI REX [ 9 ] SONVS ISTE [ 9 ] 1624 [ ⛢ 1. ]
3. IH'2 : NAZARENVS [ 9 ] REX : IVDEORVM [ 9 ] FILI : DEI [ 9 ] MISERERE : MEI [ 9 ] 1624 [ ⛢ 1. ]
4. CVM · SONO · SI · NON · VIS [ 9 ] VENIRE [ 9 ] NVNQVAM · AD · PRECES [ 9 ] CVPIES · IRE [ 9 ] 1624 [ ⛢ 1. ]

On Sundays the 1st bell is rung at 8 a.m.: the 1st and 2nd at 9 a.m.

# ASFORDBY.

ALL SAINTS.                                                    5 BELLS.

1.  GOD : SAVE [9] THE : kING [9] ANTHONY HILL
    1631 [9] [ ▽ 1. ]
2 and 3.  IH'S : NAZARENVS [9] REX : IVDEORVM [9]
    FILI : DEI MISERERE : MEI [9] 1630 [9] [ ▽ 1. ]
4.  CELORVM CHRSTE [9] PLATIAT TIBI REX [9] SONVS
    ISTE 1630    [ ▽ 1.]
5.  CVM · SONO · SI · NON · VIS [9] VENIRE [9] NVNQVAM
    AD · PRECES [9] CVPIES ·' IRE 1630 [ ▽ 1. ]
        (Nine coins near the mouth.)

After the ringing of the Death-knell each bell is tolled thrice for a
male, twice for a female.


# ASHBY-DE-LA-ZOUCH.

S. HELEN.                                                     8 BELLS.

1.  THE TWO TREBLE BELLS WERE GIVEN BY VOLUN-
    TARY SUBSCRIPTION IN COMMEMORATION OF
    THE PEACE OF 1814. JOHN BRIANT HERTFORD
    FECIT 1814.
2.  The Same.
3.  GLORIA DEO. SOLI T. EAYRE. THE GIFT OF THE
    INHABITANTS OF ASHBY 1741.
4.  J. BRIANT HERTFORD FECIT 1817.
5.  GOD [12] SAVE [12] HIS [12] CHVRCH [12] JOHN
    DICKINSON [12] WARDEN [12] ,1698.
6.  [ + 42 ] JHC [ □ 43 ] NAZARENVS [ □ 43 ]
    REX [ □ 43 ] IVDEORVM
7.  THE REV. WM. MAC DOUALL VICAR : J. TOMPSON
    AND WM. DEVENPORT C. W. J. BRIANT HERTFORD
    FECIT 1822.

8. ✠ SONORO : MEO : SONO : RESONO : DEO.

JO TAYLOR AND SON BELLFOUNDERS LOUGHBO
IN THE YEAR OF OUR SALVATION 1849.

In 6 Ed. VI. there were "fyve belles and a hande belle."

The ancient tenor bell dated 1571 and recast in 1849 weighed 14 cwt. 3 qrs. 2 ℔.; the present one weighs 17 cwt. 3 qrs. 0 ℔.

Tradition says a former inhabitant of this place having lost his way was, after wandering about nearly the whole night, and when nearly exhausted, enabled to find his way home by hearing the sound of the clock of S. Helen's Church. To mark his gratitude for this deliverance he conveyed to the trustees of the Grammar School certain property, since called the "Day-Bell Houses," upon trust, among other things, that they should cause one of the church bells to be rung for a quarter of an hour at four o'clock every morning. This direction was carried out, and the "four o'clock bell" was regularly heard every morning until the year 1807, when upon the authority of a Decree of the Court of Chancery, this custom, "useless and annoying" to the inhabitants, was discontinued. Instead of this early bell, one is now rung daily at 9 a.m. and at 2 p.m. for the purpose of assembling the boys in the Grammar School.

The Pancake-bell is rung on Shrove-Tuesday. On Sundays one bell is rung at 7 a.m., two bells at 8 a.m.

## ASHBY-DE-LA-ZOUCH.
HOLY TRINITY.                                                    1 BELL.

No inscription.

## ASHBY FOLVILLE.
S. MARY THE VIRGIN.                                            5 BELLS.

1.  GOD SAVE THE CHVRCH [ ▢ 10 ] 1652.
                    (Diam. 29 in.)

T

2. GOD SAVE THE CHVRCH [ ▫ 10 ] 1653.
(Diam. 30¼ in.)

3. IH'Ƨ : NAZARENVS [9] REX : IVDEORVM [9] FILI :
DEI [9] MISERERE : MEI [9] 1626 [ ▽ 1. ]
(Diam. 32 in.)

4. GOD [9] SAVE [9] THE [9] kING [9] RALPH PICK [9]
HENRY MOORE [9] CW [9] 1637 [ ▽ 1. ]
(Diam. 36 in.)

5. OMNIA FIANT AD GLORIAM DEI. THO. EAYRE KETT.
JOHN   BLACK   AND   JOSEPH   STEVENSON   C.
WARDENS ·∴· 1739 ·∴·
(Diam. 40¼ in.)

The Rev. J. Godson informs me that about two hundred years ago
a lady having lost her way, and regained it by the sound of the Ashby
bells, left the proceeds of a piece of land to the poor of the parish.  The
boundaries of the land were marked by three large stones, and the
produce brought to the church to strew it with hay to keep the people's
feet warm : afterwards the corn produced was for many years brought
to the church and divided amongst the poor.   It is said that from time
to time the ancient landmarks have been removed further in, till now
the once fair piece of land is but a small piece yielding to the Churchwardens about six shillings a year.

At the death-knell three tolls are given for a male, two for a female,
both before and after the knell.

## ASHBY MAGNA.

S. Mary.                                                        3 Bells.

1. ✠ SOLI DEO GLORIA PAX HOMINIBVS 1655 I. M.
2. JOHN BRIANT HERTFORD FECIT 1817 † † † † †
3. 𝕻𝕽𝕬𝕴𝕾𝕳 𝕿𝕳𝕰 𝕷𝕺𝕽𝕯𝕳 1613 [ ▽ 1. ]
(On top of bell the letters H. B.)

The 2nd bell was previously inscribed : " Jesus Nazarenus Rex
Judeorvm."

## ASHBY PARVA.

S. PETER. 3 BELLS.

1. [ + 2 ] SERVE [ ⬜ 4 ] THE [ ⬜ 4 ] LORDE 1591.
2. NEWCOMBE · OF · LEICESTER · MADE · MEE · 1607 [ 13 ].
3. [ + 22 ] BE · YT · KNOWNE · TO · ALL · THAT · DOTH · ME · SEE
   THAT · NEWCOMBE · OF · LEICESTER · MADE · MEE · 1605.

## ASTON FLAMVILLE.

S. PETER. 2 BELLS.

1. [ + 2 ] PRAYSE THE LORD 1596.
   (Diam. 31 in.)
2. Sča enterinn ora p nobis [ ⬸ 5.]
   (Diam. 37 in.)

## AYLESTON.

S. ANDREW. 4 BELLS.

1. [ + 45 ] WILELMUS : FILIUS : JHOHANNIS : RESEYVOUR .
   [ + 45 ] FECIT : ME : IN : HONORE : BEATE : MARIE.
2. [ + 3 ] JOHN : COTH IOHN : BAKER
   [ ⬜ ⬜ 62 repeated ] [ + 3 ] THOMAS . . .
   THA . . . EE [ + 3 twice ] [ ⬜ 62 four times. ]
3. [ + 22 ] BE · YT · KNOWNE · TO · ALL · THAT · DOTH · ME · SEE
   THAT · NEWCOMBE · OF · LEICESTER · MADE · MEE · 1609.
4. The same dated 1602.

The inscription on the 1st bell is in two lines round the bell as shown above. For specimens of letters used on this bell see figs. 84, 85, and 46—the latter being Y. That *William Reseyvour* was the donor, and the same person as the *John Rekevour* mentioned in the following transaction is highly probable: and so the approximate date of the bell is fixed:

"May 1, 1412. Roger de Cosyngton Vicar of S. Martin's Leicester granted one messuage, four virgates and three acres of land and twenty-seven acres of meadow with the appurtenances in Aylestone to *William son of John Rekevour*, Richard de Leicester and John de Scotton a capellan, to hold to the said William Richard and John and to the heirs of the said William, and in default of issue from the said William, the remainder to Maud his sister; which grant was confirmed by the King's letters patent dated as above."— *Pat.* 13 *Hen.* IV. 2 *m.* 26 quoted by Nichols.

The Pancake-bell is rung on Shrove-Tuesday.

## BAGWORTH.

THE HOLY ROOD.                                  3 BELLS.

1. THOMAS MEARS AND SON LONDON 1810.
       (Diam. 25¼ in.)
2. GOD SAVE THE CHVRCH N SMITH T. JOHNSON
   CHVRCHWARDENS 1720.
       (Diam. 27 in.)
3. IHS. NAZARENVS REX 1668.
       (Diam. 30 in.)

## BARKBY.

S. MARY.                                        5 BELLS.

1. THIS BELL WAS GIVEN BY THE INHABITANTS OF
   BARKBY 1631. RECAST BY W. A. POCHIN ESQ.
   1854. JOHN TAYLOR AND SONS BELLFOUNDERS
   LOUGHBOROUGH.

2. IH'2 : NAZARENVS REX : IVDEORVM FILI : DEI
   MISERERE : MEI 1634 [ ▽ 1. ]
3. [ + 64 ] 𝕬𝖁𝕰 𝕸𝕬𝕽𝕴𝕬 : 𝕲𝕽𝕬 𝕻𝕷𝕰𝕹𝕬
   𝕯𝕹𝕾 𝕿𝕰𝖀𝕸 (sic.)
4. GLORIA DEO IN EXCELSIS JNO. ILLSON AND THOS.
   HENSON C : WARDENS. JNO. BRIANT AND B.
   CORT HERTFORD FECERUNT : 1803.
5. GOD SAVE THE KINGE 1608 [ ▽ 1. ]
   (Weight 15 cwt.)

## BARKESTON.

SS. Peter and Paul.                                    4 Bells.

1. JOHANNES CLARKE MINISTER [ □ 10. ]
   (Diam. 30 in.)
2. 𝕾𝕬 .. 𝕺𝕽𝕿𝕳𝕿𝕸𝕰 (?)
   (Diam. 33 in.)
3. GOD SAVE HIS CHVRCH · R. HICKSON WARDEN 1710.
   (Diam. 36 in.)
4. I TO THE CHURCH THE LIVING CALL AND TO
   THE GRAVE DO SUMMONS ALL. GEORGE
   HEDDERLY FOUNDER NOTTINGHAM 1787. STE.N
   WILDERS CHURCHWARDEN.
   (Diam. 38¼)

In 6 Edward VI. there were " iij great bells j sanctus bell."
The Tenor bell was previously inscribed :—
> " My roaring sound doth notice give
> That men cannot here always lyve."

## BARLESTON.

S. Giles.                                          2 Bells.

1. JOHNATHAN GIBSON C W THO. HEDDERLY
   FOVNDER 1755.
   (Diam. 25 in.)

2. [ + 39 ] 𝔄𝔙𝔈 𝔐𝔄ℜ𝔍𝔄 𝔊ℜ𝔄𝔊𝔍𝔄 ℌℒ𝔈ℜ𝔄 ℌℜ𝔖 𝔗𝔈𝔊𝔙𝔐
(Diam. 27¼ in.)

## BARROW-ON-SOAR.

HOLY TRINITY.                                          5 BELLS.

1. Blank.  (Cast in 1822.)
          (Diam. 31¼ in.)
2. F E D C B A        L K I H G        W V T S R Q
   F E D C B A        M L K I H G        1642.  [ ꒱ 1. ]
          (Diam. 33¾ in.)
3. F E D C B A        M L K I H G        X W V T S
   R Q P O N        Q R S T V W  1642  [ ꒱ 1. ]
          (Diam. 37 in.)
4. [ + 27 ] 𝕀 sweetly toling men do call to taste on meuts that feeds the
   soole  1620  [ ▢ 7. ]
          (Diam. 39½ in.)
5. ALL THEM THAT HEAR MY MOURNFUL SOUND
   REPENT BEFORE YOU LIE IN GROUND 1692
          (Diam. 42 in.)

The Curfew is rung at 8 o'clock p.m.
The Pancake-bell is rung on Shrove-Tuesday at 10-45.
The custom is not to ring the Passing-bell after dark.
The bells are rung backwards to give notice of a fire.

## BARWELL.

B. V. MARY.                                          4 BELLS.

1. THOMAS PAGET RECTOR HVMPHREY PAGET ꝺANIELL
   CHAWNER CHVRCHW. 1675.
2. ℙℜ𝔄𝔍𝔖𝔈 𝔗ℌ𝔈 𝕷𝔒ℜꝺ𝔈 1601.

3. IH'Ƨ : NAZARENVS [9] REX : IVDEORVM [9] FILI :
   DEI [9] MISERERE : MEI [9] 1628 [9] [ ▽ 1. ]`
4. CVM · SONO · SI · NON · VIS [9] VENIRE [9]
   NVNQVAM AD · PRECES [9] CVPIES · IRE [9]
   1628 [9] [ ▽ 1. ]

Thomas Paget was instituted 3 Jan. 1670, and buried 31 July 1680.
Humphrey Paget was patron of the living.

Nichols relates that Mrs. Anne Power of Barwell died Sep. 29th
1785. She was, he says, a wealthy maiden lady, and at her funeral
" agreeably to the custom of the country on the interment of a spinster,
the corpse was welcomed to the church with a merry peal; and an
elegant entertainment was distributed to a numerous circle of friends
and neighbouring dependents." ! !

# BEEBY.

ALL SAINTS.                                                    3 BELLS.

1. [ + 71. ]  A B C E D (?)
   (Diam. 32 in.)
2. A B C D E F          G H I K L M
   N O P Q R S.
   (Diam. 34 in.)
3. [ + 45 ]  THE : NAZARENUS : REX :
   IUDEORUM
   (Diam. 36 in.)

# BELGRAVE.

S. PETER.                                                      5 BELLS.

1. GOD [9] SAVE [9] THE [9] kING [9] 1631 [ ▽ 1. ]
   (Diam. 30 in.)
2. CELORVM CHRSTE [9] PLATIAT TIBI REX [9] SONVS
   ISTE [9] 1631 [9] [ ▽ 1. ]
   (Diam. 31½ in.)

3.  IH'S : NAZARENVS [9] REX : IVDEORVM [9] FILI :
    DEI [9] MISERERE : MEI [9] 1631 [9] [ ▽ 1. ]
               (Diam. 34¼ in.)
4.  CVM · SONO · SI · NON · VIS · [9] VENIRE [9]
    NVNQVAM · AD · PRECES [9] CVPIES · IRE [9]
    ' 1631 [9] WH [9] GO [9] IT [9] [ ▽ 1. ]
               (Diam. 38 in.)
5.  J TAYLOR AND CO FOUNDERS LOUGHBOROUGH 1871
                    1871
           RICARDUS STEPHENS B.D.
              ÆTAT 86 MAR. 29.
           ECCLESIAM CONSERVAT DEUS
    (Diam. 44 in.   Weight 14 cwt. 2 qrs. 14 ℔.   Key F.)

In 1709 there appear to have been only four bells; Nichols mentions
five in 1795.

The Curfew is rung at 8 p.m. during Winter, and a morning bell at
6 a.m. during Summer. The Pancake-bell is rung at 11 a.m. on Shrove-
Tuesday; after which a peal on all the bells is rung. The rule is that
the bells shall not then again be rung (only chimed) until Easter Day,
so avoiding all ringing during Lent. Formerly the Pancake-bell was
rung by the oldest apprentice in the parish. At the death-knell thrice
three tolls on three different bells are given for a male and thrice two on
three different bells for a female. A morning bell is rung at 7 o'clock
on Sundays.


# BELTON.

S. JOHN BAPTIST.                                    3 BELLS.

1.  Blank.
         (Diam. 29½ in.: from the Nottingham foundry.)
2.  ABC     DEF     IHG     [ ▽ 1. ]
               (Diam. 32 in.)

3. Ḥec Campana Sacra Ḟiat Ḟrinitate Beata.
GEO WAITE WILL TOONE WARDENS GEO' HALL OVEERSER 1730.

( Diam. 35 in. )

There were formerly 4 Bells here, for in 6 Edward VI. the Commissioners say: "Belton Itm tow belles and a saunce bell. Itm tow belles sould anno R. B. Edwardi Sexti secudo all the peryshe beinge of counsayll."

On Sundays a "first peal" is rung at 8 a.m.; "second peal" at 9 a.m. After morning service another "first peal" is rung; and a "second peal" at 2 p.m.

The Pancake-bell is rung on Shrove-Tuesday, which day is kept as a general holiday.

## BILLESDON.

S. JOHN BAPTIST.                                         4 BELLS.

1. IH'S : NAZARENVS : REX : IVDEORVM : FILI : DEI : MISERERE : MEI : 1628 [ ∪ 1. ]
( Diam. 31¼ in. )

2. The same dated 1624.
( Diam. 34¼ in. )

3. J. TAYLOR AND SON FOUNDERS LOUGHBOROUGH
( Diam. 39¼ in. )

4. [ + 55 ] Stella Marin Maris Sucurre Piissima Nobis
( Diam. 42 in. )

The Pancake-bell is rung on Shrove-Tuesday. At death-knell thrice three tolls are given for a male, thrice two for a female.

## BIRSTALL.

S. JAMES.                                                3 BELLS.

1. GOD SAVE HIS CHVRCH 1656 [ ☐ 10. ]
( Diam. 26 in. )

v

2. IH'Ƨ : NAZARENVS [9] REX : IVDEORVM [9] FILI :
   DEI [9] MISERERE : MEI [9] 1625 [ ▽ 1. ]
                    (Diam. 30 in.)

3. [ + 55 ] IHC̄ [ ◻ 59 ] 𝕹𝕬𝕾𝕬𝕽𝕰𝕹𝖄𝕾 [ ◻ 59 ]
   𝕽𝕰𝕾 [ ◻ 59 ] 𝕴𝖁𝕯𝕰𝕺𝕽𝖁𝕸
                    (Diam. 33¼ in.   Cracked.)

In 6 Edward VI. there were "three belles and a saunctes bell."


## BITTESWELL.

S. Mary.                                    4 Bells.

1. HENRY PENN HE MADE ME 1706.
2. H. P. 1706.
3. H. P. HE MADE ME 170⁶ WILLIAM PALLATT WILLIAM
   CRISPE CHVRCHWARDENS
4. H. P. 1706.


## BLABY.

All Saints.                                3 Bells.

1. [ + 22 ] ROBART TILLEY AND THOMAS VARNAM
   CHVRCH [ + 22 ] NEWCOMBE OF LEICESTER
   MADE MEE 1611 WARDENS
2. IH'Ƨ : NAZARENVS [9] REX : IVDEORVM [9] FILI :
   DEI [9] MISERERE : MEI [9] 1634 [ ▽ 1. ]
3. THOMAS MEARS & SON OF LONDON FECIT 1807.

The Curfew is rung at 8 p.m. during the winter months.   The Clerk
receives a small sum annually, the rent of a piece of land, given by the
Rev. E. Stokes in 1761, for this service.—*Charity Commissioners' Report,*
1837, p. 298.

The Pancake-bell is rung at noon on Shrove-Tuesday.

# BLACKFORDBY.

S. MARGARET.                                           2 BELLS.

1.  GOD SAVE HIS CHVRCH 1724.
                    (Diam. 16 in.)
2.  [ □ 7 ] 1663.
                    (Diam. 18 in.)

Both cracked; the smallest unhung, the second with broken wheel.

The parish clerk—George Baker—succeeded his father, who was clerk for fifty years. He is eighty-three years of age. He has been clerk for sixty years, and can now (1874) mount the belfry stairs, and go up a ladder to the bells, as actively as a middle-aged man.

## BLASTON S. GILES.

S. GILES.                                             1 BELL.

GLORIA PATRI ET FILIO ET SPIRITUI SANCTO 1720.

When the above bell was cast by Thomas Eayre the following entry was made in the Register:

"The frame of the Bell belonging to S. Giles' royal donative at Blaston had an old date on it of 1116 so that it was aged 604 years in this present year of salvation by Jesus."

This was clearly a misreading for 1516 or 1556; the figure 5 being at that time written very like the figure 1.

## BLASTON S. MICHAEL.

S. MICHAEL.                                           1 BELL.

Blank.

## BOTTESFORD.

S. MARY.                                              6 BELLS.

1.  J BRYANT HERTFORD 1810.
                    (Diam. 35 in.)

2. PEACE AND GOOD NEIGHBOURHOOD A.D. 1713 [ □ 27. ]
   (Diam. 38 in.)

3. [ + 34 ] CÆLORVM CHRISTE PLA-
   CEAT TIBI REX SONVS ISTE
   1615 [ □ 8. ]
   (Diam. 42 in.)

4. In Multis Annis Resonat Campana Iohannis [ + 17 ] [ □ 31 ]
   [ ▽ 23. ]
   (Diam. 41 in.)

5. MISSI DE CÆLIS HABEO NOMEN GABRIELIS 1612.
   (Diam. 46 in.)

6. REV J THOROTON VICAR J VINCENT JNO. DERRY CH.
   WARDENS J BRYANT HERTFORD FECIT 1809.
   (Diam. 55 in.)

In 6 Edward VI. there were "v. bells."

The 1st bell was formerly inscribed "Ex dono hon͞s dni Iohannis Roos fili comitis Rutlandiæ 1675." It was cracked, and recast with the same inscription in 1791. Recast again, as now shown in 1810.

The ancient tenor bell was inscribed "Hæc sit sanctorum campana in laude bonorum." When ringing for victory over the Rebels in 1715 the clapper of the 5th bell flew out, and cracked this tenor bell, which was soon after recast, and inscribed, "Laus Domini nostra mobilitate viget." At the close of the last century this bell was again cracked, and recast by G. Hedderly of Nottingham, who placed upon it:

"The fleeting hours I tell; I summon all to pray,
    I toll the dead man's knell, and hail the festal day."

The weight of this bell is said to have been upwards of 27 cwt. Again, as is shown by its present inscription, it was recast in 1809.

In 1791 when the treble and tenor, as we have just seen, were cracked, George Hedderly of Nottingham being applied to for an estimate tried to persuade the churchwardens to enlarge their ring to eight bells, but they were "No Ways inclined" to do so. The following estimate, and letter from him, are preserved amongst the Parish Papers:

I am indebted to The Rev. Canon Norman for permission to copy them:

"An Estemate By Mr. Geo Hedderly Bellfounder And Bell-hanger of Nottingham For the purpose of Recasting the first and Tennor Bells in the parish Church of Bottesford in Leicestershire Allso for New Hangin and Compleating the peal With all New Metarial Carridg Excepted.

"For Recasting the first and Tennor Bells Being About 35 hundred weight at £1. 5s. p hundred.

"For New hanging the Six Bells £32.

"New Mettall if any wanted £5. 12s. pʳ hundred weight.

"Mr. Hough,

Sir,

As you seemed No Ways inclined to have Eight Bells think it Needless to say much on that Subject but If you Should be so inclined the casting Ma be taken at about 2 shillings pʳ hundred Less than the above the hanging in proportion with the above. Shold the Above Estemate Meet your Approbation you ma Depend on yr Business Being Done In the Best Manner and after the Most Modern taste Wich Gives Great Ease to the Steples And should happen to be imployed In your job the Greatest attention shall be paid to your steple When Ever i May happen to travel that way And the favor Be Greatfully acnoledged by your

Most Obedᵗ Obⁱᵈ Servᵗ.

George Hedderly."

"Nottingham the 4 Feby

1791."

The following Agreement—also preserved with the Parish Papers—was subsequently entered into:

"Agreed by Mr. Thos. Hough and Mr. Thos. Brown Church Wardens of Bottesford and Mr. Geo. Hedderley Bellfounder of Nottingham—That Mr. Hedderley is to recast the Treble and Tenor Bells as nearly of the same size and sound as may be, and to be allowed 25s. an Cwᵗ. the old and new Bells to be weighed—if the new ones are heavier than the old ones, an allowance to be made after the rate of £6. an Cwᵗ. to Mr. Hedderley for the overplus; on the contrary if lighter—an allowance by Mr. Hedderley to the churchwardens after the rate of £4. 15s. an Cwᵗ. It is also agreed that Mr. Hedderley new hang all the 6 Bells with Wood, Iron, Brasses, Wheels, Clappers and Every thing belonging to Bell-hanging (except ropes) all new—at £5. a bell or £30. the whole and all the wood to be heart of oak : and that Mr. Hedderley take all the old Materials for his own use (if it be hereafter Agreed that the Church Wardens find wood for the Yokes Mr. Hedderley is to allow according to the value) The Church Wardens are to be at all expence of carriage backwards and forwards but no further excepting repairing the Frames if wanted, propping the Beams or securing anything that may be thought necessary by Mr. Hedderley for taking the old Bells down and the new ones up. And it is further agreed that Mr. Hedderley shall be accountable for all risks and accidents whatever and that Every thing shall be done in a workmanlike manner—that the 2 new Bells shall be Tuneable with the other 4, and the Tenor a sufficient cover for all the rest—and that the whole shall be a fine Peal of 6 Bells according to the opinion of good judges.

Thos. Hough.      Geo. Hedderley.<br>Thos. Brown.

Witness
   Wm. Moursey."

The Rev. Canon Norman further informs me that " The Staunton property which is held with the tenure of providing a guard for Stanton Tower at Belvoir Castle is bound to provide a rope each year for our big bell, no doubt to warn the country of the want of the guard." Nichols alluding to this custom says: " By an old custom the owner of Staunton Hall in Notts. is annually obliged to find a new rope for the great bell, which is done at Christmas, when the clerk or sexton and ringers carry the old rope to Staunton and bring back a new one. An ancestor of the family was a great ringer, and entailed this custom as a Legacy on his descendants."

The Curfew-bell is rung at 8 p.m. throughout the year excepting during Whitsun-week. A day-bell is rung at 1 p.m., and the Pancake-bell on Shrove-Tuesday.

A few years ago when the Tower and Spire of Bottesford Church were taken down and rebuilt, a very small bell was found under the foundations of the Tower. This ancient bell was without the handle, which was broken off—it had apparently been a ring one—and clapper. It was at first supposed to have been a sacryng bell; but its small size (1¾ and $\frac{7}{8}$ inch in diameter and 1¾ inch in height) hardly fitted it for that purpose. It probably had been attached to a Funeral pall or to a vestment.

## BOWDEN MAGNA.

S. PETER.                                                              5 BELLS.

1. 𝕮𝖀𝕸 𝕮𝖀𝕸 𝕬𝕹𝕯 𝕻𝕽𝕰ₜ 𝕬𝕹𝕹𝕺 𝕯𝕺𝕸𝕴𝕹𝕴 1599 [ ∪ 1. ]
2. OMNIA FIANT AD GLORIAM DEI : : GLORIA DEO SOLI T : EAYRE 1737.
3. OMNIA FIANT AD GLORIAM DEI 1739 GLORIA DEO SOLI · T · EAYRE KETT
4. IH'S : NAZARENVS [9] REX : IVDEORVM [9] FILI : DEI [9] MISERERE : MEI [9] 1621 [ ∪ 1. ]
5. The same dated 1624.

At the death-knell three tolls are given for a male, two for a female: for children under twelve years of age, the 4th bell is used instead of the tenor.

Sunday ringing: 1st bell at 7 a.m. 2nd and 3rd bells at 8 a.m. When Evensong is in the afternoon the same two bells are rung at 1 p.m., when it is in the evening they are rung at 3.30 p.m.

Richard Kestin by will dated August 7th 1674, and proved at Leicester in 1675, gave to the poor people of Great Bowden, the rent of his house where Wm. Chester then inhabited, excepting one shilling yearly out of it, which the ringers were to have for their pains in ringing on the 17th day of November for ever, in thankful remembrance of restoring the Gospel, and removing Popish Idolatry, and bringing in Queen Elizabeth.—*See Charity Commissioners' Report*, 1837, p. 223. This shilling is still paid to the ringers.

On a Tablet on the Belfry walls is the following:

"If you get Drunk and hither Reel,
Or with your Brawl Disturb the Peal,
Or with mumlungeous * horrid Smoak,
You cloud the Room, and Ringers Choak;
Or if you dare prophane this Place
By Oath, or Curse, or Language Base,
Or if you shall presume in Peal
With Hatt, or Coat, or armed Heel:
Or turn your Bell in careless way,
For each Offence shall Two Pence pay;
To break these Laws if any hope
May leave the Bell, and take the Rope.
        Edward Englehern churchwarden.

N.B.   He who plucks his Bell over when turned shall pay Six Pence."

## BRANSTONE.

S. Guthlac.                                          3 Bells.

1.  GOD SAVE HIS CHURCH 1623.
2.  GOD SAVE THE KING 1662.
3.  OMNIA FIANT AD GLORIAM DEI GLORIA DEO SOLI 1738.

The church being under repair, and the floor of the bell chamber rotten and unsafe, only portions of the inscriptions on 1 and 2 can be read.

---

* Mundungus *i.e.* stinking tobacco.

# BRAUNSTONE.

S. JOHN BAPTIST.                                            3 BELLS.

1, 2, and 3.  ROBERT TAYLOR St NEOTS FECIT 1812.

The 2nd and 3rd bells were formerly inscribed "James Winstanley esquier A.B.M.E. fecit 1654." He was the first of the name that owned the Manor: he died 13 Nov. 1666.

In 1809 there were but two bells hanging, and one of them so damaged as to be useless. The parish paid, in consequence, an annual fine for several years to the Archdeacon's Court at Leicester.—*Nichols.*

# BREEDON.

SS. MARY AND HARDULPH.                                      4 BELLS.

1.  I sweetly toling men do call to taste on meats that feeds the soole
       1604  [ □ 8. ]
2.  GOD 2AVE THE CHVRCH 1604 [ □ 8 ] R. P. R. H. I. H.
3.  + AVE MARIA (?)
               (I am not certain as to this.)
4.  JOHN TAYLOR & SON FOUNDERS LOUGHBOROUGH
       1847.
                    (Weight 10 cwt.)

In 6 Edward VI. there were "three bells."

# BRENTINGBY.

S. . . .                                                    2 BELLS.

1.  [ + 55 ]  A V E  [ □ 59 ]  M A R I A
2.  [ + 41 ]  AVE  MARIA  GRACIA
       PLENA

In 6 Edward VI. there were "ij bells."
The 1st bell is cracked.

W

The following local doggrel describes and compares these bells with those in adjacent churches:

> " Brentingby pancheons,
> And Wyfordby pans;
> Stapleford organs,
> And Burton ting-tangs."

.

## BRINGHURST.

S. NICOLAS.　　　　　　　　　　　　　　　　　　　3 BELLS.

1. PACKE AND CHAPMAN OF LONDON FECIT 1776.
2. IHS NAZARENE REX IUDÆORUM FILI DEI MISERERE
   MEI.  GLORIA PATRI FILI ET SPIRITUI SANCTO
   1724.
3. [ + 72 ] DISSI [ □ 67 ] MORE [ □ 67 ] NOSTRI [ □ 67 ]
   VIVERE [ □ 67 ] DISSE [ □ 67 ] SONO [ □ 67 ]
   1618 [ □ □ 67. ]


## BROOKSBY.

S. MICHAEL.　　　　　　　　　　　　　　　　　　　1 BELL.

*THOS HEDDERLY FOUNDER* 1749.
(Diam. 12¼ in.)


## BROUGHTON ASTLEY.

S. MARY.　　　　　　　　　　　　　　　　　　　5 BELLS.

1. GOD [ 9 ] SAVE [ 9 ] THE [ 9 ] kING [ 9 ] 1637 [ ▽ 1. ]
   (Diam. 32 in.)
2. IH'Ƨ : NAZARENVS [ 9 ] REX : IVDEORVM [ 9 ] FILI :
   DEI [ 9 ] MISERERE : MEI [ 9 ] 1637 [ 9 ] [ ▽ 1. ]
   (Diam. 35 in.)

3.  The same.
> ( Diam. 37¾ in. )

4.  Z    DVCKETT    F    WALE    C    W    TOBY
    NORRIS    CAST    ME    1680.
> ( Diam. 41¼ in. )

5.  𝕬𝕭𝕮𝕯𝕰𝕱𝕲 [ 9 ] 𝕳𝕴𝕶𝕷 [ 9 ] 𝕸𝕹𝕺𝕻 [ 9 ]
    𝕼𝕽𝕾𝕿𝖀𝖃 [ 9 ] 1637 [ 9 ] 𝕬𝕭𝕮𝕯𝕰𝕱
    [ 9 ] [ ▽ I. ]
> ( Diam. 43½ in. )

The Pancake-bell is rung on Shrove-Tuesday. A morning-bell is rung on Sundays at 8 a.m. A Peal is rung in the evening on Nov. 5th.

[Broughton Nether—see Nether Broughton.]

## BRUNTINGTHORPE.

S. Mary.                                                          3 Bells.

1.  [ + 3 ] 𝕬𝕭𝕮𝕯𝕰𝕱𝕲𝕳𝕴.
> (Cracked.)

2.  S. B. RUSSELL RECTOR JOHN SEAL CHURCHWARDEN
    EDWD. ARNOLD FECIT 1788.

3.  CELORVM CHRSTE [ 9 ] PLATIAT [ 9 ] TIBI REX [ 9 ]
    SONVS ISTE [ 9 ] 1615 [ 9 ] [ ▽ I. ]

## BUCKMINSTER.

S. John Baptist.                                                  6 Bells.

1.  TO THE GLORY OF GOD AND IN MEMORY OF
    HARRIET SUSAN RABBETTS. GIVEN TO THE
    PARISH OF BUCKMINSTER-CUM-SEWSTERN BY
    THE REV. F. D. RABBETTS M.A. VICAR 1873.
    MEARS AND STAINBANK FOUNDERS, LONDON.

2. The same excepting the name of donor:
   CAPTAIN N. G. RABBETTS 1873.
3. + EX DONO RICHARDI HARTOPP ARMIGERI 1657.
4. GOD [12] SAVE [12] HIS [12] CHVRCH [12] HT [12]
   MB [12] WARDENS [12] 1691.
5. 1649.
6. ALL YOU THAT HEAR MY MOURNFULL SOUND
   REPENT BEFORE YOUR LAYD IN GROUND
   THOS. HEDDERLY FOUNDER NOTTINGHAM JOHN
   BOYFIELD CHURCHWARDEN 1778.

In 6 Edward VI. there were "iij bells."

Richard Hartopp, who was born in 1614 and died in 1667, appears to have been one of the numerous children of Sir Edwd. Hartopp, who was created a baronet in 1619.

The tenor was previously inscribed: "Jhesvs be ovre spede 1596." Thomas Hedderly, the founder of the present bell, made the following entry respecting it, after recasting, in his note-book: "Buckminster Tenor 39½ (inches) wide; 28 high, bare; 2 and 3¼ thick. Note on A."*

## BURBAGE.

S. CATHARINE.                                                5 BELLS.

1. TEMPUS SED TACITUM SUBRUIT SIT NOMEN DOMINI
   BENEDICTUM. THOS. EAYRE 1761.
   (Diam. 28½ in.)
2. JOHN MILLER THOS. FREEMAN CHURCH WARDENS 1813 T. MEARS
   OF LONDON FECIT
   (Diam. 29 in.)
3. RICHARD WEIGHTMAN 1071.
   (Diam. 30½ in.  Date reversed.)

---

* Communicated by W. P. W. Phillimore, Esq.

4. [ + 72 ] NON CLAMOR SED AMOR CANTAT IN AVRE
    DEI 1761.
                      ( Diam. 34 in. )
5. WILLIAM BROWNE THOMAS GAMBLE ϽHVϽH
    WARϹENS 1701.
                      ( Diam. 36 in. )

The Curfew (3rd bell) rings during the winter months. This bell is
also rung on the Court Leet day of the Lady of the Manor.


## BURROUGH.

S. MARY.                                          - 4 BELLS.

1. WM. BROWNE RECTOR DANIEL BARKER C W →
    E. ARNOLD LEICESTER FECIT 1798.
                      ( Diam. 26 in. )
2. WM. BROWNE RECTOR DANIEL BARKER CHURCH-
    WARDEN EDWD. ARNOLD FECIT 1798.
                      ( Diam. 28 in. )
3. IH'S : NAZARENVS [9] REX : IVDEORVM [9] FILI :
    DEI [9] MISERERE : MEI [9] 1619 [ ᴜ 1. ]
                      ( Diam. 30¼ in. )
4. ROBT. PEAKE CH WARDEN 1813.
                      ( Diam. 33¼ in. )

Previous to 1798 the bells were inscribed :—
              1.  Hugh Wattes made me 1600
              2.  IH'S &c. (the present third bell)
              3.  Praise the Lord 1609
              4.  God save the King 1730.


## BURTON LAZARS.

S. JAMES.                                          2 BELLS.

1. JOHN BRIANT HERTFORD FECIT 1804.

2.  T. MEARS OF LONDON FECIT 1823.

In 6 Edward VI. there were "ij bells and a sanctus bell." See p. 154 for local doggerel respecting these bells.

## BURTON OVERY.

S. ANDREW.                    •                        3 BELLS.

1.  CVM · SONO · SI · NON · VIS [ 9 ] VENIRE [ 9 ] NVNQVAM · AD · PRECES [ 9 ] CVPIES IRE [ 9 ] 1632 [ ⛉ 1. ]
>                      ( Diam. 32 in. )

2.  CELORVM CHRSTE PLATIAT TIBI REX SONVS ISTE 1616 [ ⛉ 1. ]
>                      ( Diam. 35 in. )

3.  The same.
>                      ( Diam. 37 in. )

The Curfew is rung ; and so is the Pancake-bell on Shrove-Tuesday.

## CADEBY.

ALL SAINTS.                                          2 BELLS.

Blanks.

## CALDWELL.

S. MARY.                                             3 BELLS.

1.  [ + 41 ] IHC : NAZARENVS : REX : IVDEORVM

2.  sᴄᴇ petri  [ ⛉ 63. ]
3.  abᴇ maria  [ ⛉ 63. ]

In 6 Edward VI. there were "three belles, a saunce bell and a hand bell."

# CARLTON-BY-BOSWORTH.

S. MICHAEL.                                                4 BELLS.

1, 2, 3, and 4.   J. TAYLOR & CO FOUNDERS LOUGH-
BOROUGH 1868.
(Diam. of treble 28 in., of tenor 34 in.)


# CARLTON CURLIEU.

S. MARY.                                                  3 BELLS.

1 and 3.  GLORIA PATRI FILIO ET SPIRITUI SANCTO
ANNO DOM 1732.
2.  OMNIA FIANT AD GLORIAM DEI · ·∴· · GLORIA
DEO SOLI AD 1732.

Nichols gives the following extract from the Register, from which it
appears there were formerly four bells:
"The fore bell having lain broken and useless near thirty years,
was new cast and all the four bells new hanged 1670, William
Roberts being then Rector, who voluntarily did give 40s. towards
casting the bell.

Robert Redley Churchwarden."


# CASTLE DONINGTON.

S. EDWARD KING AND MARTYR.                                5 BELLS.

1.  I WILL PRAISE THEE O GOD WITH ALL MI HART
W E 1675.
2.  JOHN BAKEWELL ROB. BRIGGS *THOMAS HEDDERLY
FOUNDER*
3.  ALL GLORY BEE TO GOD ON HIGH 1661 [ ▢ 7. ]
4.  [ + 63 ] omnium sactorum

5. [ + 34 ] I WILL SOUND AND RE-
     SOUND TO THY PEOPLE
     LORD WITH MY SWEET
     VOICE TO CALL THEM TO
     THY WORD 1616 [ □ 8.]

In 6 Edward VI. there were "three belles in the stepell."

The mark of contraction on the 4th bell is placed in the wrong place. "*Omnium sanctorum.*"

## CATTHORPE.

S. MARY AND ALL SAINTS.             3 BELLS.

1. [ + 40 ] WORCHEPE BE TO GOD.
         (Diam. 24 in.)

2. [ + 65 ] IOHANNES.
         (Diam. 27½ in.)

3. CUM VOCO VENITE JOSEPH EAYRE FECIT 1770.
         (Diam. 31½ in.)

## CHURCH LANGTON.

S. PETER.             8 BELLS.

1. OMNIA FIANT AD GLORIAM DEI E.D.G. HANBURY
     1762. LET US CALL UPON THE LORD WHO IS
     WORTHY TO BE PRAISED
         (Diam. 28 in.)

2. NOS SUMU$^s$ CONSTRUCTI AD LAUDEM DOMINI E.D.G.
     HANBURY ANNO DOM 1762 PRAISE HIM UPON
     THE LOUD CYMBALS
         (Diam. 30 in.)

3. JOSEPH EAYRE S. NEOTS FECIT. LAUS TIBI SIT
     TRINE TIBI GLORIA SIT SINE FINE 1763. LET
     EVERYTHING THAT HATH BREATH PRAISE THE
     LORD
         (Diam. 32 in.)

4. THOMAS NORRIS MADE MEE 1676.

> (Diam. 34 in.)

5. The same.

> (Diam. 36 in.)

6. [ + 34 ] JESVS BE OVR SPED

Under which are in ornate Gothic characters the letters ℏ ℥
[ □ 37 and 38 ] the C being placed upside down to serve for D.

> (Diam. 38 in.)

7. OMNIA FIANT AD GLORIAM DEI. WILLIAM BUSWELL
   AND JOHN BUZZARD C. WARDENS THO. EAYRE
   KETT

> (Diam. 42 in.) ˙

8. OMNIA FIANT AD GLORIAM DEI. HENRY WARD AND
   THOMAS BUZZARD C. W. THO. EAYRE K. 1741.

> (Diam. 48 in.)

The ring consisted of five bells until the year 1763.

In his First Proposals with regard to the Foundations at Church Langton issued in 1758, the Rev. W. Hanbury included amongst the intended "decorations" of the church there, "three bells, to be added to the five, to make a peal of eight."

These bells were ordered by him in the winter of 1761-2. He says in his History &c.:—"I therefore sent for Mr. Joseph Cayne* of S. Neots in Huntingdonshire, who engaged to cast three entire new bells, and complete the peal of eight, to be in time and ready for ringing, all in new frames, by the Michaelmas following. Though this was engaged for, it was not done, for they were not finished before the summer after; which was reckoned by some to have been short enough for such an undertaking."†

A description of the bells, with their mottos as given above, will be found in Mr. Hanbury's History, p. 169, as also an amusing account of the dispute he had with the two ladies of the manor, Mrs. Byrd and Mrs. Pickering, relating to these bells, and to other of his proposals

---

* A printer's blunder for Eayre.    † Pp. 17, 137, 138.

X

connected with his gigantic scheme for the Foundations at Church Langton.

The bells are rung on Shrove-Tuesday at noon. At the death-knell three tolls are given for a male, two for a woman, one for a child, both before and after the knell.

## CLAYBROOKE.

S. PETER.                                                   4 BELLS.

1. IH'S : NAZARENVS [9] REX : IVDEORVM [9] FILI :
   DEI [9] MISERERE : MEI [9] 1618 [ ▽ 1. ]
   (Diam. 35¼ in.)

2. The same dated 1626 [ ▽ 1. ]
   (Diam. 39 in.)

3. ALL GLORY BEE TO GOD ON HIGH 1672 ○ ○ ○
   (Diam. 42 in.)

4. ḥuins sce petre [ ☐ ☐ 28 and 29 ] [ ☐ 61 ] [ ▽ 63. ]
   (Diam. 46¼ in.)

In 1611 the clerk had 8s. yearly for ringing the Curfew, and 3d. for ringing a Passing-bell. The Pancake-bell was then rung on Shrove-Tuesday.—*Macaulay's Hist. of Claybrooke*, pp. 94 and 128. This bell is still rung: the Curfew is discontinued. At the death-knell, three tolls are given thrice for a male; two tolls thrice for a female.

On Sundays the tenor bell is rung at 8 a.m. Before the Services the tenor bell is again rung for fifteen minutes, after which all the bells are chimed for fifteen minutes.

## COALVILLE.

CHRIST'S CHURCH.                                            1 BELL.

1. THOMAS MEARS, FOUNDER, LONDON, 1838.

# COLD OVERTON.

S. John Baptist.                                     3 Bells.

1.  J TAYLOR & SON FOUNDERS LOUGHBOROUGH 1857.
(Weight 7 cwt. 0 qrs. 5℔.  The ancient bell weighed 5 cwt. 2 qrs. 24 ℔.)
2.  + 𝔑omen 𝔐agdalene  ampana 𝔊erit 𝔐elodie ▽
              ( The founder has omitted the capital C. )
3.  THOMAS NORRIS MADE MEE 1664 H.G. H.B.

In 6 Edward VI. there were " iij bells and a saint's bell.

# COLE-ORTON.

S. Mary.                                            6 Bells.

1, 2, 3, 4, 5.  T. MEARS OF LONDON FECIT 1826.
6. REV. F. MEREWETHER RECTOR EDWARD BUTT
       KNIGHT THOMAS AYRE CHURCHWARDENS GOD
       SAVE THE CHURCH.  T. MEARS OF LONDON
       FECIT 1826.

Previous to 1826 there were only three bells.

# CONGERSTONE.

S. Mary.                                            5 Bells.

1.  JOHN TAYLOR BELLFOUNDER OXFORD & LOUGH-
       BOROUGH 1841.
                   ( Diam. 27 in. )
2.  JOHN TAYLOR FECIT OXFORD & LOUGHBOROUGH
       1841.  GOD SAVE THE QUEEN.
                   ( Diam. 28 in. )
3.  JOHN TAYLOR BELLFOUNDER OXFORD & LOUGH-
       BOROUGH J SANDS E BAXTER CHURCHWARDENS
       1841.
                   ( Diam. 28⅛ in. )

4. JOHN TAYLOR BELLFOUNDER OXFORD & LOUGH-
    BOROUGH.   F. M. KNOLLIS M.A. RECTOR J. M.
    COX B.A. CURATE 1841.
                    ( Diam. 32 in. )
5. J. TAYLOR BELLFOUNDER LOUGHBRO & OXFORD
    WHEN WEDDED HEARTS THEIR CONTRACT SEAL
    I RING FOR THEM THE MERRY PEAL
    WHEN FRIENDS LAMENT THE PARTING SOUL
    HERALD OF DEATH MY DIRGE I TOLL
    FOR YOUNG AND OLD FOR GRAVE AND GAY
    MY CHIME RESOUNDS EACH SACRED DAY.
            ( Diam. 35½ in.   Weight 7 cwt.   Key A. )

Previous to 1841 (when the Right Honourable the Earl Howe gave
the present ring) there were two bells only.


# COPT OAK.

S. PETER.                                                    I BELL.

One small modern bell.


# COSBY.

S. MICHAEL.                                                  3 BELLS.

1. ABCDE   FGHIK   LMNO 1612 [ ▽ 1. ]
                    ( Diam. 29 in. )
2. CELORVM CHRSTE PLATIAT TIBI REX SONVS ISTE
    161 (?) [ ▽ 1. ]
                    ( Diam. 32 in. )
3. [ + 3 ] S   M A R I A  [ □ 16 ] [ ▽ 6. ]
                    ( Diam. 35 in. )

A morning bell is rung at 8 a.m. and again at 9 a.m. on Sundays.
Pancake-bell is rung on Shrove-Tuesday.

## COSSINGTON.

ALL SAINTS. 4 BELLS.

1. [ + 74 ] 𝕊 [ + 74 ] 𝕊 [ + 74 ] 𝕊
2. [ + 83 ] 𝕳𝖎𝖈 𝕮𝖆𝖒𝖕𝖆𝖓𝖆 𝕮𝖊𝖑𝖎𝖘 𝕽𝖊𝖘𝖔𝖓𝖊𝖙 𝕾𝖆𝖓𝖈𝖙𝖎 𝕸𝖎𝖈𝖍𝖆𝖊𝖑𝖎𝖘
   [ □ 52 ] over the inscription on 3rd bell.
3. 𝕮𝖊𝖑𝖔𝖗𝖚𝖒 𝖝𝖏𝖊 𝖕𝖑𝖆𝖈𝖊𝖆𝖙 𝖙𝖎𝖇𝖎 𝖗𝖊𝖝 𝖘𝖔𝖓𝖚𝖘 𝖎𝖘𝖙𝖊
4. IH'𝕊 : NAZARENVS [9] REX : IVDEORVM [9] FILI :
   DEI : [9] MISERERE : MEI [9] 1619 [ ⛁ 1. ]

## COSTON.

S. ANDREW. 2 BELLS.

1. GRATA SIT ARGUTA RESONANS CAMPANULA VOCE
   ANNO DOM 1729 + ○ ○ ○
   ( Diam. 25¼ in. )
2. GOD  SAVE  THE  KING  1671
   ( Diam. 28 in. )

In 6 Edward VI. there were "iij bells of a corde."

The 1st was previously inscribed :—" God save the Church 1638." The 2nd was cast by Norris of Stamford. There were formerly three bells. The ancient tenor was inscribed " Cœlorum Christe placeat tibi Rex sonus iste." It was lying many years ago, cracked, at the foot of the tower: it long ago disappeared.

The Pancake-bell is rung on Shrove-Tuesday.

## COTES.

In 6 Edward VI. there were here " tow belles and a small belle : a hand belle."

## COTTESBACH.

S. MARY.                                                    2 BELLS.

1. Blank and cracked.
2. [ + 55 ] IN [ □ 59 ] HONORE [ □ 59 ] SCE
   [ □ 59 ] TRINITATIS.

## COUNTESTHORPE.

S. ANDREW.                                                  4 BELLS.

1. EDWARD ARNOLD ST. NEOTS FECIT 1773.
2. J. HALL C : WARDEN.  J. BRIANT HERTFORD FECIT
   1816.
3. GOD [ 12 ] SAVE [ 12 ] HIS [ 12 ] CHVRCH [ 12 ] 1704.
4. W. WOOD 1686.

## CRANOE.

S. MICHAEL.                                                 2 BELLS.

1. [ + 42 ] SCĪ [ □ 43 ] PETRI
                    ( Diam. 22 in. )
2. [ + 42 ] AVE MARI
                    ( Diam. 24 in. )

## CROFT.

S. MICHAEL.                                                 3 BELLS.

1. EDWd ARNOLD ST. NEOTS HUNTINGDONSHIRE FECIT
   1777.
                    ( Diam. 29 in. )
2. The same dated 1776.
                    ( Diam. 32 in. )

3. 〔symbols〕 [ ∪ 6. ]
(Diam. 34 in.)

On the 2nd April 1605 the Churchwardens delivered to their successors among other things:—" Three bells with their furniture in the steeple and one ladder there." In 1664 they charge " Paid for ringing the bells on Nov' 5<sup>th</sup> o 2*s.* 6*d.*"

## CROXTON KERRIAL.

S. JOHN.                                                                 5 BELLS.

1. ✠ MEROREM : MESTIS : LETIS : SIC : LETA : SONABO
   1613.
2. [ + 52 ] JHESVS BE OVR SPEDE
   [ ℞ 37 ] [ ∪ 32 ] [ ℬ 38 ]
   ( The last initial is C reversed to do duty for D. )
3. AVE MARIA [ ∪ 63 ]
   ( Fine Gothic capitals like Melton 4th. )
4. GOD    SAVE    THE    KING    B    GOLDING
   TOBIE    NORRIƧ    CAƧT    ME    1674.
5. CELORVM CHRSTE PLATIAT IBE REX SONVS ISTE
   [ ∪ 1. ]

In 6 Edward VI. there were " iiij bells of a ryng and a sauntys bell."
Some years ago the sanctus bell was discovered on the floor of the bell-chamber. It is now used as a priest's bell.

[ CROXTON SOUTH—see South Croxton. ]

## DADLINGTON.

S. JAMES.                                                                 2 BELLS.

1. A O ( on rim of bell. )
                              ( Diam. 20¼ in. )
2. E. ARNOLD FECIT 1793.
                              ( Diam. 23 in. )

## DALBY MAGNA.

S. Swithun.                                                    5 Bells.

1. THIS AND THE FIFTH WAS RECST BY SUBSCRIPTION
   1784. JOHN WARTNABY CHURCHWARDEN THOS.
   HEDDERLY FECIT NOT^M.
   (Diâm. 30¼ in. )

2. GOD [ 12 ] SAVE [ 12 ] HIS [ 12 ] CHVRCH [ 12 ] 1684 [ 12 ]
   ( Diam. 32¼ in. )

3. FRANSIS [9] GOODWIN [9] ANNO
   [9] DOMINI 1598 [9] [ ⛉ 1. ]
   ( Diam. 33 in. )

4. ABCDEFGHIKLMNO [ ⛉ 1. ]
   ( Diam. 33¼ in. )

5. I TO THE CHURCH THE LIVING CALL & TO THE
   GRAVE DO SUMMONS ALL
   JOHN WARTNABY CHURCH WARDEN THO. HEDDERLY
   FECIT NOTTINGHAM 1784.
   ( Diam. 38¼ in. : a band [ 12 ])

The Pancake-bell is rung on Shrove-Tuesday. A Gleaning-bell is
rung during harvest. At the death-knell three tolls are given for a
male, two for a female, both before and after the knell.

Nichols says: "The Rev. Philip Hacket, twenty-five years Curate
of this parish and Rector of South Croxton, was a great promoter and
subscriber to this work (*i.e.* the recasting of the 1st and 5th bells) and
by the help of Mr. Wartnaby, a gentleman of good estate in Great
Dalby, brought it to a completion."

## DALBY ON THE WOLDS.

S. John Baptist.                                              4 Bells.

1. GOD    SAVE    THE    CHVRCH    1631.
   ( Diam. 29 in. )

2. THOMAS MEARS OF LONDON FOUNDER 1835.

(Diam. 33 in.)

3. [ + 52 ] ANDREW NOWEL ESQUIER ANO D 1584 [ □ 50. ]
[ *Donor's* ▽ *Arms.* ] [ ▽ 32 ]

(Diam. 33 in.)

4. [ + 36 ] all men that heare my mornfull sound repent before you lye in ground 1608.

(Diam. 38 in.)

Sir Andrew Noel was lord of the manor. He married Mabel, 6th daughter of Sir James Harington, sister and heir of John Lord Harington, of Exton, and died, at his seat, Brook House, in Rutland, 9th October, 1607.

His brother, Henry Noel, was one of the gentlemen pensioners of Queen Elizabeth, and lived in such magnificence—considering the smallness of his estate—as to call forth what Burton calls this "Ænigmaticall Distich" upon his name from his royal mistress:

"The word of deniall and letter of fifty
Is that gentleman's name that will never be thrifty."

*Burton's Leic.* (1622) p. 87.

## DALBY PARVA.

S. JAMES. 3 BELLS.

1. IH'S : NAZARENVS [ 9 ] REX : IVDEORVM [ 9 ] FILI : DEI [ 9 ] MISERERE : MEI [ 9 ] 1627 [ ▽ 1. ]

(Diam. 32 in.)

2. [ + 58 ] ISTA [ □ 57 ] CĀPANA [ □ 57 ] EST [ □ 57 ] CŌPOSITA [ □ 57 ] IN [ □ 57 ] HONORE [ □ 57 ] BTE [ □ 57 ] MARIA [ □ 57 ] VIRGĪS.

(Diam. 35 in. The mark of contraction placed over the four words is engraved fig. 66.)

3. [ + 45 ] AVE : MARIA : GRACIA : PLENA : DOMINVS : TECVM
(Diam. 34 in.)

In 6 Edward VI. there were "iij bells j sanctus bell."


# DESFORD.

S. MARTIN.                                                    3 BELLS.

1. GOD SAVE THE KING 1675.
(Diam. 28 in.)
2. JESVS BEE OVR SPEED 1658.
(Diam. 29¼ in.)
3. [ + 22 ] NEWCOM OF LEICESTER MADE MEE 1609.
(Diam. 33 in.)


# DISEWORTH.

S. MICHAEL.                                                   4 BELLS.

1. R. SOWTER & T. HASTINGS C. W. JOHN BRIANT
HERTFORD & B. CORT LEICESTER FECERUNT
1803.
(Diam. 32 in.)
2. IH'2 NAZARENVS REX IVDEORVM 1672 [ □ 10. ]
(Diam. 36 in.)
3. GOD SAVE THE CHVRCH 1626.
(Diam. 39 in.)
4. [ + 34 ] GOD SAVE HIS CHVRCH
1619 [ □ 8. ]
(Diam. 40½ in.)

In 6 Edward VI. there were "Three bells and one of them broken."
The Pancake-bell is rung on Shrove-Tuesday, and a morning bell on
Sundays at 7 and 9 a.m.

# DISHLEY.

ALL SAINTS.                                                    1 BELL.

1. 1813.

   The church in ruins.


# DUNTON BASSETT.

ALL SAINTS.                                                   3 BELLS.

1. IH'S : NAZARENVS [9] REX : IVDEORVM [9] FILI :
   DEI [9] MISERERE : MEI [9] 1619 [ ▽ 1. ]
2. BE IT KNOWNE TO ALL THAT DOTH ME SEE
   THAT CLAY OF LEICESTER MADE ME
   NICH: HARALD AND JOHN MORE CHURCHWARDENS
   1711.
3. The same as 1st dated 1621.


# EARL'S SHILTON.

S. PETER.                                                     3 BELLS.

1. [ + 22 ] NEWCOMBE OF LEICESTER MADE MEE 1606.
2. THO · BERNARD · AND · THO · WILEMAN · CHVRCH-
   WARDENS · THO · CLAY · MADE · ME · 1711.
3. [ + 22 ] BE · YT · KNOWNE · TO · ALL · THAT · DOTH
   ME · SEE · THAT · NEWCOMBE · OF · LEICESTER ·
   MADE · MEE · 1612.

   At death-knell thrice 3 are tolled for a male; thrice 2 for a female.
The bells are rung at midnight on the Eves of Christmas and the New
Year.

*⁎* Since the above inscriptions were taken the 2nd bell has been recast, all rehung, and two new bells added from the Loughborough foundry, at the cost of Mr. Thomas Holyland of Leicester.

## EAST NORTON.

ALL SAINTS.        3 BELLS.

1. GOD SAVE THE kING [ ∪ 1. ]
   (Diam. 22 in.)
2. GOD SAVE HIS CHURCH W EAGLEFIELD
   C. W O HEDDERLY FOUNDER 1779
   (Diam. 24 in.)
3. [ + 3 ] ଲ୍ [ + 3 ] ଲ୍ [ + 3 ] ଲ୍ [ ∪ 6 ]
   (Diam. 26¼ in.)

## EASTON GREAT.

S. ANDREW.        5 BELLS.

1, 2. HENRY BAGLEY MADE MEE 1684.
3. MATTHEW BAGLEY MADE MEE 1684.
4. RICHARD WIGNELL AND JOHN COLIN CHURCH-WARDENS 1684.
5. I TO THE CHURCH THE LIVEING CALL AND TO THE GRAVE DO SUMMON ALL 1684.

## EASTWELL.

S. MICHAEL.        1 BELL.

1. GOD [ 12 ] SAVE [ 12 ] HIS [ 12 ] CHVRCH [ 12 ] 1691 [ 12 ]

There is also a priest's bell without inscription.
In 6 Edward VI. there was "j small bell j sanctus bell."

## EATON.

S. DENYS.                                                          4 BELLS.

1. [ + 36 ] 𝕬𝕷𝕷 𝕲𝕷𝕺𝕽𝖄 𝕭𝕰𝕰 𝕿𝕺 𝕲𝕺𝕯 𝕸𝕺𝕾𝕿 𝕳𝕴𝕲𝕳 [ □ 8 ] 1618.
   𝕽.𝕾.
2. GOD SAVE HIS CHVRCH 1628.
3. TAYLOR & SON LOUGHBOROUGH S. THOROLD 1858.
4. [ + 34 ] 𝕵𝕳𝕰𝕾𝖁𝕾 𝕭𝕰 𝕺𝖁𝕽 𝕾𝕻𝕰𝕰𝕯 1589.
   [ □ 8. ]

In 6 Edward VI. there were "iij belles with oon lytyll bell in the stepull."

## EDMONTHORPE.

S. MICHAEL.                                                        3 BELLS.

1. [ + 3 ] 𝕬 𝕭 𝕯 𝕯 𝕰 𝕱 𝕲 𝕳 𝕴 [ □ 49 ] [ □ 62. ]
2. GLORY BE TO GOD ON HIGH 1776. SAMUEL FARMER
   ROBINSON C.W. THOS. HEDDERLY : FOUNDER :
   NOTTᴹ
3. GOD SAVE THE KING 1665.

In 6 Edward VI. there were "iij belles."

## ELMSTHORPE.

S. MARY.                                                           1 BELL.

There is one small bell founded by Taylor and Co. of Loughborough.
It was given by the Rector (the Rev. E. Tower) when he recently
restored the church, which had been for many years in ruins and
desecrated.

Mr. Richard Fowke, formerly a resident here, in his MS. History of Elmsthorpe, written in 1783, remarks: "Tradition says there were two bells, one bell hanging . . . . sixty or seventy years ago."


# ENDERBY.

S. JOHN.                    •                    5 BELLS.

1, 2, 3, 4, 5. JOHN TAYLOR & CO FOUNDERS LOUGH-
BOROUGH 1868.

This ring was the gift of the late Charles Brook Esq. The weight of tenor 10 cwt. Key G. There were only three bells previously.


# EVINGTON.

S. DENIS.                                        3 BELLS.

1.  IH'S : NAZARENVS [9] REX : IVDEORVM [9] FILI`:
DEI [9] MISERERE : MEI [9] 1637 [ ∪ 1. ]

2.  HUGH BATES MADE MEE
1605 [ ∪ 1. ]

3.  REVᴅ. RICHᴅ. COLTMAN VICAR RICHᴅ. GODDARD
CHURCHWARDEN EDWᴅ. ARNOLD FECIT 1797.

The Vicar's correct name was Richard *Colton.*

The Pancake-bell is rung on Shrove-Tuesday.

The Rev. W. B. Moore informs me that there is a tradition that a certain lady being lost in the neighbourhood of Evington found her whereabouts by the ringing of the church bells. To show her gratitude she purchased a piece of land and bequeathed it for the benefit of the Evington ringers for ever: certain it is there is still a field in the parish called "The Ringers' Close," but no benefit accrues from it to the ringers.

## FENNY DRAYTON.

S. Michael.                                              4 Bells.

1. [ + 42 ] IN HO [ □ 43 ] NORE [ □ 43 ] MICHAEL [ □ 43 ] ARCHANGEL
   (Diam. 30 in.)

2. GEORGE [ + 44 ] PUREFIE ESQUIER [ + 44 ] ANNO D 1596 [ ♈ 1. ]
   (Diam. 31 in.)

3. Hec Campana Sacra Fiat Trinitate Beata 1684.
   (Diam. 34 in. from the Nottingham foundry, as is shown by an
   ornamental border.)

4. THE GIFT OF SIR HENRY PURIEFOY BARONET 1684
   RECAST 1710 T. BOWNE WARDEN.
   (Diam. 36 in.)

The Purefeys were settled here as early as the reign of Richard II.

## FLECKNEY.

S. Nicolas.                                              1 Bell.

1. A.B.C. + 1604.

Tradition says there were formerly two bells. The Pancake-bell is
rung on Shrove-Tuesday at 11 a.m. The bell is rung at 8 a.m. on
Sunday mornings. The Death-knell is rung between sunrise and sun-
set only.

## FOSTON.

S. Bartholomew.                                         1 Bell.

1. IH'S : NAZARENVS · REX : IVDEORVM · FILI : DEI ·
   MISERERE MEI · 1617 [ ♈ 1. ]
   O O O

There were formerly three bells.  Two were sold about fifty years ago to pay for the repair of the tower: "a great and lasting disgrace" (remarks the present Rector) "to those then in power."

## FOXTON.

S. ANDREW.                                                         5 BELLS.

1. CELORVM CHRSTE [9] PLATIAT TIBI REX [9] SONVS
   ISTE [9] 1629 [9] [ ᴗ 1. ]
2. IH'2 : NAZARENVS [9] REX : IVDEORVM [9] FILI :
   DEI [9] MISERERE : MEI [9] [ ᴗ 1. ]
3. [ + 39 ]    𝕾𝕬𝕹𝕮𝕿𝕰𝕾𝕷𝕰𝕱𝕬𝕹𝕰𝕻𝕽𝕺𝕿𝕰
   𝕸𝕬𝕽𝕿𝕴𝕽𝕺𝕽𝕬𝕻𝕽𝕺𝕹𝕺𝕾𝕴𝕾
4. IH'2 : NAZARENVS [9] REX : IVDEORVM [9] FILI :
   DEI [9] MISERERE : MEI [9] 1632 [ ᴗ 1. ]
5. The same dated 1630.

The 3rd bell is dedicated to S. Stephen Proto-Martyr.  There are some founder's blunders in the letters.

## FREEBY.

S. MARY.                                                           3 BELLS.

1. GOD [9] SAVE [9] THE [9] kING [9] 1631 [9] [ ᴗ 1. ]
2. GOD [13] SAVE [13] HIS [13] CHVRCH [13] W [13] T
   [13] [ ☐ 10 ] 1658.
2. CELORVM CHRSTE PLATIAT TIBE REX SONVS ISTE
   1614 [ ᴗ 1. ]

In 6 Edward VI. there were "in the chapell of ffrebye a member of the churche of Melton iij bells in the stepell."

## FRISBY-ON-THE-WREAKE.

S. Thomas a Beckett.                                         3 Bells.

1. 𝕻𝕽𝕬𝕴𝕾𝕰 𝕿𝕳𝕰 𝕷𝕺𝕽𝕯𝕰 1600 [ □ 15]
   (Diam. 30¼ in.)
2. GOD [12] SAVE [12] HIS [12] CHVRCH [12] W SWIFT
   J IRELAND CHVRCHWARDENS 1711 [12]
   (Diam. 32 in.)
3. SUSCITO VOCE PIOS TU JESU DIRIGE MENTES [12]
   (Diam. 36¼ in.)

At the death-knell three "tellers" are given for a male; two for a female, both before and after the knell.

Previous to 1842 funerals were chimed to church : now the tenor bell only is tolled.

## FROLESWORTH.

S. Nicolas.                                                   3 Bells.

1. IH'S : NAZARENVS [9] REX : IVDEORVM [9] FILI :
   DEI [9] MISERERE : MEI [9] 1638 [9] [ ▽ 1. ]
   (Diam. 33 in.)
2. CŒLORUM CHRISTE PLACEAT TIBI REX SONUS
   ISTE + JOHN WRIGHT C.W. T. EAYRE KETT.
   FECIT 1749.
   (Diam. 36 in.)
3. [ + 76 ] 𝕾um 𝕽osa 𝕻ulsata 𝕸undi 𝕸aria 𝖁ocata.
   (Diam. 40 in.)

The Pancake-bell rings on Shrove-Tuesday.

## GADDESBY.

S. Luke.                                                      3 Bells.

1. GOD [12] SAVE [12] THE [12] KING [12] 1701.

   z

2. [ + 3 ] SANCTA MARIA
   [ ▽ 6. ]
3. GOD [ 12 ] SAVE [ 12 ] HIS [ 12 ] CHVRCH [ 12 ] B. REEVE
   S HVTTON WARDENS 1701.


## · GALBY.

S. Peter.                                              6 Bells.

1. OMNIA FIANT AD GLORIAM DEI ANNO DOMINI 1741.
   GLORIA DEO SOLI.
2. GRATA SIT ARGUTA RESONANS CAMPANULA VOCE
   GLORIA DEO SOLI.  T. EAYRE 1741.
3, 4, 5.  OMNIA FIANT AD GLORIAM DEI.  GLORIA PATRI
   FILIO ET SPIRITUI SANCTO 1741.
6. OMNIA FIANT AD GLORIAM DEI.  GLORIA  PATRI
   FILIO ET SPIRITUI SANCTO.  T. EAYRE KETT.
   1746.

(Weight 12 Cwt.)

The Tower and body of the church were rebuilt in 1741 by the
bounty of Mr. Fortrey, who at the same time gave the bells.—*Nichols.*


## GARTHORPE.

S. Mary.                                               3 Bells.

1. [ + 3 ] S A N N A [ □ 28 ] [ ▽ 26 ]
2. [ + 36 ] JHESVS BE OVR SPEED
   1608 [ □ 8 ]
3. [ + 21 ] GOD SAVE THE CHVRCH OVR QVEENE AND
   REALME AMEN 1600 [ □ 8. ]

In 6 Edward VI. there were "iij bells."

# GILMORTON.

ALL SAINTS. 5 BELLS.

1. WILLIAM BURDIT ROBART COULTMAN CHURCH-
   WARDENS JOSEPH EAYRE ST. NEOTS 1766.
2. TAYLOR & CO FOUNDERS LOUGHBOROUGH 1871.
3. GLORIA DEO SOLI : · T : EAYRE Wm. COALMAN &
   GEO ⁞ CARR : · C : · WARDENS 1738.
4. WILLIAM COLTMAN AND HERBERT RODGERS
   CHURCH W. 1861. JOHN TAYLOR & CO FOUND-
   ERS LOUGHBOROUGH.
5. GLORIA PATRI FILIO & SPIRITUI SACTO ·:· OMNIA
   FIANT AD GLORIAM DEI ✠ THO EAYRE KETT.
   FECIT : · ✠ 1749 ✠ ·
   (Weight 11 cwt.)

The 4th was previously inscribed " Richard Bvrdit Edward Whit-
head Wardens 1671."

# GLENFIELD.

S. PETER. 1 BELL.

1. GOD [9] SAVE [9] THE [9] KING [9] 1636 [9] [ ℧ 1. ]

There were three bells at the beginning of this century.

# GLEN-MAGNA.

S. CUTHBERT. 5 BELLS.

1. Wm. BURTON THO. HOBSON CHURCHWARDENS
   EDWd. ARNOLD FECIT 1785.
   (Diam. 28½ in.)
2. IH'S : NAZARENVS [9] REX : IVDEORVM [9] FILI : DEI
   (9) MISERERE : MEI [9] 1625 [ ℧ 1. ]
   (Diam. 29¼ in.)

3. Like 1st.

(Diam. 31 in.)

4. The same.

(Diam. 33¾ in.)

5. [ + 45] ISTA : CAMPANA : FACTA :
EST : IN : HONORE : SCI :
CUTHBERTI

(Diam. 37¾ in.)

The Pancake-bell is rung on Shrove-Tuesday.   The Curfew is lately discontinued.

At the death-knell thrice three tolls are given for a male, thrice two for a female.

On Sundays a morning bell is rung at 7 a.m.; it is rung again after morning service when Even-song is to be said.

## GLOOSTON.

S. John.                                                    2 Bells.

1. GLORIA PATRI FILIO ET SPIRITUI SANCTO 1730 +
2. + 1686 RECAST 1866 BY J. TAYLOR & CO.

## GOADBY.

1 Bell.

Blank.

(Diam. 16 in.)

## GOADBY-MARWOOD.

S. Denis.                                                   3 Bells.

1. THE CHVRCHS PRAISE I SOVND ALLWAYS 1775 THOs.
HEDDERLY FOVNDER.
2. GOD SAVE HIS CHVRCH [12] LEO DAVIS WARDEN
[12] 1710.

3. IH'S : NAZARENVS [9] REX : IVDEORVM [9] FILI :
   DEI [9] MISERERE : MEI [9] 1625 [ ▽ 1. ]

In 6 Edward VI. there were " iij bells."

The treble was previously inscribed "T. N. cast me 1694 W. Whalley
Churchwarden."

[ GREAT EASTON—see Easton Great. ]

[ GREAT ASHBY—see Ashby Magna. ]

[ GREAT BOWDEN—see Bowden Magna. ]

[ GREAT DALBY—see Dalby Magna. ]

[ GREAT GLEN—see Glen Magna. ]

[ GREAT PEATLING—see Peatling Magna. ]

[ GREAT WIGSTON—see Wigston Magna. ]

## GRIMSTONE.

S. JOHN.                                                          3 BELLS.

1. THIS BELL WAS RECAST TO SING BY FRIENDS TO
   COUNTRY AND KING.  GLOVER AND THOMAS
   AUSTIN CHURCHWARDENS THOs. HEDDERLEY
   FOUNDER NOTTINGHAM 1780.

2.  ANTHONY HEMSLEY CHURCHWARDEN.

3.  Ḣ̇ec Ꙭⰼⰰⰿⰲⰰⰿⰲⰰ [ 12 ] Ꙭⰰⰿⰼⰰ Ḟⰲⰲⰲ [ 12 ] Ꙭⰲⰲⰲⰲⰲⰲ [ 12 ] Ꙭⰲⰲⰲⰲ
    1749 *THOMAS HEDDERLEY FOUNDER.*

In Thomas Hedderley's Pocket Book (1780) still preserved are notes respecting these bells :*

"Grimstone Tenor note Lyeth betwixt A and G.   38¾ wide.
24 High.   2⅜ thick full. .

|            |              | H. | Q. | ℔  |
|------------|--------------|----|----|----|
| "Treble.   | Before Cast  | 5  | 2  | 7  |
|            | After Cast   | 6  | 0  | 18" |

## GROBY.

S. . . . . .                                           5 BELLS.

1, 2, 3, 4, 5.   THOMAS MEARS FOUNDER LONDON 1840.
(Diams. 23 in. to 30 in.)

## GUMLEY.

S. HELEN.                                              3 BELLS.

1.  IH'Ƨ : NAZARENVS [ 9 ] REX : IVDEORVM [ 9 ] FILI :
    DEI [ 9 ] MISERERE : MEI 1625 [ ▽ 1. ]

2.  † O IHS NAZARENVS REX IVDEORVM FILI DEI
    MISERERE MEI GLORIA DEO SOLI ANNO DOM : ·
    1721 ✠

3.  · [ + 39 ] Ꙭ꙾ꙍ꙾Ꙍ : ꙮꙏꙐꙑꙒꙓ : ꙔꙕꙖꙗꙘ :
    ꙙꙚꙛꙜꙝ : ꙞꙟꙠ : ꙡꙢꙣꙤꙥ

## HALLATON.

S. MICHAEL.                                            5 BELLS.

1.  THOMAS NORRIS MADE ME 1655 RG. JB.

─────────────────────────────────────────────

* Extracted for me by W. P. W. Phillimore, Esq.

2. THOMAS NORRIS MADE ME 1655.
3. PEACE AND GOOD NEIGHBOURHOOD 1772.
4. THOs. GIBBINS CHURCHWARDEN EDWd. ARNOLD 1772.
   (This inscription is incised.)
5. THOs. GIBBINS CHURCHWARDEN EDWd. ARNOLD St.
   NEOTS FECIT 1772.

There are chimes which play every third hour. The Pancake-bell is rung on Shrove-Tuesday. Thirty years ago there was a curious custom allowed here on S. Andrew's Day:—the school children locked the master out of the belfry and jangled the bells: this custom was discontinued upon the death of the then aged master.

## HARBY.

S. MARY.                                                4 BELLS.

1. [ + 36 ] JHESVS BE OVR SPEED
   1610 [ ☐ 8. ]
2. [ + 36 ] GOD SAVE THE CHVRCH 1610 [ ☐ 8. ]
3. GOD [ 12 ] SAVE [ 12 ] HIS [ 12 ] CHVRCH [ 12 ] R WHITTLE
   [ 12 ] J BROOKBANK WARDENS 1701.
4. [ + 34 ] 1614 GLORY BE TO GOD ON
   HIGH [ ☐ 8. ]

In 6 Edward VI. there were "iij bells a saynts bell yn ye stepull."

## HARSTON.

S. MICHAEL.                                             3 BELLS.

1. GOD SAVE OVR QUEENE 1602 [ ☐ 8. ]
   (Diam. 26 in.)
2. THOMAS NORRIS MADE ME 1662.
   (Diam. 28 in.)
3. THE PARSON AND HIS PEOPLE GAVE ME 1873.
   (Diam. 30 in.   Weight 5 cwt. 2 qrs. 11¼ ℔.)

The tenor bell, which bore the same inscription as the 2nd, was (being cracked) recast as shown in 1873, by Messrs. Warner and Sons of London.

## HATHERN.

S. PETER.                                                    5 BELLS.

1. WAS RAISED BY 'VOLUNTARY SUBSCRIPTION G. HEDDERLEY NOTTM. 1791.
2. EDWARD DEANE AND THOMAS HARRIMAN CHURCH- WARDENS G. HEDDERLEY FECIT NOTTM. 1791.
3. THOMAS THRONE AND THOMAS BERRINGTON 1618 [ □ 8. ]
4. THOMAS BERRINGTON J. O. THRONE 1620 [ □ 8. ]
5. EDWARD DEANE AND THOMAS HARRIMAN CHURCH- WARDENS EDWARD ARNOLD FECIT 1792.

In 6 Edward VI. there were "three belles and tow hand belles." The above ring was "opened" 18 July 1792.

## HEATHER.

S. JOHN.                                                    3 BELLS.

1. JOHN EVERARD RECTOR 1734.
                    (Diam. 25¼ in.)
2. GOD SAVE HIS CHVRCH 1734  W. BAILIE
                    (Diam. 28 in.)
3. IH'Ƨ : NAZARENVS [9] REX : IVDEORVM [9] FILI : DEI [9] MISERERE : MEI [9] 1630 [9] [ ▽ 1. ]
                    (Diam. 31 in.)

A Gleaning-bell is rung during Harvest.

## HIGHAM-ON-THE-HILL.

S. Peter.                                    5 Bells.

1. JAMES BARWELL FOUNDER BIRMINGHAM 1872.
   (Diam. 29¼ in.)
2. IH'2 : NAZARENVS [9] REX : IVDEORVM [9] FILI : DEI
   [9] MISERERE : MEI [9] 1629 [ ꙍ 1.]
   (Diam. 31 in.)
3. [ + 3 ] 𝕻𝕽𝕬𝕴𝕰𝕾 [ □ * ] 𝕲𝕺𝕯 [ □ * ] 𝕬𝕷
   [ □ * ] 𝖂𝕬𝕴𝕰𝕾 1589.
   (Diam. 33¼ in. * a fleur-de-lys.)
4. [ + 42 ] 𝕾𝕬𝕹𝕮 [ □ 43 ] 𝕿𝕬 [ □ 43 ] 𝕻𝕳 [ □ 43 ]
   𝕿𝕽𝕳 [ □ 43 ] [ ꙍ 6.]
   (Diam. 38 in.)
5. JAMES BARWELL FOUNDER BIRMINGHAM 1872
   (Diam. 40¾ in. Weight 11 cwt. 2 qrs. 10 ℔. Note A flat.)

Previous to 1872 there were only three bells.


## HINCKLEY.

S. Mary.                                     8 Bells.

1. REVᴅ JOHN COLE GALLAWAY A M VICAR THOs
   TOWLE CHURCHWARDEN EDWᴅ ARNOLD FECIT
   1792.
   (Diam. 30 in.)
2. The same.
   (Diam. 31 in.)
3. BY THE VOLUNTARY CONTRIBUTIONS OF THE
   FRIENDS OF CHURCH AND KING Wᴍ. TURNER
   THOs. MEWIS CHURCHWARDENS 1782 † E.
   ARNOLD FECIT
   (Diam. 33 in.)

2 A

4. The same as 1st.
(Diam. 35 in.)

5. CELORVM CHRSTE PLATIAT TIBI REX SONVS ISTE
1617 [ ▽ I. ]
(Diam. 36 in.)

6. The same.
(Diam. 38 in.)

7. IH'S : NAZARENVS⸱ REX : IVDEORVM FILI : DEI
MISERERE : MEI 1617 [ ▽ I. ]
(Diam. 41 in.)

8. .:. J RUDHALL GLOUCESTER FECт .:. REVᴅ MATTᴡ
BROWN VICAR THOs NEEDHAM SENʀ & Wᴍ
TOMLINSON C. W. 1825.
(Diam. 47 in.)

Burton mentions that Hinckley possessed "a very tuneable ring of
five bells" in 1622. These bells, says Nichols, were cast "in the reign
of James I. in commemoration of purchasing the manor" by the town
of Hinckley from the Earl of Nottingham in the year 1604. Judging
from the present 5th 6th and 7th bells, this ring of five was cast by
Hugh Watts in 1617. A treble bell (the present third) was added by
public subscription in 1777 (making the ring six in number). This bell
was soon afterwards cracked by lightning and recast. The tenor was
recast in 1779, and again in 1825. In 1792 two more trebles were added,
and so the present ring of eight was completed.

Unfortunately there are no Parish Records preserved in the church
from which to learn any particulars about the bells.

Messrs. Harrold and Baxter have kindly supplied the following notes:

The Curfew (5th bell) is rung during the winter months: at its close
the day of the month is tolled on the tenor bell. The parish clerk
formerly received for this service the rent of a small field which was
awarded to him by the Commissioners on the inclosure of the common
fields in 1761. *(See also Charity Commissioners' Report*, 1837, p. 174.)
The Pancake-bell (the 3rd) is rung at 11 a.m. on Shrove-Tuesday:
after which any one was allowed on payment of one penny to go into

the belfry and to ring the bells. This reprehensible privilege is now withdrawn.

On the 29th May the ringers (in addition to ringing merry peals) used to place large boughs of oak over the doors of the houses occupied by the principal inhabitants, and always fixed a large bough on the battlements of the church. This custom is now discontinued.

For "the Ringers' Call" for a wedding the treble bell is tolled three times three; then pulled up and down again very quickly: three times three is then repeated.

At the death-knell three tolls are given on each bell for a man; two tolls for a woman both before and after the knell: for a boy under ten years of age thrice three tolls are given on the tenor bell both before and after the knell: for a girl thrice two tolls. During the procession to the cemetery and whilst the Office is being said the tenor bell is tolled.

The Sunday use is:—At 7 a.m. the treble bell is rung: at 8 a.m. the 4th and 5th bells are rung for ten minutes, after which a peal on all the bells is generally rung for half-an-hour. For Divine Service the bells commencing with the treble are tolled round separately a few times; when a sermon is to be preached the tenor is then rung for ten minutes; after which the other bells are chimed twice round, the tenor is "lowered," then chiming is continued for a time; the treble or parson's bell is next rung to call the vicar, and it is "lowered" at the proper time for commencing the service. At 1 p.m. the 4th and 5th bells are again rung.

## HOBY.

ALL SAINTS.                                4 BELLS.

1. ABC   DEF   GHI.
2. THOMAS NEWCOMBE OF LEICESTER MADE ME 1604.
3. COME COME AND PRAYE
4. CELORVM CHRSTE PLATIAT TIBE REX SONVS ISTE
   1613 [ ∇ 1. ]

Nichols says: "Susannah and Dorothy Danvers (probably during the latter part of the seventeenth century) having been on a visit at the village (Thrussington) and staying a little too late were lost on the wolds, and at length regained their path to the grange on hearing the great bell of Hoby ring at eight o'clock; in commemoration of which they jointly settled from each of their fortunes a piece of land containing about four or five acres in a meadow in Thrussington lordship, appointing the said bell to be rung at the same hour to the end of time, and made the Vicar of Thrussington and Rector of Hoby trustees and guardians of the performance. On the inclosure of Thrussington fields a proportionate quantity of land was allotted to the Rector of Hoby as near as conveniently might be to the ring fence of his own parish. This laudable custom is still observed."

I am informed that this small field is now reckoned as part of the Hoby Glebe. The bell has not been rung for forty years.

# HOLT.

S. MARY.                                                    1 BELL.

1.  1833.

# HOLWELL.

S. LEONARD.                                                1 BELL.

1.  HOLWELL CHAPEL D.D. H. C. B. 1850 C. & G. MEARS
    FEC.
                        ( Diam. 11 in. )

In 6 Edward VI. there were "ij bells."

The above bell was the gift of the late H. C. Bingham, Esq., as the initials indicate. The report is that when that gentleman restored Holwell Church he brought the ancient bell away to his residence, Wartnaby Hall; this is probable; but if so it was afterwards recast, for the Dinner-bell at Wartnaby Hall is now inscribed:—"Cast by Taylor & Son Loughborough for H. C. Bingham Esq. of Wartnaby Hall, August 1856." It is 18 inches in diameter.

# HORNINGHOLD.

S. PETER.                                                      3 BELLS.

1. [ + 78 ]  AVE  [ □ 77 ]  MARIA  [ □ 77 ]
   ORA PLENA
2. IH'Σ : NAZARENVS [9] REX : IVDEORVM [9] FILI :
   DEI [9] MISERERE : MEI [9] 1628 [ ∪ 1. ]
3. ABCD EFG HIKL


# HOSE.

S. MICHAEL.                                                    5 BELLS.

1, 2, 3, 4. JOHN TAYLOR & SON FOUNDERS LOUGH-
   BOROUGH 1858.
   (Diam. of 1st 30 in.)
5. JOHN TAYLOR & SON FOUNDERS LOUGHBOROUGH.
   JAMES ROUSE & HENRY SHILCOCK CHURCH-
   WARDENS 1858.
   (Diam. 36¼ in.  Key G.)

In 6 Edward VI. there were "iij bells j sanctus bell."

Before 1858 there were still three bells.  Nichols says the first was
inscribed, "God save his church 1613," and the second " + Scī Nicholai."
The third he has not preserved.

The cost of the present ring, including new frames and fixing, was
£193. 13s. 5d. and the metal of the old bells.

The Pancake-bell is rung on Shrove-Tuesday, and the Gleaning-bell
during Harvest.


# HOTON-BY-PRESTWOLD.

S. . . . . .                                                   1 BELL.

1. T. MEARS OF LONDON FECIT 1833.

There were formerly two bells here

# HOUGHTON-ON-THE-HILL.

S. CATHARINE.                                                    5 BELLS.

1. THIS BELL WAS ADDED TO THE PEAL 1771. JOHN
   SEWELL CHURCHWARDEN.
                        [ ▽ 1 ]

2. 𝕿 𝖉 𝕰 𝕱 𝕺 𝕾 𝕲 [ ▫ 53 ] [ ▫ 49. ]
                ( In ornate Gothic capitals. )

3. WILLIAM ⦂ TOMPSON ⦂ GENT ⦂ A ⦂ RIGBY ⦂ MADE ⦂
   ME ⦂ 1706 ⦂ JOHN ⦂ HAMES ⦂ CH ⦂ W ⦂

4. IH'S ⦂ NAZARENVS [9] REX ⦂ IVDEORVM [9] FILI ⦂
   DEI [9] MISERERE ⦂ MEI [9] 1638 [ ▽ 1. ]

5. OMNIA FIANT AD GLORIAM DEI.  JOHN SEWELL
   CHURCHWARDEN 1771.

Previous to 1771 (when the 1st bell was given by Wm. Fortrey, Esq.,
of King's Norton) the ring consisted of four bells only.
"William Tompson gent." was lord of the manor.
The Pancake-bell is rung on Shrove-Tuesday.

# HUGGLESCOTE.

S. JAMES.                                                        1 BELL.

1. J TAYLOR & CO BELLFOUNDERS LOUGHBOROUGH
   1866.
                    ( Diam. 21 in. )

The bell had previously been recast in 1837.
When the chapel at Donington-le-Heath was taken down, in 1766,
its single bell was transferred to Hugglescote, making two bells there.
These with £20. in money were exchanged for the present bell in 1866.

# HUMBERSTONE.

S. MARY.                                                         5 BELLS.

1. JANE BOSE GAVE ME 1673 [ ▫ 10. ]
                    ( Diam. 28 in. )

2. OMNIA : FIANT : AD : GLORIAM : DEI : GLORIA :
   DEO : SOLI : T. EAYRE 1743.
   ( Diam. 30 in. )
3. CVM · SONO · SI · NON · VIS · VENIRE · NVNQVAM ·
   AD · PRECES · CVPIES · IRE · 1628 [ ᔕ 1. ]
   (Diam. 33 in. )
4. GOD SAVE THE kING 1620 [ ᔕ 1. ]
   (Diam. 35 in. )
5. I.H.S. NAZARENE · REX · JVDÆORUM · FILI · DEI ·
   MISERERE · MEI · GLORIA · PATRI · FILIO · ET ·
   SPIRITUI SANCTO · T. EAYRE KETTERING.
   (·Diam. 40 in. )

The family of Bose, Boose, or Bowes, had been settled at Humberstone for some years when the above gift was made to the church. The Manor passed to Richard Bowes, son of Sir John Bowes of Elford Co. Stafford, Knight, upon his marriage with the heiress of Walter Keble of Humberstone. In 1593 Jane Boose (or Bowes) of Humberstone was fined £55—for absenting herself from the parish church for three months following 1 April 34th Eliz.; and £20 more for a like absence from Tuesday in the 4th week in Lent, to the 24th of April following, (being one month) in 35th Eliz. It appeared by Inquisition taken before Sir George Hastings Knight and Francis Monk Esqr. that the said Jane Boose possessed property in Humberstone and elsewhere all which was seized into the Queen's hands till she should make submission.— *Burton and Nichols.*

A peal is rung on Sunday morning after the first Publication of Banns of Marriage.

The death-knell is tolled for fifteen minutes, and then rung for ten minutes, after which each bell is tolled thrice for a male or twice for a female.

# HUNGARTON.

S. JOHN BAPTIST.                                    3 BELLS.

1. [ + 22 ] NEWCOMBE · OF · LEICESTER · MADE · MEE · 1603.
   ( Diam. 29½ in. )

2. [ + 39 ] ISTA : CAMPANA : FACTA : EST : IN : HONORE : SANCTI : BOTULPHI :
(Diam. 32 in.)

3. [ + 55 ] ISTA [ ▢ 59 ] CAMPANA [ ▢ 59 ] EST [ ▢ 59 ] FACTA [ ▢ 59 ] IN HONORE BĒ PERTIT
( Diam. 35¼ in. )

The dedication of the tenor bell is uncertain : the stop ceases after the word "facta," the founder being apparently pressed for room, and he has made a blunder with the letters " BĒ PERTIT "—perhaps he meant BĒ PETRE.

The Pancake-bell is rung on Shrove-Tuesday.

## HUSBAND'S BOSWORTH.

All Saints.                                                    5 Bells.

1. ABCDEFG
( Diam. 30 in. )

2. ABCDE FGHIK LMNO 1611 . . . .
( Diam. 32 in. )

3. [ + 22 ] BE · YT · KNOWNE · TO · ALL · THAT · DOTH · ME · SEE · THAT · NEWCOMBE · OF · LEICESTER · MADE · MEE . . .
( Diam. 34 in. )

4. · · · · · · T. EAYRE KETTERING 1730.
( Diam. 37 in. )

5. CVM · SONO · SI · NON · VIS · VENIRE · NVNQVAM . AD · PRECES · CVPIES · IRE 1631 [ ▽ 1. ]
( Diam. 41 in. )

These large bells (owing to a dispute with the ringers some time ago) are not now rung, but are struck by hammers, by a machine, which is worked by one man. They are so placed that complete rub-bings cannot be taken.

# IBSTOCK.

S. DENYS.                                           4 BELLS.

1. SOLI DEO GLORIA PAX HOMINIBUS 1632 [ 12 ]
   (Diam. 33 in.)
2. THOMAS O CARVER O CHVRCH O WARDEN O 1711.
   (Diam. 35 in.)
3. + SOMROSA  POLSATA  MONDE  MARIA  VOCATA
   [ □ 67 ] 1632 [ □ 67 ] H [ □ 67 ] W. [ □ □ ]
   (Diam. 38¼ in.)

This, like the 1st, is from the Nottingham foundry. The inscription is a rude copy of the ancient one before the bell was recast. The stamps at the end are the letters T H and an anchor within a heart, and a rude elevation of a single gabled building with side towers, within a circle.

4. S̄cā  Elenn  ora  pro  nobis  [ ▽ 63. ]
   (Diam. 41¼ in.)

# ILSTON-ON-THE-HILL.

S. MICHAEL.                                         3 BELLS.

1. EDWARD NEWGWN [▽ 1.] MADE
   [ + 3 ] ME [ □ □ 49 *repeated.*]
2. ABCDE [ + 44 ] E [ ▽ 1.] M [ + 44.]
3. IH'2 : NAZARENVS : REX : IVDEORVM : FILI : DEI :
   MISERERE : MEI W.A. 1641 R.B.C [ ▽ 1. ]

[ ISLEY WALTON—see Walton Isley. ]

# KEGWORTH.

S. ANDREW.                                         5 BELLS.

1. PRAISE [ 9 ] THE [ 9 ] LORDE [ 9 ] 1613
   [ ▽ 1. ]

2 B

2. [ + 70 ] [ �□ 49 ] [ �□ 49 ] 𝕳𝖂𝕬𝕳𝕾𝕽𝕳𝕻𝕷𝖂𝕺
   [ + 53 ] 𝕾𝕬𝕸𝕺𝕿
   ( Perhaps intended for " Thomas Oldershawe." Read backwards. )

3. [ + 60. ] 𝕴𝔥𝔢𝔰𝔲𝔰 𝔑𝔞𝔷𝔞𝔯𝔢𝔫𝔲𝔰 𝕽𝔢𝔵 𝔍𝔲𝔡𝔢𝔬𝔯𝔲𝔪 𝕱𝔦𝔩𝔦 𝔇𝔢𝔦 𝔐𝔦𝔰𝔢𝔯𝔢𝔯𝔢 mei
   ( The capitals are crowned.)

4. 𝕴𝕳𝕾 𝕹𝕬𝖅𝕬 𝕽𝕰𝕹𝖁𝕾 [ + 25 ] 𝕽𝕰𝖃
   𝕴𝖁𝕯𝕴𝕺𝕽𝖁𝕸 [ �□ 79 ] [ �□ 29 ] [ �□ 28 ]
   [ �□ 19 ] [ �□ 8 ]

5. 𝕲𝕺𝕯 [ 9 ] 𝕾𝕬𝖁𝕰 [ 9 ] 𝕿𝕳𝕰 [ 9 ] 𝕶𝕴𝕹𝕲𝕳
   [ 9 ] 1613 [ ▽ 1. ]

In 6 Edward VI. there were "foore great belles in the stepell." The Curfew is rung every evening, Sundays excepted, during the winter months at eight o'clock, excepting on Saturday nights, when it is rung at seven o'clock, after which the day of the month is tolled. The Pancake-bell is rung on Shrove-Tuesday. After the Passing bell thrice three is tolled on three separate bells for a male; and thrice two on two separate bells for a female; after which the age of the deceased is tolled. On Sunday a morning bell is rung at 7 a.m.

*\*\** Since the above inscriptions were taken the bells have been taken down, and sent to Messrs. Taylor & Co. for recasting.

## KEYHAM.

ALL SAINTS.                                              3 BELLS.

1. Ṗ [ 12 ] SVMARFEILDE [ 12 ] C. WARDEN [ 12 ] 1705.
2. GOD [ 12 ] SAVE [ 12 ] HIS [ 12 ] CHVRCH [ 12 ] 1705.
3. EDWd. ARNOLD LEICESTER 1784.

## KIBWORTH.

S. WILFRID.                                              6 BELLS.

1. [ + 34 ] 𝕽𝕬𝕻𝕳 𝕮𝕺𝕿𝕰𝕾 𝕴𝕳𝕺𝕹 𝕾𝕸𝕴𝕿𝕳
   𝕮𝕳𝖁𝕽. 𝖂𝕬𝕽𝕯 1618.

2. SAUVIUS IN NULLIS VOX CONCINIT ÆNEA CAMPIS IN GYRUM GLOMERATA MELOS. R. HAYMES. R. CARTER J. PACKWOOD C. WARDENS 1732.

3 and 4. IH'S : NAZARENVS [9] REX : IVDEORVM [9] FILI : DEI [9] MISERERE : MEI [9] 1621 [ ♒ 1. ]

5. TINNITUS RAPIDOS SCINTILLANS SPARGO PER AURAS T. EAYRE PYROTECHNUS FECIT PRO W. FORTREY 1732.

6. CYMBALA DULCILOQUO DEMULCENT CARMINE CAMPOS ROBERT HAYMES RICHARD · CARTER JOSEPH PACKWOOD CHURCHWARDENS 1732.′

In 1825 the Tower, Spire, and westernmost bays of the Nave fell down. The treble bell was the only one injured: it was cracked and has so remained.

The Pancake-bell is rung on Shrove-Tuesday. A bell is rung at 8 a.m on Sundays.

## KILBY.

S. MARY MAGDALEN. · 1 BELL.

One small bell in an inaccessible turret.


[ KILWORTH NORTH—see North Kilworth. ]

[ KILWORTH SOUTH—see South Kilworth. ]


## KIMCOTE.

ALL SAINTS. 4 BELLS.

1, 2. [ + 22. ] BE · YT · KNOWNE · TO · ALL · THAT · DOTH ME · SEE · THAT · NEWCOMBE · OF · LEICESTER · MADE · MEE 1612.

3.  IH'Ƨ : NAZARENVS [9] REX : IVDEORVM [9] FILI :
    DEI [9] MISERERE : MEI [9] 1642 [ ▽ 1. ]
4.  CVM · SONO · SI · NON · VIS [9] VENIRE [9] NVNQVAM
    AD · PRECES [9] CVPIES · IRE [9] 1631 [▽ 1.]

## KING'S NORTON.

S. John Baptist.                                                    8 Bells.

1.  OMNIA FIANT AD GLORIAM DEI
2.  PEACE AND GOOD NEIGHBOURHOOD
3.  STATUTUM EST OMNIBUS SEMEL MORI MORTE
    BEATA NIHIL BEATIUS GLORIA DEO SOLI THOS.
    EAYRE 1760.
4.  IH'Ƨ : NAZARENVS : REX : IVDEORVM : FILI : DEI :
    MISERERE : MEI  W A 1641 R B C [ ▽ 1. ] ·
5.  LAUDATE DOMINUM CYMBALIS SONORIS CŒLORUM
    CHRISTE PLACEAT TIBI REX SONUS ISTE *(a bell)*
    1760.
6.  The same as 3rd but dated 1761.
7.  T. EAYRE ST. NEOTS FECIT IN ANNO DOM 1764.
8.  OMNIA FIANT AD GLORIAM DEI JOSEPH EAYRE ST.
    NEOTS HUNTINGDONSHIRE FECIT 1764.

Nichols tells us that Wm. Fortrey, Esq., gave a peal of ten bells to
this church when he rebuilt it, but finding the weight dangerous he
reduced them to eight.  The present 4th is of course one of the previous
ring. ·

## KIRBY BELERS.

S. Peter.                                                          5 Bells.

1.  PRAISE THE LORDE 1614 [ ▽ 1. ]
    ( Diam. 32 in. )

2. SIT * NOMEN * DOMINI * BENEDICTUM * JONATHAN
   FOX & SAMUELL HAYNES C. Ws. 1755 THOMAS
   EAYRE → FECIT
   ( Diam. 34 in. )

3. IH'Ƨ : NAZARENVS REX IVDEORVM FILI DEI MISE-
   RERE MEI 1617 W F J B C [ ▽ 1. ]

4. IHS NAZARENE REX IVDÆORVM FILI DEI MISERERE
   MEI → ANNO DOMINI 1730 *(a bell and coin of Queen Anne)*
   ( Diam. 38 in. )

5. GOD SAVE THE KINGE 1614 [ ▽ 1. ]
   ( Diam. 42 in. )

In 6 Edward VI. there were "iiij bells."

There is a tradition that a bell intended for the neighbouring parish
of Asfordby was brought by mistake to Kirby.

## KIRBY MUXLOE.

S. Bartholomew.                                        3 Bells.

1. [ + 22 ] BE · YT · KNOWNE · TO · ALL · THAT · DOTH
   ME · SEE · THAT · NEWCOMBE · OF · LEICESTER
   MADE · MEE · 1609.

2. IH'Ƨ : NAZARENVS [ 9 ] REX : IVDEORVM [ 9 ] FILI :
   DEI [ 9 ] MISERERE : MEI [ 9 ] 1636 [ 9 ] [ ▽ 1. ]

3. [ + 22 ] BE · YT · KNOWNE · TO · ALL · THAT · DOTH ·
   ME · SEE · THAT · NEWCOMBE · OF · LEICESTER ·
   MADE · MEE · 1606.

## KIRKBY MALLORY.

All Saints.                                            3 Bells.

1. [ + 3. ] S A M M

2. GOD SAVE HIS CHVRCH 1658 [ ◻ 10. ]
   ( Cracked. )

3. IH'Ƨ : NAZARENVS [ 9 ] REX : IVDEORVM [ 9 ] FILI :
   DEI [ 9 ] MISERERE : MEI [ 9 ] 1629 [ ᙦ 1. ]

## KNAPTOFT.

The church here is in ruins. Nichols says it was standing in 1630, and that in 1625 the inhabitants bought a new bell, which was afterwards transferred to Shearsby Chapel. See under Shearsby as to this bell.

## KNIGHTON.

S. Mary Magdalen.                                            4 Bells.

1. ROBERT SMITH CHURCHWARDEN EDWd. ARNOLD
   LEICESTER FECIT 1796.
            ( Diam. 33 in. )
2. WILLIAM BEATES CHURCHWARDEN JOSEPH EAYRE
   ST. NEOTS FECIT 1770.
            ( Diam. 34 in., cracked. )
3. WILLIAM BEATES CHURCHWARDEN JOSEPH EAYRE
   FECIT 1769.
            ( Diam. 36¼ in. )
4. IH'Ƨ : NAZARENVS [ 9 ] REX : IVDEORVM [ 9 ] FILI :
   DEI [ 9 ] MISERERE : MEI [ 9 ] 1627 [ ᙦ 1. ]
            ( Diam. 41 in. )

## KNIPTON.

All Saints.                                                 3 Bells.

1. [ □ 52 ] JHESVS BE OVR SPEDE
   ℣ [ □ 37 ] [ ᙦ 32 ] ℐ [ □ 38 ]
2. ROBERT   JONES   RECTOR   RICHARD   MARRIOTT
   CHURCHWARDEN   ANNO   DOM   1731   T.   EAYRE
   FECIT

(Under which is apparently a coronet and a crest, the latter a boar's head erased close.)

3. GOD SAVE HIS CHVRCH C WRIGHT RECTOR
   W. HARVEY WARDEN 1717.

In 6 Edward VI. there were "iij bells and a sanctus bell." The Pancake-bell is rung on Shrove-Tuesday at 11 a.m.

## KNOSSINGTON.

S. PETER.        1 BELL.

1. COME COME AND PRAY. ALEXr. HALLSAL RECTOR
   Rd MARTIN CHURCHWARDEN 1731.
   ( Diam. 31 in. )

The Inscription is probably a repetition of that on a former bell cast by Watts of Leicester.

There is also a small Priest's Bell—13 inches in diameter—bearing the date'only, "1735," which is rung for five minutes before the commencement of Divine Service.

There is a tradition that one or more bells were removed many years ago from this church to its neighbour at Owston.

[ LANGTON—see Church Langton. ]

## LAUGHTON.

S. LUKE.        1 BELL.

1. EDWD ARNOLD ST. NEOTS FECIT 1777 Wm. JOHNSON
   WARDEN.
   ( Diam. 24 in. )

# LEICESTER.

**ALL SAINTS.**       5 BELLS.

1. WILLIAM RVDIARD MINISTER 1595.
2. Campana Melodie geret nomen
3. [ + 22 ] BE · YT · KNOWNE · TO · ALL · THAT · DOTH · ME · SEE · THAT.· NEWCOMBE · OF · LEICESTER · MADE · MEE · 1611.
4. [ + 44 ] ROBARTE NEWCOME MAD ME 1586.
5. [ + 45 ] IOHANNES : DE : STAF-FORD : FECIT : ME : IN : HON-ORE : DE : MARIE *the*

William Rudiard was descended from a Staffordshire family. See his Pedigree in *Visitation of the Co. of Leicester*, 1619, published by the Harleian Society, p. 202.

The inscription on the 2nd bell is incomplete.

A morning bell is (or was until recently) rung daily at 6 o'clock a.m., and an evening bell at 7 p.m. during the winter months.

Sunday ringing:—1st bell is rung at 7 a.m. 1st and 2nd bells at 8 a.m. For services the bells are tolled irregularly for ten minutes, chimed ten minutes, and then the sermon bell is rung for ten minutes.

# LEICESTER.

**S. MARGARET.**       10 BELLS.

1. T. EAYRE EX DONO GUIL. FORTREY DE NORTON IN AGRO LEICESTRIENSI ARMIG : 1738.
2. The same.
3. T. EAYRE KETT : RICH : DENSHIRE AND ROB : PAGE : C.W. 1738 · OMNIA · FIANT · AD · GLORIAM · DEI

4. T. EAYRE KETT : RICH : DENSHIRE AND ROB :
   PAGE : CHURCHWARDENS ANNO · DOM : 1738.

5. CREDE RESIPECE MORI
   MEMENTO 1633.

6. HUGH WATTS OF LEICESTER THE FOREMOST IN
   HIS ART CAST THE 6 LARGEST BELLS 1633. T.
   EAYRE KETT : RECAST THIS 1739. MORTE BEATA
   NIHIL BEATIUS.

7. STATUTUM EST OMNIBUS
   SEMEL MORI 1633.
   (On the top of the bell are the letters M V + B. W.)

8. IHS NASAREUS REX JUDE-
   ORUM FILI DEI MISERERE
   MEI 1633 [ ⛿ 1. ]

9. FEARE GOD OBAIE THE KING
   GEORGE PALMER 1633.

10. CUM · SONO · SI · NON · VIS ·
    VENIRE · NUNQUAM · AD ·
    PRECES · CUPIES · IRE 1633 [ ⛿ 1. ]
    (Weight 30 cwt.)

Brand says :—" The noblest peal of ten bells, without exception, in
England, whether tone or tune be considered is said to be in S.
Margaret's, Leicester." This opinion was confirmed by that of the
Rev. W. Ludlam.*

Unfortunately there are no parochial records to tell anything about
the early history of the ring.

Nichols† says that Thomas Newcombe " who cast the six great bells
of S. Margaret's" was buried 20 May 1594. It has already been shown
(p. 52) that Thomas Newcombe was buried 7 Feb. 1579-80. Presuming Nichols to be correct in his statement as to the casting of the
bells of S. Margaret's by Thomas Newcombe, they were cast some time
prior to 1579 and were at that time six in number.

---

* See Nichols' *Leicestershire*, under King's Norton.      † Vol. i, part 2, p. 552.

2 C

These bells could not have been satisfactory, for within sixty years, that is in 1633, the whole six were recast by Hugh Watts as is recorded on the sixth bell of the present ring. The 5th, 7th, 8th, 9th, and 10th bells were from Watts' foundry.

For an anecdote relating to the casting of the tenor bell see p. 65.

In 1711 two treble bells were added to the ring from the foundry of Abraham Rudhall, of Gloucester: towards the cost of these the Corporation subscribed £20., as is recorded in the Chamberlains' Accounts. They were inscribed:

1.  A. R. 1711.
2.  Prosperity to all our benefactors 1711.

In 1738 the ring was made up to ten bells by a gift of two more treble bells by Wm. Fortrey, Esq., of Norton by Galby. Eayre at the same time recast the then 1st and 2nd bells, recently added, and the whole ring was rehung, Mr. Fortrey bearing the greater portion of the expense.

In 1739 the sixth bell was recast by Thomas Eayre, who placed upon it his testimony to the great reputation attained by its previous founder.

The Pancake-bell is rung on Shrove-Tuesday from 11 to 12 a.m.

Sunday ringing:—Treble from 7.15 to 7.30 a.m. for early celebration. For services: all the bells are tolled consecutively (commencing with ten or twelve strokes on the treble) for ten minutes, then chimed for ten minutes, after which the sermon bell is rung for ten minutes.

# LEICESTER.

S. MARTIN.                                                          10 BELLS.

1.  JOHN TAYLOR AND SON FOUNDERS OXFORD AND LOUGHBOROUGH 1854.
    (Diam. 28 in.)

2.  The same.
    (Diam. 29¼ in.)

3. JOHN TAYLOR AND SON BELLFOUNDERS LOUGH-
   BOROUGH LATE OF OXFORD, BUCKLAND
   BREWER, DEVON, AND ST. NEOTS HUNTS.;
   SUCCESSORS TO THE OLD AND CELEBRATED
   FOUNDERS NEWCOMBE, WATTS, EAYRE AND
   ARNOLD OF LEICESTER, NAMES OF HIGH
   REPUTE, DATING AS EARLY AS 1560.
   ( Diam. 30¼ in. )

4. JOHN TAYLOR AND SON FOUNDERS OXFORD AND
   LOUGHBOROUGH 1854.
   ( Diam. 31¼ in. )

5. LET EVERYTHING THAT HATH BREATH PRAISE THE
   LORD.
   ( Diam. 34 in. )

6. PRAISE HIM UPON THE WELL TUNED CYMBALS :
   PRAISE HIM UPON THE LOUD CYMBALS.
   ( Diam. 37½ in. )

7. H. WATCHORNE ESQUIRE MAYOR. J. NICHOLS AND
   W. CAPP CHURCHWARDENS. EDWD. ARNOLD
   FECIT 1781.
   ( Diam. 38½ in. )

8. The same.
   ( Diam. 40¼ in. )

9. The same.
   ( Diam. 43¾ in. )

10. The same.
    ( Diam. 52¼ in. )

In the time of Henry VIII. there were five bells. The charges for
ringing at Burials and Obits never mention more than that number.

From the Churchwardens' Accounts I make the following extracts :—

1544. Buryals of wyche the bels be not p^d for [Here follows a list
      of receipts for the burials of many persons. The payment
      for three bells was 8*d.*, for four bells 20 pence, for five bells

5*s*. 4*d*.  For burial in the church 6*s*. 8*d*.] More oying to ye
chirche ye same Day for the bels as aperyrith on this syde
of this Leffe ............................................................. x̧xxvij*s*. iiij*d*.

### Obbytts of the gylde.

Mr. Parsons obbit v bels .................................. iiij*s*.

Mr. Lyles obbyt iiij bels.................................... xx*d*.

Mr. Suyks obbyt iij bels.................................... viij*d*.

Mr. Davers obbit iij bels ................................. viij*d*.

Mr. Baylies obbit iiij bels ................................ xx*d*.

Mr. Hursts obbit iiij bels ................................ xx*d*.

Mr. Whitwels obbit iij bels .............................. viij*d*.

### Other obbytts.

Rychard Fynnes obbyt iiij bels........................... xx*d*.

Itm̄ Thoms Draks obbyt iiij bels ....................... xx*d*.

Itm̄ Mr. Ihon Wigstons obbit v bels .................. iiij*s*.

Itm̄ Mr. Wymeswolds obbyt iiij bels .................. xx*d*.

Itm̄ to Syr Will<sup>m</sup> Boroughe for the cloke & chime viij*d*.

1546-7.  Itm̄ p<sup>d</sup> to the ryngers for Kynge Henry the eyght xij*d*.

Itm̄ p<sup>d</sup> to the belman the same tyme* ................. ij*d*.

Itm̄ p<sup>d</sup> for medynge of the barrell that the chyme
goyth w<sup>th</sup> to the smyth at the west brydge............ xij*d*.

1547.  Solde to Mr. Newcome iiij hundrith and a qr of
bras at xix*s* the hundrith Summa................. iiij*li*. ix*s*.

Sold to Mr. Newcome l. pound waight of the
Organe pypes .................................................. xvj*s*.

Itm̄ for iij bell ropps one catche cope rope............ iij*s*. iiij*d*.

1549-50.  Itm̄ rec of Will<sup>m</sup> Taylor S<sup>r</sup>gant (?) in ernest of
the iij catch coppe bells aft<sup>r</sup> xxv*s* a hundryth ...... xij*d*.

Itm̄ p<sup>d</sup> to Thomas Wylmore for hys qrt wags for
rynging of the day bell .................................... xx*d*.

Itm̄ p<sup>d</sup> to W<sup>m</sup> Smyth for mendyng ye gret bell
clapp<sup>r</sup> .............................................................. ij*s*.

---

\* *i.e.* for summoning the people to church to hear mass for the late King's soul.

Itm̄ pᵈ to Robt Sekerston & Rog. Johnson for takyn
downe the iij catche coppe bells ........................ xij*d*.

1550-1. Itm̄ rec. of Mr. Lambt (?) & Mr. Herek for the
leyst catche cope bell .................................. xxvijs. xj*d*.

Itm̄ rec. of Willᵐ Tayllor & Willm Syngylton for
tow of the same bells .............................. iij*li*. xjs. viij*d*.

1558-9.  pᵈ for ale to the Ryngers when the quenes grace
was p̄clamyd .................................................. viij*d*.

1560-1.  [ A Gable rope sold. ]

1561-2.  [ Another Gable rope sold. ]

1585-6.  Reseaved of the pishners of S. Martins for the charges
and castinge of the forr * bell as followethe :
[ Here follows a list of donations; the Mayor and nine of
his brethren, or Aldermen, giving 6s. 8*d*. each, twenty-one of
the company of forty-eight, or Common Councillors, 3s. 4*d*.
each, several individual donors sums from 5s. to 1s. each,
and the commoners in each of the five wards various small
sums; the whole producing £11. 18s. 6¼*d*. ]
Charges for castinge the forr bell of the parishe of Saynt
Martin in Leicester, in the yeare of our lord 1585, Master
James Clarke then beinge Mayor :
Imprimis payd for c̄astinge the forr bell to the bellfounders ...................................................... v*li*.
Itm̄ payd for a hundred wayght of mettell in the bell
more than it wayed before at vj*d*. the pounde ...... lvjs.
Itm̄ payd for fourescore and too pounde of mettell
that was wasted in the castinge at vj*d*. the pounde xljs.
Itm̄ payd for takinge downe the bell out of the
steeple ........................................................ xx*d*.
Itm̄ payd for a baudrike † for the same bell ......... xij*d*.
Itm̄ payd for gettinge the bell out of the churche
into yᵉ carte .................................................. iiij*d*.

---

* Fore or treble bell.

† A thong of whit-leather with which the clapper was fastened to the bell.

Itm̄ payd for a beridge* when the bell was meltinge at Mr. Newcomes...................................... ijs.　vjd.

Itm̄ payd to the belfounders servantes when the bell was taken out of the grounde and finished ...... 　　xvjd.

Itm̄ bestowed of them in ale and bread at the same time.................................................... 　　vjd.

Itm̄ payd to John Harris for carrtinge the bell to the founders ...................................... 　　iiijd.

Itm̄ payde to robart talor for bringeinge the bell to the church agane....................................... 　　iiijd.

Itm̄ payde for gettinge the bell into the steeple agayne ...................................................... 　　xvjd.

Itm̄ payde to john bayly for takinge downe the bell and hanginge it up in his frame agayne ............... ijs.

Itm̄ payd to john bayly for mendinge the for bell frame ......................................................... 　　xd.

Itm̄ payd to Christopher Needam for an Iorne† band for the same ......................................... 　　vjd.

Itm̄ payd for the belfounders bounde ‡ makinge ... 　　xijd.

Itm̄ payd to Christopher Needam for braddes to hange the for bell in his frame and for setinge the chime in order ................................................ 　　xijd.

The whole sum of the payments for the bell is £10. 11s. 8d.

1588-9 [ and following years the bells were rung on S. Hugh's Day. ]

1597-8. Pᵈ for 3 yards great wyer to make a Soon Dyall with which master Belgrave made to set the clock by at the end of the New Ospitall §.................... 　　xijd.

1603-4. Item payd to the Ringers when her Maᵗⁱᵉ was in this town ...................................... ijs. iiijd.

1604-5. Item leade forth when the greate Bell fell downe...................................................... xxijs. xjd.

---

* Probably a corruption of bever or beverage, *i.e.* drink. Mr. Walcott informs me that "Bever" was until recently used at Winchester for a measure of College ale in the summer season.　　† Iron.　　‡ Bond.　　§ Wiggeston's Hospital

Item payd for mendinge the chyme when the greate
bell fell downe ................................................. ij*s.*

The bell was rehung by Mr. Newcomb.

1610-11. Item payde for takeinge the seconde bell downe
out of the steeple ............................................. ij*s.* ix*d.*

Item given to the bellfounders at the wayinge of
the bell to drinke ............................................. vj*d.*

Item given to them for their beridge at the castinge
of the bell ...................................................... ij*s.* vj*d.*

Item to drinke at the wayinge of the bell againe
[i.e. *after the recasting.*] ..................................... vj*d.*

Item payde to William Symson for hanginge of
the bell .......................................................... x*s.*

Item in drinke to the workemen that hunge the
bell .............................................................. xij*d.*

1611-12. Item to Robte Newcome* ...................... vij*li.* ix*s.*

Item payde to Mr. Mortin for old Mr. Edwarde
Newcome in full payment for castinge of the
seconde bell .............................................. vj*li.*

1612-13. [Payments for "4 notes for the chymes."]

Item p*d* to the Ringers for Ringinge 3 days when
the Kinge and prince was here ........................ xviij*s.* vj*d.*

1614-15. Item payde to the Ringers for Ringinge when
his Ma^{tie} came to Leicester ............................. xiij*s.*

1616-17. [A similar payment.]

1617-18. M̄. That if the seckerston shall Ringe at any
tyme when any nobleman cometh to the towne he
must have ij*s.* vj*d.* from the churchwardens if he have
nothinge sent him from the Inn where they lye.

1618-21. [The clock face or dial placed.]

1621-2. To Mr. Wattes for a brasse for the bell ............ ......

ffor ringeinge to praiers every sabboth and holie
daie .............................................................. iij*s.*

---

* Son of Edward next mentioned.

1624-5. Paid for 5 Ringers for Ringinge at the first and
second time pclaiminge the Kinge ..................... vs.

In 1629-30, a new frame being required for the bells, nine shillings
were spent in going to Lutterworth to view the frame there. The
timber was bought at Beaumanor: ten pounds is charged in part payment thereof to Mr. John Hericke and three shillings was expended
for work at "beamaner."  •

1630-1. Paid for Ringinge of the Bells when newse was
brought the Queene was brought to bed .............. ijs. vjd.
1634-5. P^d the ringers beeing viij for the tyme that his
maiestie stayed in Leic. .................................... xvs.

Thus far I have given the extracts from the manuscript Accounts of
the Churchwardens of the parish;* for the next few I am indebted to
the pages of Nichols and Throsby, the originals for those years
being missing.

1640. Paid for Bow-bell when Cockle lay sick ......... o . o . 6d.
[ see page 115.]
1651. Paid for casting the third bell and charges
in Court .................................................. £11 . 11 . 10

In the year 1657 the ring of five bells was converted into one of six.
It was agreed in that year "that the ring of bells be made into six
tuneable bells; the treble and tenor to be cast into three bells tuneable
under the other three, and the fourth bell that now is, to be made a
tuneable tenor without casting." This business was undertaken by Mr.
Norris (Thomas, I suppose) of Stamford, but he failing to please the
ears of the churchwardens or of the parishioners of S. Martin's, the
bells being perhaps not "tuneable," an agreement was made with Mr.
George Oldfield, of Nottingham, to recast the whole six for £50.

---

* For a full account of this interesting collection see North's *Chronicle of the Church
of S. Martin in Leicester.*—Crossley and Clarke, Leicester.

1687. A new clock was made at the charges of the parish, the old clock being sold the following year to Mr. Wilkin, a local clock maker, for 20*s.*

1689. July 1. Agreed that all the bells be rehung.

1700. The fifth bell was recast by William Noone of Nottingham, for the doing of which he was to receive 20*s.* per cwt.

1702. New chimes were again ordered this year, and the tenor bell being cracked, it was sawn at a cost of £1. 4s. od.

1704. Mr. Noone of Nottingham was engaged to recast the tenor bell, which had been cracked for some time previously. Upon being taken down the bell was found to weigh 19 cwt. 1 qr. 16 lbs. The casting cost £26. 8s. od.

The extracts that now follow are from the original accounts of the churchwardens preserved in the church chests:

> 1747. April 21. It is agreed that the Prayer bell from Lady day to Michaelmas shall begin to ring at Ten in the morning and three in the afternoon; and from Michaelmas to Lady day at Eleven in the Forenoon and Two in the afternoon, and to ring each time a quarter of an hour.

> 1754. Oct 16. Agreed to take down the Ringing loft and make a new Ringing loft with a ceiling under; at a cost not exceeding £20—and the old materials.

> 1765. Jany 24 Agreed that the churchwardens be fully empowered to take down the second Bell which is become crakt and unfit for use, and that they cause the same to be recast and replaced at y* expence of y* Parish, and do therein what further repairs shall appear necessary.

> Feb 6. Postage to and from St. Neots about the bell ...................................................... 0 . 1 . 4
>
> Mar. 4 Spent at the Cranes on account of Mr. Ayres...................................................... 0 . 3 . 0
>
> Paid for carriage of a bell to St. Neots ........... 1 . 7 . 6
>
> Paid porterage for Do. ................................. 0 . 3 . 0
>
> May 5. Paid Mr. Eyre his bill ...................... 21 . 13 . 0

2 D

In 1781 Edward Arnold of Leicester recast the whole ring: the six heaviest of the present bells are of this date. The Churchwardens' Accounts for the year 1780-1 are unfortunately missing. It is fair to presume that Arnold cast the six old bells into eight, to which were added two more in 1787, thus making a ring (as Nichols describes it) of ten light bells. This idea is corroborated by the following note of the weight of S. Martin's bells taken about this time by Thomas Hedderly, a Nottingham Bellfounder, and preserved in a Pocket Book formerly belonging to him and now in existence:—

### S. Martin's, Leicester.

| | | | | | | |
|---|---|---|---|---|---|---|
| 1. | .... | 7 | . | 2 | . | 12 |
| 2. | .... | 8 | . | 0 | . | 3 |
| 3. | .... | 7 | . | 3 | . | 24 |
| 4. | .... | 9 | . | 1 | . | 23 |
| 5. | .... | 10 | . | 0 | . | 11 |
| 6. | .... | 11 | . | 3 | . | 6 |
| 7. | .... | 14 | . | 2 | . | 3 |
| 8. | .... | 21 | . | 3 | . | 6 |

Tons 4 . 10 . 3 . 20*

1786. July 13. The clock and chimes being apparently worn out, it was resolved to have new ones. It was reported at a meeting that £150 had been raised by subscription for that purpose, and that much more was expected. Mr. Edward Arnold was contracted with to make a clock and chimes, immediately, for the sum of £240. Soon after having passed this resolution it appeared necessary to some of the inhabitants of the parish to have an addition of two bells to the ring "in order that the set of chimes now making may be the more perfect."

---

* For this transcript I am indebted to W. P. W. Phillimore, Esq. It may be noted that the 3rd bell is given as lighter than the 2nd, and that the total weight is not correct.

As, however, they were to be "erected and set up at the expense of the parish by monies to be collected by levy," there was some opposition to this proposal, which, nevertheless, was carried by a large majority at a public meeting of the parishioners held 10 July, 1787. These two treble bells making a ring of ten were inscribed, according to *Nichols :—*

1.  EDWD. ARNOLD, LEICESTER FECIT.
2.  T. LOCKWOOD, E. WEBB, J. MALLETT CHURCHWARDENS 1787.
    E. ARNOLD FECIT.

In 1791-2. There are payments to Mr. Arnold probably for keeping the clock in order, and that gentleman's name occurs again every year in the Churchwardens' Accounts until the year 1798-9.

In 1854. The four lightest bells were recast by Messrs. John Taylor & Son of Loughborough: upon them was found the following inscriptions :—

1 & 2.  As just given.
3.  OMNIA FIANT AD GLORIAM DEI
    EDWD. ARNOLD FECIT.
4.  PRAISE HIM UPON THE WELL TUNED CYMBALS.
    PRAISE HIM UPON THE LOUD CYMBALS.

In this way the present ring of ten bells was completed. The chimes are not now used.

- The morning bell rings at six o'clock in the summer and at seven o'clock in the winter. The curfew (8th bell) rings at nine in the evening. At the death-knell thrice 3 tolls are given for a man ; thrice 2 for a woman ; thrice 1 for a boy, and twice 1 for a girl. The same custom is universal at the old parish churches of Leicester. Sunday ringing :— The treble bell is rung at 7 a.m. Two bells at 8 a.m., excepting when there is a Celebration of the Holy Communion, when they are rung at 7.35, after which the 6th bell is rung. For services:—The bells are tolled irregularly for ten minutes, then chimed for ten minutes, after which the sermon bell is rung for ten minutes.

# LEICESTER.

S. MARY.                                                    8 BELLS.

1. T. MEARS OF LONDON FECIT 1830. JOHN MOORE
   BORN JUNE 19, 1787.
2. T. MEARS OF LONDON FECIT 1830. JOHN WARBURTON
   BORN AUGUST 20, 1778 PARISHIONER JOHN
   BAXTER BORN OCTOBER 14, 1774 PARISHIONER.
3, 4. T. MEARS OF LONDON FECIT 1830. W. L. FANCOURT
   D.D. VICAR. SIMEON MORRIS THOMAS DEXTER
   CHURCHWARDENS.
5, 6, 7. T. MEARS OF LONDON FECIT 1830.
8. IH'Ƨ : NAZARENVS [9] REX : IVDEORVM [9] FILI :
   DEI [9] MISERERE : MEI [9] 1631. T.W ISC [ ꓯ 1. ]
   ( Weight 18 cwt. Key F. )

The Church Records are lost. Nichols preserves a few entries in
the Churchwardens' Accounts from which we learn that there were five
bells only in 1495 :—

> 1495. The frames for the five bells made this year: wages to
> workmen were :—
>
> Carpenters per diem ................. 6*d.*
> Inferior servants under them ......... 3*d.*
> Labourers ............................ 4*d.*

> Wm. Gibson subscribed four shillings and fourpence "to
> the frames of the bells for Margaret his wife's soul."
> 1504. Paid to the bellringers quarterly ...................... 10*d.*
> 1507. Paid to Henry Yerle Pye bellringer for his quarter
> of Michaelmas ............................................... 20*d.*
> 1509. Paid to the ringers of all the bells for our King
> Harry the Seventh, the which deceased the  £ *s. d.*
> 25th April..................................................  0 . 1 . 2

In 1830 one of the ancient ring of five bells being cracked, it was agreed that the 4th should be retained as the tenor for a new ring of eight bells, the other four being taken away. Mr. T. Mears of London cast the new bells, which, when hung, completed the present ring. It was "opened" on Monday, 7th March, 1831, by the ringing of a complete peal of 5040 grandsire triples in three hours and three minutes.

The Curfew at 8 p.m. and the morning bell at 6 a.m. regularly sounded here until Easter 1856, when both were discontinued. The Pancake-bell is rung on Shrove-Tuesday. Sunday ringing: For services the bells are tolled irregularly for ten minutes, chimed ten minutes, and sermon bell rung for ten minutes. The early Sunday morning peals have lately been discontinued.

## LEICESTER.

S. NICOLAS.        3 BELLS.

1. IH'2 : NAZARENVS REX 1656 G. OLDFIELD
   ( Diam. 28 in. )
2. GOD SAVE HIS CHVRCH  HENRY SMITH RICHARD
   HVNT WARDENS 1710.
   ( Diam. 28 in. )
3. CELORVM CHRSTE PLATIAT TIBI REX SONVS ISTE
   1617 [ ⛉ 1. ]
   ( Diam. 32 in. )

There were bells here in 1321, see p. 8.

Sunday ringing:—For services the bells are tolled singly a few minutes, then chimed, after which the sermon bell is rung.

## LEICESTER.

CHRIST'S CHURCH.        1 BELL.

1. Blank. ( Diam. 24 in. )

## LEICESTER.

HOLY TRINITY.                                                      1 BELL.

1.  THOMAS MEARS OF LONDON FOUNDER 1837.  THOMAS
    FREWEN ESQR. 1837.
                         ( Diam. 29¾ in. )

## LEICESTER.

S. JOHN.                                                           1 BELL.

1.  J. WARNER & SON CRESCENT FOUNDRY LONDON.

## LEICESTER.

S. ANDREW.                                                         1 BELL.

Small bell in external turret.   Church consecrated 20 Feb. 1862.

## LEICESTER.

S. LUKE.                                                           1 BELL.

1.  1707 A. R. *(two bells.)*

This is a second-hand bell, which has had a further inscription, now
carefully filed off.

## LEICESTER.

S. GEORGE.                                                        6 BELLS.

1.  JOHN   TAYLOR   &   SON   BELLFOUNDERS   LOUGH-
    BOROUGH 1856.
                         ( Weight 5 cwt. 3 qrs. )
2.  The same.
                         ( Weight 6 cwt. )

3. The same.
> ( Weight 6 cwt. 2 qrs. )

4. The same.
> ( Weight 7 cwt. )

5. The same.
> ( Weight 8 cwt. 2 qrs. )

6. The same.
> ( Weight 12 cwt.   F sharp. )

The cost (according to the newspapers of the day) was £320. exclusive of the old bell.

Sunday ringing:—Treble bell at 7 a.m.  Treble and second bells at 8 a.m.  For services the bells are irregularly tolled for ten minutes, chimed for ten minutes, and sermon bell is rung for ten minutes.

# LEICESTER.

S. PAUL.                                                              1 BELL.

1.  J. TAYLOR & CO FOUNDERS LOUGHBOROUGH 1871.
> ( Diam. 32 in. )

# LEICESTER.

S. PETER (Modern).                                                   1 BELL.

A small bell in temporary external turret.

# LEICESTER.

S. MARK.                                                            8 BELLS.

1.  J. TAYLOR & CO BELLFOUNDERS LOUGHBOROUGH 1872.
> ( Weight 7 cwt. 0 qrs. 8 lbs. )

2. The same.
> ( Weight 7 cwt. 2 qrs. 18 lbs. )

3. The same.
                              ( Weight 8 cwt. 3 qrs. o lbs. )
4. The same.
                              ( Weight 9 cwt. 1 qr. 18 lbs. )
5. The same.
                              ( Weight 11 cwt. 2 qrs. 24 lbs. )
6. The same.
                              ( Weight 12 cwt. 1 qr. 12 lbs. )
7. The same.
                              ( Weight 16 cwt. 3 qrs. o lbs. )
8. The same.
                              ( Weight 22 cwt. 3 qrs. 24 lbs. )

The total weight of this fine ring of bells (the gift of the munificent founders of the church, W. Perry-Herrick, Esq., and the late Miss Herrick,) is 96 cwt. 2 qrs. 20 lbs ; the Key E flat. The cost was about £960. The Pancake-bell is rung on Shrove-Tuesday. At the death-knell thrice 3 tolls are given for a man, thrice 2 for a woman, twice 3 for a boy, and twice 2 for a girl, after which the age is tolled.

Sunday ringing:—Treble and second bells at 8 a.m. For services the bells are irregularly tolled for five minutes, chimed for fifteen minutes, the first and second bells are then rung for five minutes, after which the sermon bell is rung for five minutes.

## LEICESTER.

WIGGESTON'S HOSPITAL (old).

1. WILLIAM WIGSTON FOUNDER JOHN PIKE WARDEN
        1689.

This bell was removed on the 1st of April, 1874, by order of the Trustees, from the ancient Hospital then standing on the west side of S. Martin's Church but since taken down.

There is a small modern bell at the New Hospital.

# LEICESTER.

S. Peter (destroyed). 4 Bells.

This church, which formerly stood in Leicester, possessed, previous to its destruction, four bells. Mr. Thompson incidentally shows the existence of a bell here in 1306. He says: *

"On Saturday 'in the vigils of the Nativity of our Lord' (Christmas Eve), 1306, and about midnight, Simon the Waleys, clerk, went to the church of S. Peter to strike the bell, early in the morning, as was his custom. He there found William the Vicar, standing in the church, who asked him why he had delayed so long before coming; and there-upon struck him on the head with a meat knife, called a 'misericorde,' the blade of which pierced to his brain. The clerk lived but two days. Matilda Brodey was with him when he died, and immediately gave the alarm to the townsmen, at the gates, and informed the coroners and bailiffs of the circumstances. An inquisition was taken before them and they said that suspicion as to the death rested upon none other than William the Vicar. He sheltered himself in the church for seven weeks. At last he gave himself up to the King's peace, and was con-fined, in prison, in the custody of Hugh the Mercer. There is not, however, any record of the punishment awarded to him."

The materials of the church were sold to the Corporation of Leicester by Queen Elizabeth for £35. paid to the Duchy of Lancaster, and on condition that it should erect a Schoolhouse with them where an old one stood before time, and the overplus, if any, to be employed in bringing a conduit of fresh water into the town.

From the Hall Book † we learn that on the Feast of S. Matthew the Apostle, 5th Elizabeth, it was notified:

> The weight of the bells of Seynt Peters weyd before Mr. Davye Mayor, Mr. Darker, Mr. Pare, Mr. Norys, Robert .... & Robert Davye Chamblyns & Thomas Newcombe w^th others

---

* Hist. Leicester, p. 108.       † In MS. vol. ii. p. 92.

2 E

The great bell weys xi<sup>e</sup>. xvj<sup>li</sup>. the third bell viij<sup>e</sup>. D qr xxvj<sup>li</sup>. the second bell vj<sup>e</sup>. D qr xviij<sup>li</sup>. the fore bell v<sup>e</sup>. x<sup>li</sup>.

Sm̄ totlis xxxij<sup>e</sup>. xiij<sup>li</sup>.

At a Common Hall, held 30th June, 1564, it was ordered that one of the bells of S. Peter's be sold for the repair of the Schoolhouse. From the Chamberlains' Accounts (in MS.) for the year 1563-4 we learn the following particulars of this sale, and from the weight observe it was the great bell which was then sold:

1563-4.  It.  Receyved of Thomas Newcombe & Mr. Norys
  for j bell of sent Peters church weying xj<sup>e</sup>. xvj<sup>li</sup>.
  xiiij*li*. xvj*s*. viij*d*.
  It.  Receyved of the same Thomas for viij brases
  weyinge xxxviij pounds & iij bell clappers of the
  same sent Peters church weying lxxxxv pounds...xxij*s*.
  It.  Receyved for j bell whele of the same church  j*s*.

Mr. Noris also bought some of the lead.   The other bells were quickly disposed of:

1564-5.  Itm̄. receyved of ffrauncis Watts for the bell
  wheles of Seynt Peters .....................................xij*s*.
1565-6.  It. of Thomas Newcom for three Bells wayinge
  xxi<sup>e</sup>. xij<sup>li</sup>. cxxxs. the hundreth ..................xxxj*li*. xij*s*.

## LEICESTER.

### The Abbey of S. Mary de Pratis.

Dugdale says* "at the time of the Dissolution the bells were valued by estimation at £88."

The great bell (and so probably the whole ring) was purchased by Robert Newcombe, of Leicester, Bellfounder (see p. 47), and shortly

---

* *Mon.* vol. vi. p. 462.

afterwards (in 1542) exchanged by him—in the way of his business—with the churchwardens of the parish church of Peterborough—S. John Baptist—for their great bell which was then "brokyn," and the difference of value in money.

A full account of this transaction is preserved in the Accounts of the Churchwardens of "the Parrysh cherche of Petborow" (*i.e.* of S. John the Baptist), and is so curious and full of interest that it is here given entire : *

| Churche Wardens | By Ryc' Morgan John German Ryc' Baylyff and Thoms Marrett | The charge for changyng the great bell in the xxxiij yer of the reigne of o' Sov'eigne Lorde Kyng Hen. the eight for the great bell of the Abbey of Leicester | | |
|---|---|---|---|---|
| Recytts | Imp'mis Receyved of the great box in the chirch at the syght of dyv'se honyst men in the pyshe as ap- peryth by a byll in the saide Chirch boxe ......................... | vij*li.* | ix*s.* | iiij*d.* |
| | It̄m Receyyed moor by the gyfte of John German by quest ............ | | xx*s.* | |
| | It̄m Recevede moor by the gyfte of Robart Tochis bequeste ............ | | xx*s.* | |
| | It̄m Receyvede at the gyfte of John Shepe ................................. | | vj*s.* | viij*d.* |

Sm̄ Recepte
ix*li.* xvj*s.*

* For this transcript from the original manuscript I am much indebted to James Cattel, Esq., of Peterborough. He informs me that the Church of S. John Baptist at Peterborough had formerly six bells, and that in 1808 these were cast into the present ring of eight, so that the ancient bell from Leicester Abbey in all probability then disappeared.

| | | |
|---|---|---|
| Payments for the change of the bell | Itm̄ payde to Robarte Newcom Bell founder in Lecyst' for the onely exchaunge of the holl bell for the brokyn ............................... | iiij*li*. |
| | Itm̄ payde moor to the sayde Robarte Newcom fôr that his bell weyde moor then o' bell by iij*ᵉ*. a qt*ʳ*. & iiij*ˡⁱ*. at iiij*d*. the pounde vj*li*. ij*s*. viij*d*. as thus on hunderde & xxxix*ˡⁱ*, of mettell that was the chirches at iiij*d*. the li. which came to xxxiij*s*. & ix*d*. & for the rest redy money | iiij*li*. iiij*s*. xj*d*. |
| | Itm̄ payde moor to hym for that his clapper weyde mor then o' clapp by xxviij*ˡⁱ*. ............................... | ij*s*. iiij*d*. |

| | | |
|---|---|---|
| Expences & chargis for the said Bell. | Itm̄ payde to the man at Wyttyllsey for a gable to tacke down the olde bell & hang up the new ............ | xx*d*. |
| | Itm̄ payde for drynk at the takyng down of the olde bell .............. | vj*d*. |
| | Itm̄ payde to John Whell wright for makyng of a carte & axlyng of the whells wᵗ o'things for ij days worke | xij*d*. |
| | Itm̄ for his meat & drynke that ii days ...................................... | · iiij*d*. |
| | Itm̄ for a Rygewyth for the same carte...................................... | ij*d*. |
| | Itm̄ for Carte clouts & naylls for the first clowtyng ...................... | xvj*d*. |

The first days charge
beyng fryday going
wᵗ the carte.

| | | |
|---|---|---|
| Itm̄ for meat & drynke for iiij men that went wᵗ the carte the sayde first day ................................ | | xiij*d*. |
| Itm̄ for the chayngyng of a strocke & for iiij carte naylls at Uppinghm̄ the first nyght ........................ | | xij*d*. |
| Itm̄ for horsmet of xv horsis that went wᵗ the bell the same first day & nyght at Uppingham ...... | ii*s*. | ix*d*. |

On Sat'day.

| | | |
|---|---|---|
| Itm̄ for meat & drynke for v men that day ................................ | ij*s*. | iiij*d*. |
| Itm̄ for bayting of horses the sam day by the way ........................ | | ix*d*. |

Sm̄ of the payments &
expences ix*li*. iij*d*.

( *The end of one page.* )

Expences
&
Charges
for the saide
Bell

On Sunday in Lecester
all day.

| | | |
|---|---|---|
| Itm̄ for iiij carte clowts and a wynd-yng for the whells..................... | | xj*d*. |
| Itm̄ the mens sop* the same nyght... | | xij*d*. |
| Itm̄ for horsmet of xv horssis for ij nyghts & a day ther in Lecester... | v*s*. | viij*d*. |

* Supper.

On Monday comyng
whom wards.

| | | |
|---|---|---|
| Itm̄ for meat & drynke for the men that day ................................. | iis. | |
| Itm̄ for horsmet that day & nyght... | iis. | xjd. |
| Itm̄ for iiij new Carte naylls & shottyng a strock & settyng hyme on agayn at Uppingham ............... | | vjd. |

On Tewisday.

| | |
|---|---|
| Itm̄ for meat & drynke for the men that day ................................. | xiiijd. |
| Itm̄ for baytyng ther horses the same day ...................................... | vjd. |
| Itm̄ for a wynding & ij dowledgs for the whells ............................ | vd. |
| Itm̄ payd for drynke for carters & other men that helpyd owt wᵗ a tree in a dycke that my lorde * gave the chirch to mack ij yeocks at Westwood ......................... | iiijd. |
| Itm̄ payd for fetchyng the same in a Carte ................................. | viijd. |
| Itm̄ payd for ij sawyers for ij days worke ..................................... | xvjd. |
| Itm̄ payde for gresse at dyv's tymes for the Carte & the burrells in the Chirch at the takyng down of the bell & wyndyng up the other bell | vjd. |

* Lord Bishop.

| | | |
|---|---|---|
| Itm̄ payde to Raffe for the takyng down the olde bell & yowkyng the new & hangyng hym up ............ | xs. | iiij*d.* |
| Itm̄ payde to John Smyth for makyng the Yronworke of the great bell... | v*s.* | |
| Itm̄ payde to John Gadney for the hyr of iiij horssis & hymselfe to goo wᵗ them for vij days ............ | vj*s.* | |
| Itm̄ payde to Robarte Allyn for vj horsys & ii men for viij days ...... | xiiij*s.* | |
| Itm̄ payde to Ryc' Hewet for mend-yng & shootyng of the Roope we borowyd at Wittyllsey.............. | xiiij*d.* | |
| Itm̄ geven to a man to cary hit to the wat'syde that shold cary whout the rope to Wyttyllsey.............. | ij*d.* | |

Sm̄

liiij*s.* vij*d.*

## LEIRE.

S. PETER.                                                    3 BELLS.

1. EVS    BEE    OVR    GOODE    SPEEDE    1654.
2. HENRICUS BAGLEY FECIT 1675.
3. RECAST + A.D. 1755 JOHN SLEATH C.W. THOS. EAYRE
   DE KETTERING FECIT.

*Round the rim :*

GIVEN BY JANE CART RELICT OF JAMES CART OF
   LEIRE, DAUGHTER OF THOMAS CHEW AND
   ELIZABETH HIS WIFE, WHICH ELIZABETH
   WAS DAUGHTER OF W. M. MARSH OF DUN-
   STABLE A°. D. 1732.

[ LITTLE ASHBY—see Ashby Parva. ]

[ LITTLE DALBY—see Dalby Parva. ]

[ LITTLE PEATLING—see Peatling Parva. ]

[ LITTLE WIGSTON—see Wigston Parva. ]

## LOCKINGTON.

S. NICOLAS. 5 BELLS.

1. Ꝟox d̄m̄i iħū xp̄i box exultacionis . . . [ ▽ 6 ] [ □ 28 ] [ + 42 ]
   [ □ 16. ]
   ( For initial letter see fig. 81. )
2. GOD [ 12 ] SAVE [ 12 ] HIS [ 12 ] CHVRCH .... 1692.
3. RVND. PHILLIP STORY VICAR T. PALMER C. W. JOHN
   BRIANT HERTFORD FECIT 1806.
4 and 5. T. MEARS OF LONDON FECIT 1832.

In 6 Edward VI. there were "foore great bells." Previous to 1832
the fourth, and then tenor, bell, was inscribed :—"William Bainbrigge
and Edward Burton Churchwardens 1650."

The Curfew is rung during the winter months at 8 p.m. A morning-
bell is rung on Sunday at 8 a.m.

## LODDINGTON.

S. MICHAEL. 3 BELLS.

Ꝯ ꝝ ꞇ
1. [ + 45. ] AVE : MARIA : GRACIA :
   PLENA : DOMINUS : TECUM.
   ( Diam. 30 in. )

2. 𝕲𝕺𝕯 𝕾𝕬𝖁𝕰 𝕿𝕳𝕰 𝕮𝕳𝖁𝕽𝕮𝕳 1602.
   ( Diam. 30¼ in.: Watts' letters. )
3. OMNIA FIANT AD GLORIAM DEI † GLORIA DEO
   SOLI  .:.  T. EAYRE KETT. 1737.
   EDMUNDUS MORRIS ARMIGER.
   ( Diam. 31¼ in. )

At death-knell thrice 3 tolls are given for a male, thrice 2 for a female.


## LONG CLAWSON.

S. REMIGIUS.                                    5 BELLS.

1. LET EVERYTHING THAT HATH BREATH PRAISE THE
   LORD. EDD. WRIGHT CH. WARDEN T. HEDDERLY
   OF NOTTINGHAM FECIT 1782.
   ( Diam. 36¼ in. )
2. IH'S : NAZARENVS [9] REX : IVDEORVM [9] FILI :
   DEI [9] MISERERE : MEI [9] 1631 [ ⛝ I. ]
   ( Diam. 37¼ in. )
3. all · men · that · heare · my · mornfull · sound · repent · before · you
   lye · in · ground 1608 [ □ 8. ]
   ( Diam. 38¼ in. )
4. [ + 55 ] 𝕴𝕾𝕿𝕬 [ □ 59 ] 𝕮𝕬𝕸𝕻𝕬𝕹𝕬 [ □ 59 ]
   𝕱𝕬𝕮𝕿𝕬 [ □ 59 ] 𝕰𝕾𝕿 [ □ 59 ] 𝕴𝕹
   𝕳𝕺𝕹𝕺𝕽𝕰 [ □ 59 ] 𝕾𝕬𝕹𝕮𝕿𝕰 [ □ 59 ]
   𝕿𝕽𝕴𝕹𝕴𝕿𝕬𝕿𝕴𝕾.
   ( Diam. 43 in. )
5. I TO THE CHURCH THE LIVING CALL AND TO THE
   GRAVE DO SUMMONS ALL. EDD. WRIGHT
   CHURCHWARDEN T. HEDDERLY OF NOTTING-
   HAM FECIT 1782.
   ( Diam. 47 in. )

2 F

There was formerly "a large Sancte's bell inscribed 'God save the King 1662.'" This was taken down and placed in the Tower of the new School in the year 1849.

In 6 Edward VI. there were "iiij bells and a saunce Bell."

The 1st bell was formerly inscribed: "Cvm sono si non vis venire, nvnqvam ad preces cvpies ire."

Nichols says:—"The inhabitants have a tradition that one of the Bozons went into France (whether with Edward III. or Henry V. they know not) and, among other spoils, brought thence four great bells which he hung up in this church. The present fourth bell is a very old one, and is yet called Bozon's bell. In 1631 the great bell of Grantham being cracked the Burgesses of Grantham gave the men of Clauston their cracked bell and twenty pounds in money for Clauston great bell, which was exactly the same note they wanted: thus the biggest of Bozon's great bells went to Grantham. With the metal of Grantham cracked bell, and the aforesaid £20., the inhabitants of Clauston procured two new bells, being the 1st and 2nd of their present peal: and thus they came to have five instead of four bells."

With reference to this tradition it may be noted that the founder of the fourth bell was Johannes de Yorke. It is hardly probable that Bozon brought four great bells from France, but it is not improbable that he brought a quantity of spoil, and from the proceeds of a portion of that paid for four new bells for the church here.

[ LONG WHATTON—see Whatton Long. ]

## LOUGHBOROUGH.

ALL SAINTS. (?)                                   8 BELLS.

1. A VOICE FROM THE TEMPLE A VOICE FROM THE
   LORD.   REVᴰ. J. PLAICE M.A. OFFICIATING
   MINISTER A.D. 1840.
        ( Weight 6 cwt. 1 qr. 11 lbs. )

2. GLORY BE TO GOD ON HIGH TAYLOR FOUNDER
   JUNE 18th 1840 LOUGHBOROUGH.
   
   REV. W. HOLME B.D. RECTOR
   
   JOHN FARMER ⎫
   DANIEL CARTWRIGHT ⎭ C. WARDENS.
   
   ( Weight 6 cwt. 1 qr. 24 lbs. )

3. REV. W. HOLME B.D. RECTOR
   
   JOHN FARMER
   
   C. WARDENS.
   
   D. CARTWRIGHT
   
   TAYLOR FECIT 1840.
   ( Weight 7 cwt. 0 qr. 2 lbs. )

4. REV. W. HOLME B.D. RECTOR
   
   J. FARMER
   
   C. W. 1840.
   
   D. CARTWRIGHT
   
   TAYLOR FOUNDER LOBORO'.
   ( Weight 8 cwt. 0 qr. 23 lbs. )

5. COMMITTEE REV. W. HOLME B.D. JOHN FARMER
   DANIEL CARTWRIGHT JOHN CARTWRIGHT
   THOMAS CRADOCK JOHN FOWLER W JOSEPH
   FRY THOMAS BURKILL JULIUS MOTT.
   
   J. TAYLOR FECIT 1840.
   ( Weight 10 cwt. 0 qr. 3 lbs. )

6. The same as to Committee.
   
   JOHN TAYLOR CAMPANARIUS 1840.
   ( Weight 10 cwt. 3 qrs. 21 lbs. )

7. REV. W. HOLME B.D. JOHN FARMER DANIEL
   CARTWRIGHT.
   COMMITTEE JOHN CARTWRIGHT THOMAS CRADOCK
   JOHN FOWLER 1840 W. JOSEPH FRY THOMAS
   BURKILL JULIUS MOTT.

OXFORD
JOHN TAYLOR BELLFOUNDER      AND
LOUGHBOROUGH
( Weight 15 cwt. o qr. 21 lbs. )

JOHN FARMER
8.   REV. W. HOLME, B.D.              CHURCHWARDENS 1840.
•  DANIEL CARTWRIGHT
W. & J. TAYLOR BELLFOUNDERS OXFORD & LOUGH-
BOROUGH.

( Weight 24 cwt. 1 qr. 12 lbs.   Diameter 52¾ inches.   Total weight of
bells 88 cwt. 2 qrs. o lbs.   Key D. )

In 6 Edward VI. the Commissioners reported that there were in the
church of " Loughborowe fyve belles."

The following duties belonging to the bellman's office in the church
here are copied from the draft of an old document, which appears to
have been drawn up *temp.* Edward VI.

Thes dootes follo'ng longs to ye bellmās offyys in ye cherch.

It. ferst to ly in ye cherch and to cō at viij of ye cloke at night
in whinter & somer to ring corfir & then to go to bed.

And every Sonday & Alliday bedforth to Ring a vij of ye
cloke at neght.

Also ye mā to leght the cādylles in ye cherch everry Allyday as
cossto has bene yowsed.

Also to blow ye orgends at matts & mas and egsong as has bene
of costo afore tyme.

Also to help to reng to sarvys if nedbe.

Also to swyp ye cherche thorow & to clen every sevtʰ day &
every allow even.

Also to swyp ye pellors to & of ye cherch as hy as he cā Rech
wᵗ a long banner poll & wher cobwebbs & dost heng on clenly and
bedforth to dow ye wth er.

Also to go every ffryday a bowt ye towne to bed pray for all crestan soles as of costo has be yowsed at vj of ye clok in somer & vij of ye clok in wenter.

Also to satt ye heres & of everry cores.*

*The Churchwardens' Accounts* are full of entries relating to the bells. The following are examples:

1583.   Imprimis payed to Joseph Byngloye for mending the great bell clappers, and to keip yt in reparatio ffor ij years after from the xv<sup>th</sup> of Aprill last ......... vjs. viijd.

Item pd to W<sup>m</sup> Wallys for makinge of viij wedges & for fynding Iron for the fourth bell .................. vjd.

1584.   Item pd for mendinge the Hand Bell .................. viijd.

Item pd to Edmund Iveson for a Bell Rope ......... ijs.

Item pd to the Ringars on St Hew Daye ............ iiijs. iiijd.

It. pd to Thomas Smith for makeing the fourth clapper now weying 49<sup>li</sup>. at iiijd. the pound ......... xvjs. iiijd.

1585.   Receved of the Townesmen of this parishe towards the payment of the Castinge of the great bell, as maye appeare by a Bill collected of every partye, which have alreddy payd whiche is in Toto......vli. vjs.   ijd.

---

* In one or two instances the items are rather unintelligible.   The paper from which they are copied is merely the *draft* of the original.   This curious document was contributed by Mr. W. G. Dimock Fletcher to the *Reliquary* in the year 1873. The Editor adds the following explanatory note which arrives at the meaning as near as can be got:—" The Bellman [or Bellmaster] it appears had to sleep in the church; to ring the curfew at eight o'clock at night on week days and seven o'clock on Sundays and holy-days all the year round; to light the candles on holy-days; to blow the organ at matins, mass and evensong; to help, if need be, to ring to service; to sweep and clean the church every Saturday and every hallow-eve; to sweep the pillars and walls of the church as high as he can reach with a long banner pole, and to take down any dust or cobwebs there may be; to perambulate the town every Friday evening at six o'clock in summer and seven in winter [? morning] to bid the people pray for all Christian souls *i.e.* private prayer in their own houses; and to prepare and set ready the hearse or bier for any corpse that had to be buried."

Item pd for ij Baldriggs for ye Bells ................... ij*s*.

Pd for Candells at takeing the bell downe ............          j*d*.

Item payed for Carridge of the greate bell to Leicest[r]
and home agayne, together w[th] the chardges about
the same, untill it was hanged upp agayne as may
appeare by the Bill of percells thereof made vidz.... liij*s*. viij*d*.

Item pd to ffrauncis Watts and Mr. Newcome the
Belfounders of Leic. for one half of the payment
for Castinge the great Bell ....................... iiij*li*.

1586.    Receyved of certayne persons towards the castinge
of the great bell as apperith by oure bill, in Toto ...xxij*s*.

Imprimis payed and layed downe for our Suppers
at Leicest[r] at the casting of the Bells .................iiij*s*. viij*d*.

Pd for our Brekefasts the next day .................... ij*s*. ij*d*.

Pd for o[r] Suppers the same daye .................... xvij*d*.

Pd for drinke for the bellfounders men ............... xvj*d*.

Pd to Mr. Newcomes maides ......................... vj*d*.

Pd for Aale ................................................ iiij*d*.

3*d*.                    4*d*.

Pd for Aalle at Mountsorrell and at home ........... vij*d*.

Pd to Georg Hardie for helpinge downe the bells... iiij*d*.

Pd to Joseph Binglaye for Iron worke ...............iiij*s*.

Paid to Thomas Smartwood for mendinge the bell
Clappers........................................................ xvij*d*.

Pd to Edward Iveson for tow new bell roopes and
for showting two bell roopes ............................. v*s*.    x*d*.

Pd to Robert Claye for takinge downe the fourthe
bell and hangine up the othere bell ..................... iij*s*.

Pd for the carte that cam from Nott for the bell ...vij*s*.

Pd to Claye for takinge downe the bell that came
from Notting' and hanging up the towe other bells iiij*s*. iiij*d*.

Pd to Kathernes and his man and libes Jesone for
a daies worke hangine the bells ....................... ij*s*. iiij*d*.

Pd for helpe in takinge downe the fourth bell ...... xiiij*d*.

Pd to W<sup>m</sup> Kathernes and his towe men for takinge
downe the greate bell ......................................... iiij*s.*   ij*d.*

Pd to Robert Claye for him and his man for mend-
inge the hingine of the great bell better .............   xviij*d.*

Pd to George Cawdwell for carringe the bell to
Nottingham ................................................. viij*s.*

Pd to the Ringars upon sainct hews daye ............ iij*s.* iiij*d.*

Pd for Yookinge the ffourth bell and for makinge
a new wheile, And for yokinge the seconde bell .... xiij*s.*

Pd for mendinge the great bell yooke .................   xiiij*d.*

Pd to Hubbard of Quorne for mendinge the great
bell clapper ....................................................viij*s.* viij*d.*

Pd to Robert Claye for makinge the Barrell for the
chyme ......................................................... v*s.* iiij*d.*

Pd to Robert Claye for makinge the great bell a
new wheile.................................................... vij*s.*

Pd to Edward Iveson shewtinge and peisinge the
chyme rope ...................................................   xx*d.*

Pd for W<sup>m</sup>. Evington's chardges goeinge to caste
the bells at Leicester ...................................... ij*s.* x*d.*

Pd to Joseph Binglaye for makinge the goodgins
and hartstaple a shanke for the fourth bell clapper
Rowndinge the oninyon, shewtinge one sheire and
a staye ......................................................... iij*s.* iiij*d.*

Paid for iij hammers v stayes iij jacks vj verty
vayles, for a C Iron pegge, for a C neales, iij lyfts, a
long pyne of Iron, for mendinge all the lyftes at the
chyme and the gaage, and for ij hoops of Iron, and
other Iron worke aboute the chyme.................... x*s.*

Payed to Richard the paynter towards his wages
for settinge the Chyme in part of his payment ...... xiiij*s.* vj*d.*

Pd to Bryan Smythe for a tang for the bauldaricke
of the seconde bell............................................   ij*d.*

Pd to John Wever for his tow dayes chardges
when he went to Nottingham for them that came
to prove the tune of ye Bells ............................ xiiij*d*.
Pd for drinke that they dronke by the waye ......... iij*d*.
Pd for a gaune of Aale for the ringars.................. vij*d*.
Pd for greace for the chyme a pynte .................. iij*d*.

It is agreed at this Accompt that John Wever shall have
from henceforthe the fee for the belman whiche Henry
Scattergood had. Doiynge his Dowtye for the same.
Allowinge widow Scattergood towards her kepinge ij*d*. every
weike for her better helpe out of the pore mens box; or
ells some other wayes.

1587. Payed for carrynge the fourthe bell to Leicester
and home agayne............................................... xiijs. iiij*d*.
Payed to George Ball for the chyme barrill and for
makinge of yt ................................................... vij*s*.

1588. Agreed at this Accompt that every marridge haveing or
reqring to have the bells rung, shall paye vj*d*. to the poremens
boxe and vj*d*. towards repairinge of the bells and the churche
and the clarke to receyce.

1613. Item paid to Oldfeild in earneste when he toke in
hand to caste the great Bell ............................. xij*d*.
Item spent in bread and Beare when the great Bell
was ffirste taken downe to them y* did helpe ......... xx*d*.
Paid for helpers to Lood the bell the first tyme ... vj*d*.
Paid for chardges att Nottingham at the first
castinge of the Greate Bell...............................xxj*s*. viij*d*.
Paid for Bread and Beare when the great bell was
first hanged upp ............................................. ij*s*.
Paid for the chardges for Mr. Ouldfeild and his
sone when we sent for them ............................. ij*s*. vj*d*.
Item pd for Bread and Beare when the Bell was
taken downe to be chipt.................................... xviij*d*.

Item spent in bread and bere when the Bell was
had up aft' she had bene chipt to them w'ʰ did help      viij*d*.
Item paid unto Mr. Oulefeild for casting the great
Bell at the first & for mettall he added unto it   xiij*li*. vj*s*. viij*d*.
Paid unto Mr. Ouldfeild for iiij'. & a half of mettall
more added unto ye great Bell at the second
casting of it ............................................ xvj*li*. xvj*s*.
Paid unto Mr. Ouldfeild towards his chardges ye
second casting of the great Bell in good will ..iij*li*. vj*s*. viij*d*.

Sum payd
xxxiiij*li*. iij*s*. x*d*.

    M. That the great Bell was in waight before it was first
new cast vidz.: xviij'. 3 qrs. 13 lbs. And now it is xxiij'. & a
half & 20 poundes.

1616. [This year the ancient ring of five bells was increased to six
as may be gathered from the Churchwardens' Accounts and
from the inscriptions presently quoted.]

    It. spent upon Ouldfeild's sonne when he came to
the towne the 17 of Septemb.............................    xij*d*.
It. Paid to John ffowler for carryeing the third bell
to Nottingham & for bringinge it & *the new bell back* xxj*s*.   vj*d*.
It. to be paid to Mr. Ouldfeild for casting of the
third bell & for adding of mettall ...............xv*li*. xvij*s*.   vj*d*.
It. spent in giveing entertainem' to the gentlemen
strangers when they came to ringe .................... xj*s*.

The six bells, at this date, bore the following inscriptions copied by
the eminent Botanist Dr. Pulteney, when he was at the free school of
the parish :

1. 𝕴 will sound and resound unto all Christian people
    And to the benefactors that gabe me to this steeple 1616.
2. 𝕴n multis annis resonet campana Johannis
3. 𝕾it nomen Domini benedictum; laudate illum cymbalis sonoris
4. 𝕹os sumus constructi ad laudem Domini 1616.

    2 G

5. 𝔖𝔦𝔯 𝔊𝔢𝔬𝔯𝔤 𝔥𝔞𝔰𝔱𝔦𝔫𝔤𝔢𝔰 𝔪𝔞𝔡𝔢 𝔪𝔢 𝔞𝔫𝔫𝔬 𝔇𝔬𝔪𝔦𝔫𝔦 1586.
6. 𝔥𝔢𝔠 𝔠𝔞𝔪𝔭𝔞𝔫𝔞 𝔰𝔞𝔠𝔯𝔞 𝔣𝔦𝔞𝔱 𝔗𝔯𝔦𝔫𝔦𝔱𝔞𝔱𝔢 𝔅𝔢𝔞𝔱𝔞 1613.

*The Churchwardens' Accounts* also contain frequent entries of sums of money paid to the ringers, thus:

|  |  | £. | s. | d. |
|---|---|---|---|---|
| 1642. | Pd to the Ringers for his majesty..................... | 0 | 10 | 0 |
|  | Pd to the same when prince Rupert went to Leicester ...................................................... | 0 | 1 | 0 |
|  | Pd to the same when prince Rupert came to view the Trayne band ............................................ | 0 | 1 | 0 |
|  | Pd to the Ringers when the King was here another tyme................................................. | 0 | 5 | 2 |
| 1645. | It. payd to ye Ringers when ye King's Maᵗʸ came by ...................................................... | 0 | 2 | 6 |
| 1646. | Spent on ye Ringers whe Sʳ Thomas ffarefax passed by ..................................................... | 0 | 1 | 0 |
| 1649. | It is agreed at this Assembly by the consent of all present that the great Bell shall not be rung at any buriall except once for the passing peale & that there shall be no other ringinge but all ye belles or 2 or 3. |  |  |  |
| 1657. | Spent on ye Ringers when the Lord Protector was proclaimed............................................. | 0 | 4 | 6 |
| 1664. | Pd to ye Ringers to drinke on St Georges day ... | 0 | 5 | 0 |

[ Entries frequently occur of sums paid to the ringers on St. George's Day; also on Candlemas Day and on November 5th. ]

In the *Account Books of Thomas Burton's Charity*, which are complete from 1570 to the present time, there are frequent entries of a similar nature. The following are instances:

| 1686. | Paid Js. Dalby for Towleing the Bell .............. | 0 | 1 | 0 |
|---|---|---|---|---|
| 1702. | Given to the Ringers & at the Burnfires Nov. 5 | 0 | 2 | 6 |
|  | Given to the Ringers on the Thanksgiving Day | 0 | 2 | 6 |
| 1713. | Given ye Ringers ye same day (May ye 3rd) ...... | 0 | 2 | 6 |
|  | July 7. Given ye Ringers of ye Thanksgiving for ye peace ................................................. | 0 | 2 | 6 |

The whole ring of six bells were recast in the year 1754 by Thomas Eayre of Kettering, the cost being defrayed by public subscription. The following particulars are preserved in *The Churchwardens' Book:*

1754. Reced of the Subscribers for recasting 5 of the Bells, and for all materials necessary for them as follows. [ Here follows a list of Subscribers' names and the amount of their subscriptions. The Total was ] .............. £111 14 . 8½

| | | |
|---|---|---|
| Pd Wm Underwood for going to Kettering to see the Bells weigh'd ............................ | £1 . 0 . 0 | |
| Pd Do for going to seek after ym | 0 . 5 . 0 | 108 . 5 . 0 |
| Pd Mr. Eayres for recasting five Bells & providing all necessaries for them &c. ....................... | 107 . 0 . 0 | |
| Balance in hand ........................ | | 3 . 9 . 8½ |

1754. Sep. 3. At a Vestry Meeting this Day held it is agreed that Mr. Eayres shall by the present churchwardens be paid at Giving up their Accounts the sum of eleven pounds seven shillings being due to him, by verbal agreement for 1c. 3qr. 16lb. of metall more than where in the old Bells.

The Six Bells where all recast by Mr. Eayres of Kettering and the Weight of them are as follows:

| | c. qr. lb |
|---|---|
| The 1st Bell ............................................ | 10 . 3 . 10 |
| 2nd ,, ............................................ | 11 . 0 . 11 |
| 3rd ,, ............................................ | 11 . 2 . 5 |
| 4th ,, ............................................ | 12 . 3 . 15 |
| 5th ,, ............................................ | 14 . 1 . 10 |
| 6th ,, ............................................ | 24 . 2 . 14 |
| | 85 . 1 . 9 |

The Weight of old Bells where as follows:

|  | c. | qr. | ℔ |
|---|---|---|---|
| The 1st Bell | 9 | 1 | 11 |
| 2nd „ | 9 | 1 | 0 |
| 3rd „ | 11 | 0 | 3 |
| 4th „ | 14 | 2 | 20 |
| 5th „ | 15 | 2 | 1 |
| 6th „ | 23 | 3 | 19 |
|  | 83 | 2 | 26 |
| The new Bells heavier than the old ones | 1 | 2 | 11 |
| The old Crown Staples | 0 | 1 | 5 |
| The whole difference is | 1 | 3 | 16 |

Which at 6 £ a Hundred is £11 . 7 . 0

1754. March 26.   Pd Mr. Stockdale for ye 5th Bell
being cracked and not recast before ye Visitation £1 . 1 . 6

The inscriptions on the six bells now cast by Eayre were:

1.  Vox mea dulcis mea scintillans vultus.
2.  Statutum est omnibus semel mori; omnia fiant ad gloriam Dei.
3.  Nos sumus constructi ad laudem Domini; in Dei gloriam; in ecclesiæ commodum.
4.  Sit nomen Domini benedictum, laudate illum cymbalis sonoris.
5.  Morte beatâ nihil beatius.   Thomas Eayre fecit; Richard Mansfield and John Warren Sidesmen.
6.  Thomas Alleyne rector; Francis Winfield and Edward Savage Churchwardens.   Thomas Eayre fecit, anno Domini 1754.

Mr. J. W. Taylor of Loughborough reports that these old bells (recast in 1840) were in E flat, and weighed 83 cwt. 1 qr. 2 ℔, showing a considerable difference between the actual weight and that quoted in the Churchwardens' Accounts.

In the year 1840 these six bells were recast and formed into the present ring of eight, by Messrs. W. and J. Taylor, who came from

Oxford for the purpose, and who finding Loughborough a central and convenient place for their calling settled there and erected their foundry.

A tablet in the belfry records the ringing of several peals.

The Curfew still rings every evening at eight o'clock, after which the day of the month is tolled on a smaller bell.

The morning bell rings every morning in summer at six, in winter at seven o'clock. The Pancake-bell rings on Shrove-Tuesday.* At the death-knell three tolls are given for a male, two for a female, both before and after the knell.

## LOUGHBOROUGH.

EMMANUEL.                                                                    1 BELL.

1. THOMAS MEARS OF LONDON FOUNDER 1837.

## LOWESBY.

ALL SAINTS.                                                                  3 BELLS.

1. GOD [ 13 ] SAVE [ 13 ] HIS [ 13 ] CHVRCH [ 13 ] 1657 [ ☐ 10. ]
   ( Diam. 34 in. )

2. IH'Ƨ : NAZARENVS [ 9 ] REX : IVDEORVM [ 9 ] FILI :
   DEI [ 9 ] MISERERE : MEI [ 9 ] 1265 [ ♉ 1. ]
   ( Diam. 37 in. )

3. 𝔸𝔹𝔺𝔻𝔼 𝔉𝔊𝔥𝕀𝕂 𝕃𝕄ℕ𝕆 1613 [ ♉ 1. ]
   ( Diam. 40 in. )

The figures of the date on the 2nd bell mean 1625.

## LUBENHAM.

ALL SAINTS.                                                                  5 BELLS.

1. IHS NAZARENE REX IUDÆORUM FILI DEI MISERERE
   MEI WILLIAM SPRIGG BENEFACTOR A.D. 1724.

---

* For the inscriptions on the Lough-borough bells, and for all the extracts from the parochial records, I am much indebted to the industry and courtesy of W. G. Dimock Fletcher, Esq.

2. IHS NAZARENE REX IUDÆORUM FILI DEI MISERERE MEI THO : · EAYRE DE KETTERING CAMPANA·RIUS 1724.

3. IHS NAZARENE REX IUDÆORUM FILI DEI MISERERE MEI GLORIA DEO SOLI T : · EAYRE : · KETTER·ING : ·

4. GLORIA DEO SOLI OD 1724 O JOHN ASHTON MINISTER OO JOHN CAVE & WILLIAM ILIFFE CHURCH·WARDENS O

5. IH'S : NAZARENVS [9] REX : IVDEORVM [9] FILI : DEI [9] MISERERE : MEI [9] 1624 [ ∇ 1. ]

Previous to 1724 there were four bells only; all—like the present tenor—from the foundry of Hugh Watts of Leicester.

The Rev. H. E. Bullivant kindly supplies the following extracts from the Churchwardens' Books:

| | | £. | s. | d. |
|---|---|---|---|---|
| 1723. | Oct. Sp^t with the Bellfounder and nabors ye first time..................................... | 0 | 3 | 0 |
| | Sp^t with nabors another time when we met ab^t the Bells..................................... | 0 | 1 | 6 |
| | for wood for the steeppel Brought from Harborough ..................................... | 0 | 8 | 0 |
| | Spent on Nabors who w^d confermd the Bargin to have the Bells Rund ..................................... | 0 | 3 | 0 |
| | for Mr. Ashton's expenses writing for the Bellfounder ..................................... | 0 | 0 | 4 |
| | Spent on ye nabors and workmen when the Bells were taken Dound and wayed ..................... | 0 | 2 | 0 |
| | Pd for Will^m Spriggs charges and men y^t helpt to unlood the Bells at Kettering .................... | 0 | 2 | 8 |
| | for a journey to Kettering when the Bells went... | 0 | 3 | 0 |
| 1724. | Pd for Bell rops wayed 27 pounds att 6d. per ℔ | 0 | 13 | 6 |

Sep. 18. Spent with the Bellfounder & nabors £. *s.* *d.*
when he came to hing the Bells and paid John
Mansfield for the Bell caps ........................... 0 . 1 . 9

1725. May 12. Pd Mr. Eayre part of his Bill............ 10  12 . 3½
[William Iliffe Churchwarden for the "open field side" of
Lubenham also charges "Pd my part of Mr. Eayre's Bill
£10 . 12 . 3½"]

1726. Jan. 12 [there are charges for additional "mettel" for the
third bell.]

For my journey and teams to fetch the new bell
from Kettering ............................................... 0  10 . 0
Pd for Bell loding at Kettering....................... 0 . 1 . 0
Pd for unloading the Bell and getting up in y*
Stepel....................................................... 0 . 1 . 6

The Ringers and "Nabors" spent 10s. amongst them—most probably
in beer.

There is a tradition that in some unexplained way the bells of Lubenham and Foxton were exchanged by the Bellfounder.

# LUTTERWORTH.

S. Mary.                                                                 6 Bells.

1.  HENRY ⁞ MERITON ⁞ RECTOR ⁞ THOMAS ⁞ ILIFFE ⁞
    AND ⁞ JOHN ⁞ WRIGHT ⁞ CHVRCH ⁞ WARDENS ⁞
    ALEXANDER ⁞ RIGBY ⁞ MADE ⁞ ME ⁞ 1705.
                    (Diam. 32 in.)

2.  J. BRIANT HERTFORD FECIT 1814.
                    (Diam. 32½ in.)

3.  MLKIHG      FEDCBA      XWVT      SRQP      ON
        MLKIHG      1640 [ ᒐ 1. ]
                    (Diam. 33 in.)

4.  FEDCBA      MLKIHG      SRQPON      XWVT
        FEDCBA      1640 [ ᒐ 1. ]
                    (Diam. 36 in.)

5.  T MEARS OF LONDON FECIT 1828.
                        (Diam. 39 in.)
6.  THE HONBLE. & REVND. HENRY RYDER RECTOR W.
    MASH & J TILLY C. W. JOHN BRIANT HERTFORD
    FECIT 1812.
                        (Diam. 40 in.)

" *Sacrament Bell.*"

   [ + 3 ]  ℙℍ  [ + 3 ]  𝕋ℍℝ.
                        (Diam. 18 in.)

The Rev. S. J. Walker has kindly made the following extracts for me
from the Churchwardens' Accounts :—

|  |  | £. | s. | d. |
|---|---|---|---|---|
| 1639-40.  Jany. 29.  To Mr. Watts in earnest for the Bells and beare which was drunkt with our neighboures | | 0 | 1 | 10 |
| June 6.  Payd for mending the bell wheele | | 0 | 0 | 4 |
| 16.  Payd to George Johnson for keeping the clocke and chymes | | 1 | 0 | 0 |
| Nov. 5.  Giuen to the Ringers | | 0 | 2 | 0 |
| December 24.  Payd to Francis Callis for 4 Bellropes | | 0 | 10 | 0 |
| 5 yard shooting to the great bell rope | | 0 | 0 | 9 |
| February 7.  Payd to John Robinson for mending the saint bell | | 0 | 0 | 4 |
| March 17.  Payd for Letting downe the 2 Bells | | 0 | 2 | 0 |
| 1640.  April 7.  Payd George Johnson for breaking and weighinge the Bells | | 0 | 1 | 4 |
| Payd to others for helpe in beare | | 0 | 1 | 0 |
| Payd Obediah Wightman for going to Mʳ Watts to Leicester about the Bells | | 0 | 1 | 0 |
| It. paid for carring yᵉ bells to Leicester and bringing them backe againe | | 2 | 0 | 0 |
| June.  It. paid for letting downe yᵉ 2 Bells | | 0 | 2 | 0 |
| It. spent at loading the 2 Bells | | 0 | 1 | 0 |

|  | £. | s. | d. |
|---|---|---|---|
| It. giuen to William Wall in earnest to hang the Bells ...................................................... | 0 | 0 | 6 |
| It. spent at Casting yᵉ bells and weaying them of my selfe and George Johnson & our horse meat & hire 2 daies & a night ................................. | 0 | 11 | 6 |
| July. It. giuen to Mr. Watts his men in beare and money at weaying and loading of yᵉ Bells ... | 0 | 4 | 6 |
| It. spent of my selfe and my partner and George Johnson at weaying and fetching away the bells & of our horses............................................... | 0 | 5 | 4 |
| It. spent of them that did help me load ye 5 bells & on the carters ......................................... | 0 | 1 | 6 |
| It. spent when we drew up the 3 first bells ...... | 0 | 1 | 0 |
| It. paid to Mr. Parker for boardes and wood for the bell wheeles ......................................... | 0 | 8 | 9 |
| It. paid to Lucas the Woodman for Postes for the new bell wheeles ..................................... | 0 | 1 | 8 |
| It. paid to Francis Callis for 3 Bell ropes for yᵉ least bells ................................................. | 0 | 5 | 6 |
| August. It. paid to Hugh Russell (?) & his son for mending ye floure which ye bells had broken | 0 | 1 | 8 |
| October. Paid to George Johnson for Ironworke mending the bell irons & a new claper and ironing the new bell ................................................. | 5 | 8 | 0 |
| Nov. 5. Giuen to Ringers............................. | 0 | 2 | 0 |
| February. Paid to Mr. Watts of Leicester ...... | 18 | 15 | 0 |
| April. It. for peicing the great bell Claper & laying iron to it............................................. | 0 | 10 | 0 |
| It. for setting ye Chimes upon ye 5 Bells ......... | 1 | 15 | 0 |
| It. for 2 new roules for ye chime rope to go on 3 irons......................................................... | 0 | 1 | 6 |
| 1641. December. Item paid to Mr. Watts for the bells | 17 | 0 | 0 |

1644. November 6. It. to George Johnson for the clock & chimes for plates and brads for the Bell wheele

2 H

|   |   | £. | s. | d. |
|---|---|---|---|---|
| | for pins and neales for a balrig & for the Steeple dore Lock & thick house dore lock ................... | 1 | 7 | 10 |
| 1645. | For Bellropes and Ringings at Gunpowd Trea. ... | 0 | 8 | 0 |
| 1647. | Paid for worke abought the Belles and the hanginge of a new Claper ..................................... | 0 | 2 | 8 |
| | Spent in beere when the bell weare taken downe and hunge up agaíne ..................................... | 0 | 1 | 6 |
| | Dec.  Paid for mending the Gudgings of the fore bell ..................................`.................................... | 0 | 0 | 6 |
| 1651. | May 21.  Paid George Johnson for a balrige for the greate Bell ............................................... | 0 | 0 | 10 |
| | Spent uppon the men that Helped to raise the greate bel ..................................................... | 0 | 0 | 6 |
| 1681. | Pd for a Bolrill for ye forth bell claper ........... | 0 | 1 | 6 |
| 1684. | Spent upon the Ringers ye Day the King was proclaimed in Lutterworth............................. | 0 | 6 | 0 |
| 1730. | Spent when all set ye bell ............................. | 0 | 6 | 0 |
| | Gave to the men that helped take it down in ale | 0 | 5 | 0 |
| | Casting ye bell and new mettle........................ | 20 | 18 | 0 |
| | Horse hire and expenses to Kettering to bring home ye Bell................................................. | 0 | 5 | 0 |
| | Pd for takeing up ye 5th bell........................... | 0 | 3 | 0 |
| | Pd for a messenger to Mr. . . . . to know when we should come for ye bells .......................... | 0 | 2 | 0 |
| | For altering 5th bell ................................... | 3 | 3 | 0 |
| 1774. | Sept'.  Paid to Mr. Jeaks for chime Rope ......... | 2 | 2 | 1 |

A Morning-bell is rung daily at 5 a.m. in summer, and 6 a.m. in winter. The Curfew is rung at 8 p.m. every night.

The Pancake-bell is rung on Shrove-Tuesday from 12 to 1. At the death-knell thrice three tolls are given for a man thrice two for a woman; the bell is then rung for an hour, after which the tolls are repeated: for a child under ten years of age the 4th bell is rung for half-an-hour.

The ancient Sanctus bell, now called "the Sacrament Bell," is rung in place of the Sermon-bell on Sunday, when there is a Celebration of the Holy Communion.

## MARKET BOSWORTH.

S. Peter.                                                         5 Bells.

1. EX DONO BELLAMONTIƧ DIXIE IN FELICCISSIMVM CAROLI REGIS ƧECVNDI REDITVM.

[ □ 7 ] 1660.
( Diam. 33 in. )

2. 𝔙or [ + 3 ] b̄ni [ + 3 ] iͫhu [ + 3 ] xp̄i [ + 3 ] box [ + 3 ] exultacionis [ □ 49. ]

□

( Diam. 36 in.   For initial letter see fig. 81. )

3. IH'Ƨ : NAZARENVS [9] REX : IVDEORVM [9] FILI : DEI [9] MISERERE : MEI [9] 1630 [ ▽ 1. ]

( Diam. 38¼ in. )

4. The same dated 1624.

( Diam. 41 in. )

5. 𝔙or [ □ 43 ] b̄ni [ □ 43 ] iͫhu [ □ 43 ] xp̄i [ □ 43 ] box [ □ 43 ] exultacionis [ □ 49. ]

𝕽 [ + 53 ] 𝖂𝖋 𝕴 [ + 53 ] 𝕻.𝖂𝖋 [ + 53 ] 𝕾 [ □ 49. ]

□ □

( Diam. 44 in.   For initial letter see fig. 81. )

Sir Beaumont Dixie (the second Baronet) was born in 1629, and died in May 1692.

The bells were rehung in 1788.   The Pancake-bell is lately discontinued.

## MARKET HARBOROUGH.

S. Dionysius the Areopagite.                                 6 Bells.

1. THOMAS MEARS FOUNDER LONDON 1841.

2. 𝕻𝕽𝕬𝕴𝕾𝕳 [ 9 ] 𝕿𝕳𝕰 [ 9 ] 𝕷𝕺𝕽𝕯𝕳 [ 9 ] 1613 [ 9 ] [ ▽ 1. ]

3. OMNIA FIANT AD GLORIAM DEI GLORIA PATRI FILIO
   ET SPIRITUO SANCTO : T : EAYRE KET : 1740.
4. ＧＯＤ ＳＡＶＥ ＴＨＥ ＫＩＮＧ 1609 [ ▽ 1. ]
5. CELORVM CHRSTE PLATIAT TIBI REX SONVS ISTE
   1614 [ ▽ 1. ]
6. ＧＯＤ [9] ＳＡＶＥ [9] ＴＨＥ [9] ＫＩＮＧＨ
   [9] 1613 [ ▽ 1. ] .
   There is also a small Priest's bell without inscription.

Nichols says five of the six bells here were recast between the years
1608 and 1614 "as appears from the town accompts" ... "by the famous
Mr. Watts and one Narum of Leicester." Unfortunately these accompts,
as I am informed by W. H. Gatty, Esq., who has kindly made a search
for me, are not now to be found. The treble bell previously to the year
1841, when it was recast, had no inscription, but bore several impressions
of coins issued in the reign of Queen Elizabeth—one clearly dated 1567.
The bells cast by Watts would therefore be the other five (four of which
are still hanging) in which work he was assisted by Newcombe of
Leicester *(Narum* being a misreading by Nichols for *Nucom).*

Rouse in his *Harborough Charities and Donations,* 1768, gives the following
dimensions of the bells:

| NO. | DIAMETER. | | FROM SHOULDER TO SKIRT. | | THICKNESS. | |
|---|---|---|---|---|---|---|
| | F. | I. | F. | I. | I. | T. |
| 1. | 2 . | 8 | 1 . | 11½ | 2 . | 0 |
| 2. | 3 . | 0 | 2 . | 2¼ | 2 . | 4 |
| 3. | 3 . | 1½ | 2 . | 2½ | 2 . | 5 |
| 4. | 3 . | 4½ | 2 . | 4½ | 2 . | 3 |
| 5. | 3 . | 8 | 2 . | 8 | 2 . | 7 |
| 6. | 4 . | 0¾ | 2 . | 11½ | 3 . | 1 |

There were chimes here at an early date, as appears by a Bond dated

14 April 1602, formerly preserved in the parish chest, by which John Lea of Lutterworth, clockmaker, bound himself, in consideration of 6s. 8d. paid to him yearly in the south porch of the chapel of Harborough, to keep the chimes "in as good, sweet, solemn and perfect tune of musick as ever the same was at the sight and judgment of a skilful man in musick to be chosen by the townsmen of Harborough."— *Nichols.*

The ringing of the Curfew has been recently discontinued. At ringing the death-knell (6th bell) three tolls are given for a man, two for a woman; for a child under twelve the 1st bell is used in a similar manner; all both before and after the knell.

A "Call-bell" rings an hour before funerals for a short time. The funeral-bell is tolled in a similar manner to the death-knell.

## MARKFIELD.

S. MICHAEL.                                                       3 BELLS.

1. GOD [12] SAVE [12] HIS [12] CHVRCH 1747.
    ( Diam. 26 in. )
2. IH'Ƨ : NAZARENVS REX : IVDEORVM FILI : DEI
    MISERERE : MEI 1617 [ ▽ 1. ]
    ( Diam. 28 in. )
3. [ + 83 ] 𝔑omen 𝔇e celis 𝔄beo 𝔐icuelis 𝔐issi.
    And round the rim :—
    [ + 83 ] robarte · arke and annis þys tuefe made me.
    ( Diam. 32 in. )

In 6 Edward VI. there were "iij belles."
The Pancake-bell is rung on Shrove-Tuesday.

## MEDBOURNE.

S. GILES.                                                          5 BELLS.

1, 2, 3. JOSEPH EAYRE ST. NEOTS 1768.

4. ARNOLD LEICESTER AND ST. NEOTS JOHN MEADOWS
   1784. CHURCHWARDEN.
5. I TO THE CHURCH THE LIVING CALL AND TO THE
   GRAVE DO SUMMON ALL.

Previous to 1768 there were four bells only.

## MELTON MOWBRAY.

S. MARY.                                                      8 BELLS.

1. TWO BELLS WERE ADDED TO THE PEAL BY SUB-
   SCRIPTION ANNO DOMINI MDCCCII THOMAS FORD
   LL.D. VICAR VINCENT WING AND JOHN MOWBRAY
   C : WARDENS JOHN BRIANT OF HERTFORD
   FECIT. GLORIA DEO IN EXCELSIS.
2. STATUTUM EST OMNIBUS SEMEL MORI. OCTO CAM-
   PANAS SACRA EXAUDIMUS IN ARCE DULCES
   ALTISONAS O HILARES HILARES. JOHN BRIANT
   HERTFORD FECIT ANNO DOMINI MDCCCII.
3. BENEFACTORS TO THIS BELL: DUKE OF RUTLAND
   SIR T. PARKENS T. BENNETT ESQ. E. SMITH ESQ.
   MRS. D. L. FOUNTAINE MRS. GREENE, MR. J.
   REEVE MR. S. STOKES MR. J. BROWNE MR. T.
   CRAVEN MR. J. BREWIN A.D. 1728.
4. ḢVIVS SAṄĊTE MARIA
   In early Gothic capitals, 2 inches high, under which is [ ▽ 68. ]
5. [ + 53. ] bt n tn mn ri n [ □ 49 ] [ ▽ 6. ]
6. GLORIA PATRI FILIO ET SPIRITUI SANCTO 1730.
   CŒLORUM CHRISTE PLACEAT TIBI REX SONUS
   ISTE.
   ( Under which is an impression of Queen Ann's groat. )
7. ROBERT WARTNABY RICHARD WORRILL CHURCH-
   WARDENS WILLIAM DURRANCE WILLIAM HILL
   MATTHEW SIMPSON OVERSEERS 1766.
   ( There is an impression of George the Second's farthing. )

8. EYRE DE KETTERING FECIT, JAMES FOWKES AND
JAMES DURRANCE C. Ws. Ao. Dɪ. 1753. WILLIAM
HOWES AND JAMES FOWKES C. Ws. Ao. Dɪ. 1754.
SIT NOMEN DOMINI BENEDICTUM. LAUDATE
ILLUM CYMBALIS SONORIS. CUM SONO SI NON
VIS VENIRE NUNQUAM AD PRECES CUPIES IRE
( Weight 35 cwt. Note E flat. )
There is also a Priest's bell without inscription but dated 1688.

In 6 Edward VI. there were "v Great bells in the stepyll wᵗʰ yᵉ sance bell."

The Churchwardens' Accounts supply some interesting particulars. I extract the following entries :—

| | | | |
|---|---|---|---|
| 1546. | Itm̄ peyde for ij bawdryckes to ye bells .............. | | xxd. |
| | Itm̄ peyde for a wele to on of yᵉ bels .................. | vs. | jd. |
| | Itm̄ peyde for medyng of the lytyll bell .............. | | vd. |
| 1547. | Itm̄ pd to yᵉ smyth of Kyrkeby for peesyng the Grett beill clapper ........................................ | vs. | |
| | Itm̄ pd to ij Ryngers wᵗʰ rong to yᵉ S'mon when the bisshop of lincoln was here.......................... | | ijd. |
| 1549. | Paid for mending the cloke and chyme .............. | ijs. | ijd. |
| 1553. | October. Itm̄ payd to John Hynmane & to Robert Bagworth for rynginge of yᵉ great bell for *master latimore** sarmon ........................................... | | ijd. |
| | Itm̄ payd to the Ryngers at the dyryge for the Kyng†...................................................... | | |
| | ⁻Itm̄ paid the x daye of Aprell to Thomas Owefeld‡ for castyng of the sants bell ............................ | xs. | |
| | Itm̄ payd for iijˡˡ & dᵃ of bell mettell for the sanctus bell .................................................. | ijs. | |
| | Itm̄ payd for a clapper for yᵉ bell...................... | | viijd. |

---

* Hugh Latimer. † Service for the Dead. Edward VI.
‡ Probably one of the Nottingham founders.

Itm̄ payedd to goodman hobbs for hangyng of the
saunce bell .................................................... vj*d.*

1557-8.   Itm̄ pd for a galland of ale to yᵉ Reyngars when
yᵉ bycchype was here ........................................ iij*d.*

1558.   Pd ffor makynge yᵉ greyt bell claper .................. vj*s.* viij*d.*

Pd for caryinge yᵉ bell clap & yᵉ fetchynge............ vj*d.*

Pd to Pykeryng ffor mendyng yᵉ for bell ............ x*d.*

1562.   Pd for drinck at the lifting up of oʳ Ladye bell ...... iiij*d.*

Pd for a bawdrick ........................................ viij*d.*

The Townwardens' Accounts tell us more about "our Lady bell"
(the fifth of the present ring).

1562.   Itm̄ to Willm̄ tille for takinge downe the bell......... x*s.*

Itm̄ to John Hindman his wife for ale at the takinge
downe of the bell............:.................................... xxij*d.*

Itm̄ to John Poley for carrying a Letter to Lester... xij*d.*

Itm̄ in earnest to the bell fovnder...................... iiij*d.*

Itm̄ to Willm freers for worke for the bell ........... xvj*d.*

Itm̄ to Albyne Alee for carrying the Bell to Lester
& bringing it home ........................................... xij*s.*

Itm̄ for ij gallons of ale for them wᶜʰ blewe the
bellows at Lester at the casting of the bell............ viij*d.*

Itm̄ at the same tyme for fishe .......................... ij*s.*   v*d.*

Itm̄ for breyd & ale .......................................... iij*s.* viii*d.*

Itm̄ for our obligacon̄ making ........................... viij*d.*

Itm̄ to Mayster Newkom the halfe of his money dew
at the casting of the bell .......................... iiij*li.*   viij*d.*

Itm̄ more to hym for mettill .............................. xlij*s.*

Itm̄ to fravncis his s'vunt ................................. viij*d.*

Itm̄ our charge at the casting of the bell at Lester viij*s.*

Itm̄ for breade & ale at the hanging up of the bell... xvj*d.*

Itm̄ to tilley for hanging up the bell..................... x*s.*

Itm̄ to Mayster Newkom for the full payment of
the bell more than was gathered ....................... vij*s.*   x*d.*

Itm̄ for a quarte of wyne at Lester ..................... v*d*.
1584. ( "five catches for y*ᵉ* chyme." )
1592-4.   Payde for mendinge the clappers at Nottingham
for castinge of them & for caringe in An° 1594 ...... xv*s*. vj*d*.

I now return to the Churchwardens' Accounts:—

1601.  Rec. of the Bell founder for mettell wᶜʰ was overplus of the forthe Bell wᶜʰ was caste by him ......... xxiij*s*.
It. pd Willᵐ Smarte and his men for hanginge the
bells & mending them ...................................... vj*s*. viij*d*.

Nichols preserves the inscription on this bell which was:—" I will sound and resound unto thi people Lord With my sweet voyse to call them to thy word.   Thomas Owndle Thomas Clowdesley Wardens 1619."
The date was miscopied.

1610.  Another levie made the x of december for castinge the third bell and other nedefull charges about the churche wᶜʰ came to x*li*. ix*s*. viij*d*.

This bell, according to Nichols, had the inscription :—" Hec campana sacra fiat Trinitate Beatâ 1610."

1612.  The Churchwardens' charge for "Yokes for the Bells"— "pynes for the greate bell"—"cappes sheres the crowne stapell and the Kayes aboute the greate bell"—"mendinge the Anselltree of the greate bell"—"ij Bavdrickes for the greate bell."
1656.  The ancient great bell of the ancient ring of five appears, from the inscription preserved by Nichols, to have been recast in 1656, and to have then had this inscription placed upon it:—" Glory be to God on high.  Roger Waite and John Hodgkins Churchwardens 1656."

2 I

In 1728 the present third bell was added as a treble making the ring six in number, and in 1802 two more trebles were added, completing the present ring of eight bells. At the latter date a new set of chimes and a clock were erected. The chimes still play every third hour.

At a town meeting held 23rd September, 1708, it was agreed "that the four of clock bell shall cease, and not be rung any longer."

The Curfew (the 5th bell) is rung from Michaelmas to Lady-day at 8 p.m., after which the day of the month is tolled.

At the death-knell three tolls are given for a male, two for a female. At the close of a funeral in the churchyard the tenor bell tolls until the mourners reach their home. This ancient custom is not followed after funerals in the cemetery. The 6th bell is tolled fifteen minutes to call Parish Meetings. On Sunday the treble bell is rung for ten minutes at 7 a.m.; the 1st and 2nd bells are rung at 8 a.m. For service the bells are chimed three times, the sermon bell (tenor) is then rung for a few minutes after which the Priest's bell calls the parson.

Nichols says :—"the great bell is traditionally supposed to have been taken from the Lazar-house at Burton," and the sanctus bell to have been "brought hither from Eye-Kettleby Chapel."

I heard the following tradition in Melton some years ago :—When the Prince Regent visited Belvoir Castle early in the present century he stayed at Melton to see the horses belonging to the many sportsmen then in that metropolis of hunting. The ringers hearing of his approach rang out a full peal, and in due time made their application to the Prince for a gratuity. This, however, not being forthcoming, they began to hint, then to say, that he was something which sounded the very opposite of a gentleman, and the townspeople being generally of the same opinion, they saluted him upon his appearance in the streets with a strong volley of snowballs, no doubt very much to his astonishment. We have dictated to several of our monarchs and beheaded one, but this is the only instance probably in which a monarch, or his representative, has been dealt with in such a style as that in which the Bell ringers of Melton, according to this tradition, expressed their opinion to the Prince Regent.

# MISTERTON.

S. Leonard.                                                    4 Bells.

1. HENRY BAGLEY MADE MEE 1675.
2. [ + 22 ] BE · YT · KNOWNE · TO · ALL · THAT · DOTH ·
   ME · SEE · THAT ·˙NEWCOMBE · OF · LEICESTER ·
   MADE · MEE · 1607.
3. IH'Ƨ NAZARENVS : REX : IVDEORVM : FILI : DEI :
   MISERERE : MEI : 1620 [ ꭣ 1. ]
4. [ + 22 ] BE · YT · KNOWNE · TO · ALL · THAT . DOTH ·
   ME · SEE · THAT · NEWCOMBE · OF · LEICESTER ·
   MADE · MEE · 1607.

# MOUNTSORRELL (NORTH).

S. Peter.                                                      3 Bells.

1. GOD SAVE HIS CHURCH 1614 R SMALLEY R HOOD
   WARDENS.
2. IH'Ƨ : NAZARENVS [9] REX : IVDEORVM [9] FILI : DEI
   [9] MISERERE : MEI [9] 1627 [ ꭣ 1. ]
3. T. MEARS OF LONDON FECIT. JOHN SPICER THOMAS
   BRIERLEY CHURCHWARDENS 1813.

In 6 Edward VI. there were "in the chapel of Saynt John Baptyste"
—now called S. Peter—"seven litell bells in the steple ther."

# MOUNTSORRELL.

S. Nicolas (destroyed).

In 6 Edward VI. the Commissioners report that there were " in the
chappell of Saynt Nicholas a sacringe bell, a hand bell, a saunce bell
wythe other tow bygger belles in the stepell."

This chapel was " wholly decayed " before 1622.

## MOUNTSORRELL (SOUTH).

CHRIST'S CHURCH.                                                  1 BELL.

One small bell cast by Taylor of Loughborough.


## MOWSLEY.

S. NICOLAS.                                                       1 BELL.

A small bell cast by Taylor and Son, Loughborough, about the
year 1856.

The Parish Register gives the following information :—

"July 1, 1659. It is agreed upon by the inhabitants of Mowsley
that having but two bells in our chapel, and the lesser of them being
cracked and of no use, we whose names are underwritten do give
our consents that the bell shall be sold, and the money laid out
upon the repairs of the church, viz.: Imprimis to build it a steeple
to hang our other bell in," &c., &c.  Signed by William Burdett
and nineteen others.


## MUSTON.

S. JOHN BAPTIST.                                                  4 BELLS.

1.  IHS MARIA  [ ▽ 51. ]
2.  GOD SAVE THE CHVRCH AND REALME AND SEND
       VS PEACE IN CHRIST AMEN  [ □ 8. ]
3.  IHESVS BE OVRE SPEED  [ □ 8. ]
       [ □* ] [ □† ] [ □ 24 ]  □ □

(* A slipped Pomegranate (like fig. 79) ensigned by the Tudor
crown.  The Pomegranate was the badge of Queen Katharine of
Arragon and so became a Tudor Badge.  † A Tudor rose ensigned in
the same way.  The two last marks are apparently Tudor Badges, but
I am unable to give them.)

4.  all men that heare my mornful sound repent before you lye in grond 1605
       [ □ 8. ]

There is also a small sanctus bell, now unhung. It is without inscription or marks.

In 6 Edward VI. there were " iiij bells of one ryng w^th a lyttell bell."

The Pancake-bell is rung on Shrove-Tuesday.

Tradition says that the Rev. Charles Holmes, who was Rector in the troublous times preceding the Commonwealth, presuming to baptize a child according to the Office in the Book of Common Prayer, was sought for to be hanged by the Roundheads, but he gave them the slip. However they caught the Parish Clerk, and trussed him up in one of the bells.

## NAILSTONE.

ALL SAINTS.                                          3 BELLS.

1.  THE GIFT OF THE RIGHT HONble EARL HOWE 1843
    J. TAYLOR FECIT LOBRo.
2.  [ + 3. ] S. KATHERINA [ □ 49 ]
    [ ▽ 6. ]
3.  THOMAS HARMON FARMER ROB. ALDRIDG WARDENS
    1611.

The Pancake-bell is rung on Shrove-Tuesday.

## NARBOROUGH.

ALL SAINTS.                                          5 BELLS.

1.  I SWETELY TOLEING MEN DOE CALL TO TASTE ON
    MEAT THAT FEEDS THE SOVLE 1672.
    (Diam. 33 in.)
2.  FEARE GOD HONOR THE KING 1672.
    (Diam. 34 in.)
3.  IH'S : NAZARENVS [9] REX : IVDEORVM [9] FILI : DEI
    [9] MISERERE : MEI [9] 1623 [ ▽ 1. ]
    (Diam. 35½ in.)

4. ℬℐ □ □ ⊙ [ □ 49 ] ℰℂ [ ▽ 1 ] [ □ 28 ] [ + 17. ]
   □

(Diam. 37½ in.   Several of the marks on this bell are too much worn
to be deciphered.)

5. 𝔄𝔅𝔠𝔇𝔈𝔉 [9] 𝔊𝔥𝔦𝔨𝔩𝔪 [9] 𝔩𝔪𝔫𝔬𝔭𝔮 [9] 𝔯𝔰𝔱𝔲𝔵 [9] 1640 [9] [ ▽ 1. ]
(Diam. 41½ in.)

## NETHER BROUGHTON.

SS. Mary and Joseph.                                         3 Bells.

1. THOMAS HILL C. W. THOMAS HEDDERLY FOUNDER
   NOTTm. 1766.
   (Diam. 30 in.)
2. [ + 21 ] GOD SAVE THE CHVRCH 1613 [ □ 8. ]
   (Diam. 32½ in.)
3. [ + 34 ] 𝔍𝔥𝔢𝔰𝔳𝔰 𝔅𝔢 𝔒𝔳𝔯𝔢 𝔰𝔭𝔢𝔡𝔢
   (Diam. 35½ in.)

The 1st bell was previously inscribed: "God save the chvrch 1639."

[ Nether Seile—see Seile Nether. ]

## NEWBOLD VERDON.

S. James.                                                   2 Bells.

1. THE CHVRCHIS PRAIS WE SOVND ALL WAYS 1754.
2. GOD [ 14 ] SAVE [ 14 ] HIS [ 14 ] CHVRCH [ 14 ] 1663 [ □ 10. ]

## NEWTON HARCOURT.

S. Luke.                                                     1 Bell.

1. [ + 20 ] 𝔍𝔥𝔠 : 𝔫𝔞𝔷𝔞𝔯𝔢𝔫𝔳𝔰 : 𝔯𝔢𝔵 :
   𝔦𝔳𝔡𝔢𝔬𝔯𝔳𝔪
   (Diam. 27 in.)

# NEWTOWN LINFORD.

ALL SAINTS.               4 BELLS.

1. ⊕ (?)
   (Diam. 26 in.)
2. THE GIFT OF THE EARL OF STAMFORD A.D. 1842.
   CAST BY JOHN TAYLOR OF LOUGHBOROUGH.
   (Diam. 29 in.)
3. CELORVM CHRSTE PLATIAT IBE REX SONVS ISTE
   1614 [ ᵥ 1. ]
   (Diam. 30 in.)
4. RECAST BY JOHN TAYLOR BELLFOUNDER LOUGH-
   BOROUGH 1842.
   (Diam. 35 in.)

In 6 Edward VI. there were " three belles and a lytell bell."

# NORMANTON-LE-HEATH.

HOLY TRINITY.           -           2 BELLS.

1. GOD SAVE THE KING     L. FARMER R. KIRKBY
   WARDENS 1677.
2. LESTER AND PACK OF LONDON FECIT 1769.

The three bells of Ravenstone, Derbyshire, 1¼ mile distant, are traditional rivals of these two at Normanton.

The first have long been supposed to say :—

Who beats us? Who beats us?

Normanton—the notes being an interval of a third—to reply :—

We do! We do!

## NORTH KILWORTH.

S. CLEMENT.                                          5 BELLS.

1, 2.  RICHARD BANBURY JOSEPH HIPWELL CHURCH-
      WARDENS 1764. WM. HUNT SEXTON  OOOO

3.  IH'S : NAZARENVS : REX : IVDEORVM : FILI : DEI :
      MISERERE : MEI 1641 [ ▽ 1. ]

4.  T. WHITEMAN C. WARDEN 1853  TAYLOR BELL-
      FOUNDER LOUGHBOROUGH.

5.  𝔄 𝔅 ℭ 𝔇 𝔈  𝔉 𝔊 ℌ 𝔍 𝔎  𝔏 𝔐 𝔑 𝔒  [ ▽ 1. ]

On 1st and 2nd bells are impressions of coins of John V. of Portugal
and of an early shilling of George III.

A daily-bell rings at one o'clock, called the dinner-bell.

The death-knell is rung as at South Kilworth.

## NORTON  BY  TWYCROSS.

HOLY TRINITY.                                       3 BELLS.

1.  IESU NAZARENE REX IUDEŌM FILI DEI MISERERE
      MEI 1640.
                ( Diam. 31 in. )

2.  GOD  SAVE  THE  CHURCH  1663.
                ( Diam. 34 in. )

3.  GLORY  TO  GOD  ON  HIGH  1663.
                ( Diam. 37 in. )

[ NORTON EAST—see East Norton ]

[ NORTON KING'S—see King's Norton. ]

## NOSELY.

S. MARY.                                                         1 BELL.

1. 𝕿homas Ᏼ𝔢𝔷𝔢𝔩𝔯𝔦𝔤 Squier made me 1596 [ ▽ 1. ]

There were formerly four bells here. The existing one is on the ground. The manor of Nosely has been in the possession of the Hazlerigg family since early in the fifteenth century. "Thomas Hazlerig" the donor of the above bell, married Ursula, daughter of Sir Thomas Andrewes, of Winwicke Co. Northampton, and died in 1605.—(*Visitation of the Co. of Leic.* 1619, *p.* 15, issued by Harleian Society).

## OADBY.

S. PETER.                                                       4 BELLS.

1. OMNIS CARNALIS VIS FORTIS CONGRUIT HERBIS :
   ·∶· · ← THOs. EAYRE FECIT ← 1754 : ·∶·
          ( Diam. 27¼ in. )

2. RICH. CLARKE IOHN HARDEY WARDENS [ 13 ] [ ▢ 10 ]
   1656.
          ( Diam. 29½ in. )

3. 𝕻𝕽𝕬𝕴𝕾𝕰 𝕿𝕳𝕰 𝕷𝕺𝕽𝕯𝕰 1600.
          ( Diam. 31¼ in. )

4. [ + 34 ] 𝕵𝕰𝕾𝖁𝕾 𝕭𝕰 𝕺𝖁𝕽 𝕾𝕻𝕰𝕯𝕰.
   (and on the rim)
     𝕴. 𝖂. 𝕳. 𝕯. ( in two ornate Gothic letters
   [ ▢ ▢ 37 & 38 ] the C being placed upside down to form a D )
   𝖂. 𝕾. 𝕿 𝕽 O O O ( *coins.* )
          ( Diam. 34 in. )

The Pancake-bell (the 4th) is rung on Shrove-Tuesday at 11 a.m. A correspondent in a local newspaper writes :—" The oldest family supposed to live in this village are the Ludlams ; and up to 1844 they claimed the distinction of having the deceased members of the family 'chimed to church,' and asserted that it had been the custom to do so

2 K

from time immemorial. I remember it being observed on three separate occasions; the last being in the case of a very old inhabitant, named Richard Ludlam, who had served his country during twenty-one years in the Peninsular war. He died in the said year 1844, and the then vicar (the Rev. F. R. Phillips) declared that such a distinguished privilege should no longer be allowed whilst he remained vicar. Tradition states that the next oldest family in the village, that of Norman, was also so distinguished, but I cannot remember any of them being so honoured."

## THE OAKS.

S. . . . . .                                                            1 BELL.

1. ARCHDEACON PARKINSON 1845.
(Diam. 27 in.)


[ OLD DALBY—see Dalby-on-the-Wolds. ]


## ORTON-ON-THE-HILL.

S. EDITH.                                                        4 BELLS.

1. GAVDETE [12] IN DOMINO [12] ET EXVLTATE [12] IVSTI [12] 1701.
(Diam. 28¼ in.)
2. MORABOR [12] IN DOMO DOMINI IN LONGITVDINEM DIERVM 1701.
(Diam. 29¾ in.)
3. PRAYSE GOD 1595.
(Diam. 32¼ in.)
4. JESVS NAZARENVS REX IVDEORVM FILI DEI MISE-RERE MEI [12] J. POYNTON T. MORHALL CHURCHWARDENS 1701.
(Diam. 36¾ in.)

# OSGATHORPE.

S. MARY.                                                              2 BELLS.

In 6 Edward VI. there were " tow belles."

The present bells are in an almost inaccessible bell turret, and are reported by the Rector to be without interest.

[ OVER-SEILE—see Seile Over. ]

# OWSTON.

S. ANDREW.                                                          3 BELLS.

1. EVERET BRITTON VICKER JOHN RIPPIN C. W. 1754.
   *THOS. HEDDERLY* FOUNDER.
   ( Diam. 30 in. )
2. 9961 · EM · TSAC · SIRRON · EYBOT · SEKWAF · NHOI.
   ( Diam. 31 in.   Reads backwards. )
3. JOHN TAYLOR & CO. LOUGHBOROUGH 1860.
   ( Diam. 34 in.   Weight 7 cwt. )

In 1860 the ancient treble—said to have been inscribed "Johannes Shevt fecit me "—was taken away, and the present tenor added, thus making the ring heavier.

It is the custom to ring a peal after service when Banns of Marriage are first published.

When new ropes are substituted for old ones, the custom is for the two churchwardens to take each one of the latter, and the parish clerk the third.

Tradition says that one or more of the bells here came originally from the neighbouring parish of Knossington.

The Revd. Everard Breton was instituted 1724, died 1755.   He was also rector of Withcote.

## PACKINGTON.

THE HOLY ROOD.                                             4 BELLS.

1.  𝕬𝕷𝕷 𝕾𝕷𝕺𝕽𝖄 𝕭𝕰𝕰 𝕿𝕺 𝕲𝕺𝕯 𝕽.𝕯.
    𝕽.𝕭. CHVRCHWARDENS 1695 [ 12. ]
    (Diam. 28 in.)

2.  𝕷𝕰𝕿 [ 12 ] 𝕿𝕳𝕰 [ 12 ] 𝕲𝕺𝕾𝕻𝕰𝕷𝕷 [ 12 ]
    𝕱𝕷𝕺𝕽𝕴𝕾𝕳 [ 12 ] 1695 [ 12 ]
    (Diam. 29 in.)

3.  GOD [ 12 ] SAVE [ 12 ] HIS [ 12 ] CHVRCH [ 12 ] 1695 [ 12 ]
    (Diam. 31 in.  Cracked.)

4.  ROBERT    HASTINGS    VICAR.    THOMAS    POTTER
    & RICHARD HARRISON CHURCHWARDENS E.
    ARNOLD LESTER FECIT 1793.
    (Diam. 34 in.)

In 6 Edward VI. there were "three belles."
The ancient tenor was cracked by lightning in 1790.


## PEATLING MAGNA.

ALL SAINTS.                                                4 BELLS.

1.  IH'S : NAZARENVS [9] REX : IVDEORVM [9] FILI :
    DEI [9] MISERERE : MEI [9] 1619 [ ▽ 1. ]
    (Diam. 33 in.)

2.  CELORUM CHRSTE PLATIAT TIBI REX SONUS ISTE
    1617 [ ▽ 1. ]
    (Diam. 35 in.  Broken and unhung.)

3.  𝖁ox [ □ 28 ] d̄n̄i [ □ 28 ] iħu [ □ 28 ] x̄p̄i [ □ 28 ] ꞗox [ □ 28 ]
    exultacionis [ □ 49. ]
    (Diam. 40 in.  For initial letter see fig. 81.)

4.  [ + 44 ]    𝕬𝕭𝕮𝕯𝕰𝕱𝕲𝕳𝕴𝕶𝕷𝕸𝕹𝕺
    ꞗ𝕴𝕷𝕷𝕴𝕬𝕸 [ + 44 ] 𝕲𝕰𝕬𝕽ꞗ𝕴𝕾
    (Diam. 43 in.)

# PEATLING PARVA.

S. ANDREW.                                                    3 BELLS.

1. [ + 70 ]    [ + 53 ]    [ + 70 ]    [ + 53 ]
   [ ▽ 6. ]
                  ( Diam. 28 in. )
2. [ + 64 ]  𝔊𝔄𝔅𝔯𝔦𝔢𝔩  [ ▽ 6. ]
                  ( Diam. 32 in. )
3.  𝔊𝔜𝔐  𝔊𝔜𝔐  𝔄𝔫𝔡  𝔓𝔯𝔢𝔞  1599  [ ▽ 1. ]
                  ( Diam. 34 in. )


# PECKLETON.

S. MARY.                                                    6 BELLS.

1. SOLI DEO O M GLORIA IN ÆTERNUM MDCCXIIII.
                  ( Diam. 27 in. )
2. RESONABO LAUDES GENTIS BOOTHBEIANÆ
                  ( Diam. 28 in. )
3. OMNE TULIT PUNCTUM QUI MISCUIT UTILE DULCI
                  ( Diam. 30 in. )
4. JOHN HARRYMAN RECT. JOHN CUTLER GEN : C :
   WARDEN J. M. HALTON. DAN : HEDDERLY CAST
   US ALL ANNO MDCCXIIII.
                  ( Diam. 31 in. )
5. MORTEM REGINE DEFLEAT ANG : COLATUR PAX
   FLOREAT ECCLESIA
                  ( Diam. 35 in. )
6. THOMAS BOOTHBY OF TOOLY ESQUIRE GAVE THESE
   SIX BELLS MDCCXIIII.
                  ( Diam. 41 in.   Weight 9 cwt. )

The Parish Register gives the following information :

"John Harryman Rect.
Mr. John Cutler churchwarden
in the year MDCCXIV.

In the beginning of this Register that Posterity should know how much it is indebted to the present age, let it be recorded that Thomas Boothby of Tooley Park Esq. . . . . . and whereas before this there was but three small bells about thirteen hundred weight belonging to the church, he caused six (above fourty hundred weight) to be made new and hung up at his own sole and proper expense."

Mr. Boothby appears to have purchased the two ancient bells from the chapel formerly standing at Stanton under Bardon, and to have used the metal in making the new ring here.

The Pancake-bell is rung on Shrove-Tuesday.

## PICKWELL.

ALL SAINTS.                                                3 BELLS.

1. &#x1D518; &#x1D51C; &#x1D516; &#x1D51C; &#x1D516; &#x1D513; &#x1D508; &#x1D517; &#x1D518; &#x1D516;

2. WILLAME CAVE [ □ 62 ] MADE THIS BELL [ □ 62 ]

3. Huius Sancti Johannis Baptiste.

The inscription on the 1st bell is in large Gothic capitals like Melton 4th bell. That on the 2nd in letters like Aylestone 2nd. William Cave was the donor, not the founder. John Cave, Esq., was patron of the Living in 1622.

## PLUNGAR.

S. HELEN.                                                2 BELLS.

1. THO. [ 12 ] HEDDERLY [ 12 ] FOVNDER [ 12 ] 1747.
2. WILLIAM [ 12 ] CAVNT [ 12 ] CHVRCHWARDEN [ 12 ] 1747.

In 6 Edward VI. there were "ij bells and j lyttell bell." The small bell hung in the west window of the tower.

Tradition says it was removed in 1829 (being then without a clapper and uninscribed) to the neighbouring village of Barkestone.

# POTTER'S MARSTON.

S. MARY.

There was formerly a bell here marked:

P

I . M   It was broken at the beginning of this century and disappeared long ago.

# PRESTWOLD.

S. ANDREW. 5 BELLS.

1. THE GIFT OF CHARLES JAMES PACKE ESQ. JUNIOR JOHN BRIANT HERTFORD FECIT 1812.
2. JOHN BRIANT HERTFORD FECIT. THE GIFT OF C. J. PACKE ESQ. JUNIOR 1812.
3. JOHN BRIANT HERTFORD FECIT 1810.
4. The same dated 1809.
5. JOHN BRIANT HERTFORD FECIT 1809. THE REVD. C. J. PACK RECTOR. E. GAMBLE AND T. SOMES C.W.

Previous to 1809 there were three bells only.

# QUENIBOROUGH.

S. MARY. 4 BELLS.

1. GOD SAVE HIS CHVRCH J SEARSON J BLACKE WARDENS 1697.
2. [ + 71 ] ⬛⬛ ⬛⬛ ⬛⬛⬛ (?)
3. REVD. SENECA WILLIAM WINTER VICAR. ANTHONY HEMSLEY JOHN WALTON STEVENSON CHURCH-WARDENS TAYLOR FOUNDER LOUGHBORO' 1858.

4. IH'ℨ : NAZARENVS [9] REX : IVDEORVM [9] FILI :
   DEI [9] MISERERE : MEI [9] 1619 [ ▽ 1. ]

# QUORNDON.

S. Bartholomew.                                    6 Bells.

1. MR. SAMUEL SCULTHORPE MR. COCK. QUODA
   PLURIBUS COLLATUM HIC ME PONIT 1777.
   (and round the rim)
   EDWARD ARNOLD St. NEOTS HUNTINGDONSHIRE
   CAST US ALL SIX.
   (Diam. 29 in.)

2. EDWd. ARNOLD St. NEOTS FECIT 1773. PATRI UNICO
   DEO SACRUM.
   (Diam. 30 in.)

3. EDWd. ARNOLD St. NEOTS FECIT 1773. FILIO DEI
   UNIGENITO SACRUM.
   (Diam. 31¼ in.)

4. EDWd. ARNOLD St. NEOTS HUNTINGDONSHIRE
   FECIT 1773. SPIRITUI SANCTO SACRUM.
   (Diam. 33 in.)

5. EDWd. FARNHAM ESQ. AND JAMES SCULTHORPE
   CHURCHWARDENS 1773. TEMPUS TRANIT DEUS
   VOCAT.
   (Diam. 36 in.)

6. EDWd. FARNHAM ESQ. AND JAMES SCULTHORPE
   CHURCHWARDENS 1773. EDWd. ARNOLD FECIT
        R
   MOS ADEST PARA.
   (Diam. 39 in.)

In 6 Edward VI. there were "three great belles and a litell bell."

The letter R in "mors" on the tenor bell is chiseled to correct the
founder's blunder.

## RAGDALE.

ALL SAINTS. 2 BELLS.

1. [ + 51 *a*. ] 𝔄𝔙𝔈 𝔐𝔄𝔕𝔦𝔄 𝔊𝔕𝔄𝔠𝔦𝔄 𝔓𝔩𝔢𝔫𝔄 𝔇𝔫𝔰 𝔗𝔢𝔠𝔲𝔪
2. No inscription and cracked.

## RATBY.

S. GEORGE. 4 BELLS.

1. [ + 22 ] BE · YT · KNOWNE · TO · ALL · THAT . DOTH · ME · SEE · THAT · NEWCOMBE · OF · LEICESTER · MADE · MEE . 1607.
   (Diam. 30 in.)
2. The same.
   (Diam. 31 in.)
3. IH'S : NAZARENVS [9] REX : IVDEORVM [9] FILI : DEI [9] MISERERE : MEI [9] 1636 [ ʊ 1. ]
   (Diam. 35 in.)
4. [ + 45] 𝔍𝔥𝔢𝔰𝔳𝔰 : 𝔫𝔞𝔷𝔞𝔕𝔢𝔫𝔲𝔰 : 𝔕𝔢𝔵 : 𝔦𝔳𝔡𝔢𝔬𝔕𝔲𝔪.
   (Diam. 39 in.)

## RATCLIFFE CULEY.

ALL SAINTS. 2 BELLS.

1. GOD [ 12 ] SAVE [ 12 ] HIS [ 12 ] CHVRCH [ 12 ] J C 1684.
2. RICHd FARRIN CHURCHWARDEN EDWd ARNOLD OF St NEOTS FECIT 1778.

There were formerly three bells: the second of that ring is missing.

## RATCLIFFE-ON-THE-WREAKE.

S. BOTOLPH. 4 BELLS.

1. THOMAS MEARS OF LONDON FECIT 1811.

2 L

2.  THOMAS MEARS OF LONDON FECIT 1814.
3.  THE THREE BELLS RECAST AND ONE ADDED AT
    THE EXPENSE OF THE Rt. HONble. EARL
    FERRERS ANNO DOMINI 1811. THOMAS MEARS
    OF LONDON FECIT.
4.  THOMAS MEARS OF LONDON FECIT 1814.

## REARSBY.

S. Michael.                                              3 Bells.

1.  𝔄 𝔅 ℭ    𝔇 𝔈 𝔉    𝔊 𝔥    1607.
              ( Diam. 29¼ in. )
2.  GOD [ 13 ] SAVE [ 13 ] HIS [ 13 ] CHVRCH [ 13 ] [ ☐ 10 ] 1652.
              ( Diam. 31¼ in. )
3.  𝔈lemens 𝔄tque 𝔓iu 𝔐iseris 𝔖uccurre 𝔐aria.
              ( Diam. 36 in. )

The Pancake-bell (2nd) was rung until recently on Shrove-Tuesday.

## REDMILE.

S. Peter.                                               3 Bells.

1.  GOD SAVE HIS CHVRCH 1613.
2.  O LORD SAVE THY PEOPLE MDCCCXLI.
3.  ROBERT HAND CHURCHWARDEN THO. HEDDERLY
    FOUNDER 1770.

In 6 Edward VI. there were " ij bells j sanctus bell."  The 2nd was
previously inscribed " God save his church 1703;" the 3rd " Jhesus
be oure spede."

## ROLLESTON.

S. John.                                                1 Bell.

1.  THOMAƧ    NORRIƧ   ˙CAƧT    ME    1629.

# ROTHERBY.

ALL SAINTS.                                    3 BELLS.

1. 𝕮𝖚𝖒 𝕮𝖚𝖒 𝕬𝖓𝖉 𝕻𝖗𝖆𝖞 1597 [▽ 1.]
2. [+ 39] 𝕬𝖛𝖊 : 𝕸𝖆𝖗𝖎𝖆 : 𝕲𝖗𝖆𝖈𝖎𝖆 : 𝕻𝖑𝖊𝖓𝖆 : 𝕯𝖔𝖒𝖎𝖓𝖚𝖘 : 𝕿𝖊𝖈𝖚𝖒 :
3. 𝕬𝕭𝕮 𝕯𝕰 𝕱𝕲 1611 [▽ 1.]

# ROTHLEY.

S. MARY.                                       5 BELLS.

1. E. ARNOLD LEICESTER FECIT 1784. LONG LIFE AND
   PROSPERITY TO OUR WORTHY SUBSCRIBERS.
2. THE FOUNDER WILL REJOICE TO HEAR
   THAT ALL OUR VOICES PLEASE THE EAR.
3. I TO THE POOR AND NEEDY AM A FRIEND
   FOR WHOSE RELIEF I CALL YOU TO ATTEND.
4. FOUR BELLS CAST INTO FIVE BEING THE FIRST
   BELLS CAST AT LEICESTER BY E. ARNOLD 1784.
5. JOSEPH NEWOLD AND DANIELL PAGETT CHURCH-
   WARDENS E. ARNOLD FECIT 1784. HENRY
   WOODCOCK VICAR.
   I TO THE CHURCH THE LIVING CALL
   AND TO THE GRAVE DO SUMMON ALL.
             ( Weight 12 cwt. )

In 6 Edward VI. there were "foore belles and a saunce bell."

The Rev. Richd. Burton kindly furnishes the following extract from the Parish-book, under date 28th September, 1784:

"Mr. Arnold's bill for recasting the Bells £95 . 7 . 9."

This outlay was met partly by a rate and partly by a subscription of £55 . 2 . 6.

The curfew has been recently discontinued, and a school bell rung at 9 a.m. instead.

The Pancake-bell is rung on Shrove-Tuesday at noon.

## SADDINGTON.

S. HELEN.                                          5 BELLS.

1. EDWD. ARNOLD St. NEOTS HUNTINGDONSHIRE FECIT 1777.
2. INTACTUM SILEO PERCUTE DULCE CANO. THOs. EAYRE KETTERING 1761.
3. VOX MEA EST DULCIS MEA SCINTILLANS VULTUS. THOs. EAYRE DE KETTERING FECIT 1760.
4. ROBERT JOHNSON & JOHN (*blank*) C. W. 1762.
5. WE ARE ORDAIN'D FOR THE PRAISE OF THE LORD. EAYRE KETTERING FECIT 1762.

(Note A flat.)


## SALTBY.

S. PETER.                                          3 BELLS.

1. THOMAS NORRIS MADE ME 1636.
2. [ + 52 ] ... pro suis (?) sonus hic honor fi't caterine.
3. HVIVS SCI PETRI [ □ 61. ] [ ▽ 63. ]

In 6 Edward VI. there were "iij bells of a corde."

The inscription on the 2nd bell is too much worn to give a perfect rubbing: a learned archæologist renders it:—"This sound becomes an honour to Catherine (and) to the gift for her (services.)" The gift being the bell itself.

The 3rd bell is traditionally believed to have been found in a pond in Croxton Park, and to have formerly belonged to Croxton Abbey.

At the commencement of the present century there was a fourth bell, a treble, inscribed "T. Willbourne Toby Norris cast me 1681." It was then broken and useless, and has, since that time, disappeared. The bells have not been rung, only chimed, for many years, and are considered to be in a very unsafe condition.

A Gleaning-bell sounds during harvest at 8 a.m. and 6 p.m.

# SAPCOTE.

ALL SAINTS.                                                      4 BELLS.

1. [ + 3 ] 𝕮𝕺𝕸 𝕮𝕺𝕸 𝕬𝕹𝕯 𝕻𝕽𝕬𝕴𝕿 1611 (13.)
   ( Diam. 30¼ in. )
2. J OVER B.H † B PERKINS C W † J BRIANT HERTFORD
   FECIT 1809 †
   ( Diam. 32¾ in. )
3. J. F. TURNER ESQ. PATRON J. E. HARRINGTON RECTOR W. SPENCER
   A. NURSE CHURCH WARDENS 1812. T. MEARS OF LONDON FECIT.
   ( Diam. 37 in. )
4. [ + 22 ] THOMAS [ + 22 ] NEWCOMBE OF LEICESTER
   MADE MEE 1611 [ 13. ]
   ( Diam. 39 in. )

There were formerly only three bells here. The following note is on the cover of the Parish Register :—

" The greate Bell of Sapcot was broke on ye feaste day of St. Michaell 1611, and cast into two Bells on the ninth day of November ye same and hunge upon the " [ *no date is here given.* ]

At the end of the same Register:—

" The bells of Sapcoate were newly hunge in a newe frame the xi^{th}. day of Auguste in the yeare of our Lord 1621 by Edward Jones a Northamptonshire man; Richard Messenger and John Kinde beinge churchwardens at the same time; John Worshipe beinge parson who dyed the xi^{th} day of January next after.

(Signed)    Thos. Adams."*

The 2nd bell was previously inscribed :

" Thomas Newcombe of Leicester made mee 1611."

---

* For these extracts I am indebted to the Rev. J. F. Norman.

The 3rd :—

"Ave Maria grā plena Dn̄s tecvm."

The Pancake-bell is rung on Shrove-Tuesday.
A Sunday morning bell is rung at 8 a.m.

## SAXBY.

S. Peter. 3 Bells.

1. ROBT. TAYLOR ST. NEOTS FECIT 1801.
2. ROBT. MIDDLETON D.D. RECTOR ROBT. KIRKBY CHURCHWARDEN.
3. THE GIFT OF ROBERT LATE EARL OF HARBOROUGH 1801.

(Weight 7 cwt.)

In 6 Edward VI. there were "iij bells and a sanctus bell."
Previously to 1801 when the bells were recast they were inscribed:

1. God save the Queene 1601.
2. Blank.
3. + S. Katerina.

The present very small bells are hung in an iron cage.

## SAXELBY.

S. Peter. 3 Bells.

1. JOHN TAYLOR & SON FOUNDERS LOUGHBOROUGH LATE OF OXFORD ANNO DOMINI 1847.

(Diam. 29 in.)

2. [+ 3] S PAULEE [ ꓴ 6.]

(Diam. 33 in.)

3. Hec Campana Sacra Fiat Trinitate Beata
T S F H WARDENS 1695.

(Diam. 35 in. From the Nottingham Foundry.)

At Funerals on the arrival of the procession at the church gates the bells are chimed until all are within the church.

## ,SCALFORD.

S. Egelwin the Martyr. 3 Bells.

1. CELORVM CHRSTE PLATIAT TIBE REX SONVS ISTE 1616 [ ▽ 1. ]
2. [ + 34 ] GOD SAVE OVR CHVRCH 1615 [ ▢ 8. ]
3. god sabe the queene 1595.

In 6 Edward VI. there were "iij bells wth a sanctes bell."

## SCRAPTOFT.

All Saints. 3 Bells.

1. [ + 3 ] GEVE [ + 3 ] THANKES [ + 3 ] TO [ + 3 ] GOD [ ▢ 49. ]
2. ABCD EFGHI KLMNOP [ ▽ 1. ]
3. GOD [ 13 ] SAVE [ 13 ] HIS [ 13 ] CHURCH [ 13 ] 1654 [ 13 ] [ ▢ 10. ]

## SEAGRAVE.

All Saints. 3 Bells.

1. [ + 34 ] GOD SAVE THE CHVRCH 1595 [ ▢ 8. ]
2. sca marcus [ ▢ 19 ] [ ▽ 63. ]
3. GOD [ 12 ] SAVE [ 12 ] THE [ 12 ] CHURCH [ 12 ] 1710.

## SEILE (NETHER).

S. Peter. 5 Bells.

1. T. GRESLEY R. MOER R. INGE REC.
2. JOHN SPEAK AND ISAAC HARE W.

3. REPENT IN TIME AND SIN NO MORE
4. DANIEL HEDDERLY . . . . . . THIS RING 1707.
5. SOLI DEO IMMORTALE SIT GLORIA R.N. R.A. I.K.OOOO

In 6 Edward VI. there were "three belles wyth a saunce bell."
The Pancake-bell is rung on Shrove-Tuesday.

## SEILE (OVER).

S. Matthew.                                                    1 Bell.

1. THOMAS MEARS FOUNDER LONDON 1841.

The Pancake-bell is rung on Shrove-Tuesday.
The bell is rung on Sunday morning at 8 o'clock.

## SEWSTERN.

Holy Trinity.                                                  1 Bell.

1. TAYLOR LOBRO' FECIT 1842.

## SHACKERSTON.

S. Peter.                                                     3 Bells.

1. IH'S : NAZARENVS [9] REX : IVDEORVM [9] FILI :
   DEI [9] MISERERE: MEI . . . [▽ 1.]
          (Diam. 31 in.)
2. GOD [14] SAVE [14] HIS [14] CHVRCH 1604 [□ 7.]
          (Diam. 32 in.)
3. + 1664 ALL GLORY BE TO GOD ON HIGH. JOHN
   TAYLOR & SON BELLFOUNDERS LOUGHBOROUGH
   A.D. 1868.
          (Diam. 36 in.)

There is a tradition that "Mr. Hodges" being Vicar when Cromwell
became Protector was ejected from the living, and that being reinstated
at the Restoration, he then "put up" the tenor bell, since recast.

There is probably truth in this tradition. According to the list of Vicars given by Nichols, John Hodges, M.A., of Exeter College, Oxford, was inducted 10 July 1630. In the Minute Book of the Committee of Sequestration, preserved in the Bodleian Library, John Hodges is called "delinquent."* The living was held by Thomas Salter, *minister*, 1649, and Samuel Oldershaw, *minister*, 1652, after which no name is given until Albion Shrigley 1680, so that probably Samuel Oldershaw turned out, and the Rev. John Hodges came to his own again, at the Restoration, held the living for several years, and recast the tenor bell in 1664, placing upon it the inscription given above, which (with the date) was preserved when the bell was again recast in 1868.

## SHANGTON.

S. Nicolas                                                      2 Bells.

1, 2. (Blanks.) .

## SHARNFORD.

S. Helen.                                                       3 Bells.

1. WILLIAM BROWN BENGAMAN ROLLSTONE CHURCH-WARDENS 1771.  THOMAS HEDDERLY FOUNDER NOTTINGHAM.
   ( Diam. 32¼ in. )
2. [ + 22 ] BE · YT · KNOWNE · TO · ALL · THAT · DOTH · ME · SEE · THAT · NEWCOMBE · OF · LEICESTER · MADE · MEE 1602.
   ( Diam. 36 in. )
3. 1827 JAMES HARRISON CHURCHWARDEN 1827.
   ( Diam. 40¼ in. )

The 3rd was previously inscribed :—" Omnia fiant ad gloriam Dei. Joseph Eayre St. Neots fecit 1764."

The Pancake-bell is rung on Shrove-Tuesday.

---

* Ex. Infor. W. G. Dimock Fletcher, Esq.

2 M

# SHAWELL.

ALL SAINTS.                                                    5 BELLS.

1. BRYANVS ELDRIDGE ME FECIT 1656.
   (Diam. 26¼ in.)
2. GOD [9] SAVE [9] THE [9] kING [9] 1632 [▽ 1.]
   ·(Diam. 28 in.)
3. [+ 3.]   S I A D O B H   [▽ 6.]
   (Diam. 31 in.)
4. Sancta Katerina Ora Pro Nobis [ □ 31 ] [ ▽ 30 ] [ + 17.]
   (Diam. 33 in.)
5. JOHN WHITMILL Wᴍ. FLVILL CHURCHWARDENS
   JOSEPH EAYRE Sᴛ. NEOTS FECIT 1770 † †
   (Diam. 37¼ in.)

# SHEARSBY.

S. MARY MAGDALEN.                                             4 BELLS.

1. IH'8 : NAZARENVS [9] REX : IVDEORVM [9] FILI :
   DEI [9] MISERERE : MEI [9] 1625 [▽ 1.]
   (Diam. 27 in.)
2. ABDC EFGHI KLMNO PQRST
   (Diam. 27 in.)
3. JOHN BRIANT HERTFORD FECIT 1796.
   (Diam. 30¼ in.)
4. IH'8 : NAZARENVS [9] REX : IVDEORVM [9] FILI :
   DEI [9] MISERERE : MEI : 1620 [▽ 1.]
   (Diam. 34¼ in.)

The 3rd bell was previously inscribed :—" Maria."

Tradition says that the first bell formerly hung in the tower of the
ruined church of Knaptoft. It being supposed to be the property of the
Duke of Rutland, the sons of his grace's tenants at Aylestone fetched it
from Knaptoft, intending to place it in the steeple of their own village ;

but stopping with their cart to drink at Shearsby, the inhabitants of that hamlet (as belonging to Knaptoft) claimed the bell, took possession of it, and sent the youths of Aylestone home without their booty.

## SHEEPSHED.

S. BOTOLPH. 6 BELLS.

1, 2, 3, 4, 5. JOHN BRIANT AND SON HERTFORD FECIT AN. DOM. 1805.
(Diams. 31 in., 32 in., 34¼ in., 36 in. and 39 in.)
6. JOHN BRIANT AND SON HERTFORD FECIT AN. DOM. 1805. T. LUDLOW AND R. THOMPSON CHURCH-WARDENS. REVᴅ. CHARLES ALLSOPP VICAR.
(Diam. 43 in.)

In 6 Edward VI. there were "three bells." Subsequently and previous to 1805 there were five bells.

The curfew (5th bell) is rung at 8 p.m. during the winter months, after which the day of the month is tolled on the 1st bell.

The Pancake-bell (4th) is rung on Shrove-Tuesday for an hour commencing at 11 a.m.

The 3rd bell is the ringer's call: the 4th is rung to call church meetings.

"First" and "second peals" are rung on Sunday morning: the treble bell at 7 a.m.; the treble and second at 8 a.m.

## SHENTON.

· · · · · · (?) 3 BELLS.

1. IH'Ƨ : NAZARENVS [9] REX : IVDEORVM [9] FILI : DEI [9] MISERERE : MEI [9] 1628 [∪ 1.]
(Diam. 26¼ in.)
2. [+ 45] ᔕᏟᎬ : ᏞᎬᎤᏁᎯᎡᎠᎬ : ᎤᎡᎯ : ᏢᎡᎤ ᏁᎤᏃᎥᔕ.
(Diam. 30¼ in.)

3.  THOs. HARDING ✛ EDWd. ARNOLD FECIT 1788.
(Diam. 35 in.)

## SHEPEY MAGNA.

ALL SAINTS.                                                  5 BELLS.

1 & 2.  FRANCIS    GADDESBY    AND    THOMAS    SMITH
CHURCHWARDENS PACK AND CHAPMAN LON-
DON FOUNDERS A.D. 1778.

3.  [ ✛ 3.]  𝔄 𝔅 𝔇 𝔇 𝔈 𝔉 𝔊 𝔥 𝔦 𝔨 𝔩 𝔪 .

4.  ℑ sweetly toling men do call to taste on meats that feeds the soole 1607 [ ☐ 8. ]

5.  [ ✛ 21] GOD ·⁝· SAVE ·⁝· THE ·⁝· CHVRCH ·⁝· OVR
·⁝· QVEENE ·⁝· AND ·⁝· REALME ·⁝· AND
·⁝· SEND ·⁝· VS ·⁝· PEACE ·⁝· IN ·⁝·
CHRIST ·⁝· AMEN ·⁝· 1601 [ ☐ 8. ]

The Curfew is rung at 8 o'clock during the winter months, excepting
during the interval between the death and burial of any parishioner,
when it is discontinued.

In a map of the lands inclosed in 1659 there are two parcels of land
(Nos. 91 & 92) marked "Bell-rope Piece," and across both is written as
the owner "Great Sheepy Parish Clerk." These lands were left to the
Parish Clerk for providing Bell-ropes and for ringing the 8 o'clock bell
at night.—(See *Charity Commissioners' Report* 1837, p. 209.)

## SIBSTONE.

S. BOTOLPH.                                                  4 BELLS.

1.  [ ✛ 22 ] BE · YT · KNOWNE · TO · ALL · THAT · DOTH
· ME · SEE · THAT · NEWCOMBE · OF · LEICESTER
· MADE · MEE 1605.
(Diam. 34 in.)

2.  OMNIA FIANT AD GLORIAM DEI.   T. EAYRE KETT.
FECIT JOHN FARMER CHURCHWARDEN 1751 ○ ○
(Diam. 36 in.)

3. OMNIA FIANT AD GLORIAM DEI : · GLORIA PATRI
   FILIO ET SPIRITUI SANCTO : · ANNO DOM.
   1733 : ·
   ( Diam. 39 in. )
4. ALL YOU THAT HEAR MY MOURNFULL SOUND :
   REPENT BEFORE YOUR LAYD IN GROUND. ○○
   THOs. BERRY & JOHN FARMER CHURCHWARDENS.
   THOs. HEDDERLY FOUNDER NOTTINGHAM 1779.
   ( Diam. 42 in. )

The following extracts from the Parish Books are kindly supplied by the Rector—the Rev. T. Douglas Page.

1750. N.B.   Agreed at the meeting when the Accounts were given up, that the Bell Ropes, when they are weared out, shall be produced by the Parrish Churchwarden at the Parrish meeting when the Accounts are given up, and be sold by Auction, and the money to be disposed of to the use of the Parrish.

|  | £. | s. | d. |
|---|---|---|---|
| 1751. Paid Mr. Eayre for Runing the Second Bell ...... | 18 | 7 | 0 |
| Spent when it was tane down ........................ | 0 | 4 | 0 |
| Spent when it was Loded ............................ | 0 | 2 | 6 |
| Paid 3 men for hanging y* second Bell ............ | 0 | 5 | 0 |
| Spent when I paid Mr. Eayre ........................ | 0 | 8 | 6 |
| John farmer for Carige ................................ | 1 | 8 | 6 |
| Tho. farmer for Carige ................................ | 1 | 0 | 0 |
| Mr. Eayres his Bill ..................................... | 6 | 1 | 0 |
| 1778. Pd at a meeting about the Bell...................... | 0 | 1 | 6 |
| To extra expence applying about the Bell & taking it down ...................................................... | 0 | 7 | 6 |
| To the Carriage of the Bell to & from Leicester by Whitmore ............................................. | 1 | 18 | 0 |
| Allow⁴ to the Ringers in helping up the Bell...... | 0 | 5 | 0 |

To Mr. Hedderly of Nottingham for recasting
the Tennor Bell weighing 13 . 1 . 7 taking from
Leicester & Returning it there again & replacing
it finished in the steeple ................................. 21 . 0 . 0

Rec* by a 5*d*. Levy...... 35 . 9 . 2
Rec* by sale of the old
   Communion cloths... 0 . 5 . 1
   ───────────
                35 14 . 3
   ───────────

The Curfew is rung during the winter months at 8 p.m. The Pancake-bell is rung on Shrove-Tuesday.

Tradition says that a field, called "the Bell Field," in Congerstone parish, was given for the tenor bell: and that a field called "Eight Lands" was given to ensure the ringing of the Curfew by a man, who having lost his way, regained it by hearing the sound of the bell. This field is said to have been afterwards bartered to the Rector by the Clerk for his Sundays' dinner. This field has formed part of the glebe from time immemorial.

## SILEBY.

NATIVITY OF B. V. MARY.                                   5 BELLS.

1. IN HONOREM GULIELMI CUMBRIÆ DUCIS REBELLES
   SCOTOS VICTRICIBUS ARMIS DEBELLANTIS 1745.
         ( Diam. 38 in. )

2. JHESVS  [ 35 ]  BE  [ 35 ]  OVRE  [ 35 ]
   SPEDE  [ 35 ]  [ □ 10. ]
         ( Diam. 40 in. )

3. CELORVM CHRSTE PLATIAT TIBI REX SONVS ISTE
   1622  [ ▽ 1. ]
         ( Diam. 41 in. )

4. HENRY · PENN · MADE . MEE 170$\frac{7}{8}$ JOHN · WOOLDRICE
   HENRY · KILBURNE · CHURCHWARDENS.
   (A rose between each word.  Diam. 46 in.)
5. CVM SONO SI NON VIS [9] VENIRE NVNQVAM AD
   PRECES [9] CVPIES IRE [9] 1622 [▽ 1.]
   (Diam. 50 in.)

A bell at Fareham, Hants., cast in the same year as Sileby, 1st, and commemorating the same event, has the following verse :

> "In vain the rebels strive to gain renown,
> Over our church, the laws, the King and crowne ;
> In vain the bold ingrateful rebels aim
> To overturne, when you support the same.
> Then may great George our King live for ever to see
> The rebellous crew hang on the gallows tree."
>
> *Sussex Bells.*

The Pancake-bell is rung on Shrove-Tuesday.

Nichols writing (A.D. 1800) of these bells says :—" They are allowed by judges to be an excellent ring of bells, and are rung by the inhabitants to astonishment."  There was formerly a set of chimes here which played "*Charles' Dragoons.*"

There is a tradition that the bells from Newstead Abbey were brought here.

## SKEFFINGTON.

S. THOMAS À BECKETT.                                              5 BELLS.

1.  ABCD EFGHI KLMNO 1610 [▽ 1.]
       (Diam. 27 in.)
2.  ABCDEF GHIK LMNO 1612 [▽ 1.]
       (Diam. 27¼ in.)
3.  ABCDE FGHIK LMNO 1612 [▽ 1.]
       (Diam. 29¼ in.)

4. ᏩLORY [ 13 ] BE [ 13 ] TO [ 13 ] GOD [ 13 ] ON [ 13 ] HIGH
   [ 13 ] 1657 Ᏼ [ □ 10 ] ᏴᏚ ESQVIRE
   (Diam. 32¼ in.)

5. [ + 44 ] 𝔚𝔦𝔩𝔩𝔦𝔞𝔪 𝔖𝔨𝔢𝔳𝔦𝔫𝔤𝔱𝔬𝔫
   𝔈𝔰𝔮𝔲𝔦𝔢𝔯 𝔤𝔞𝔳𝔢 𝔪𝔢 1601.
   ( Under which is the crest of the Skeffingtons, see below. )
   (Diam. 36 in.)

William Skeffington, Esq., was knighted 23 April, 1603, and died, without issue, 19 December, 1605. Burton in his *Description of Leicestershire* (1622) has something to say as to his peculiarities. The Skeffingtons were seated here 31 Edward I. Their crest was "a mermaid proper, crined or, holding in the dexter hand a looking glass of the last, and in the sinister a comb (untinctured)."—*Visitation of Leicestershire*, 1619, published by Harleian Society, p. 7. This is the crest on the above tenor bell.

At the death-knell thrice three tolls are given for a male, thrice two for a female.

## SLAWSTON.

ALL SAINTS.                                                3 BELLS.

1. THOMAS NORRIS MADE ME 1660.
   ( Diam. 30 in.)

2. JOHN TAILBY CHURCHWARDEN JOSEPH EAYRE St.
   NEOTS 1768.
   ( Diam. 32¼ in.)

3. The same.
   ( Diam. 34 in.)

Nichols says :—" In the north aisle on the floor is a large blue stone stripped of all its brass . . . . [which] is said to have been used for the purpose of paying part of the expence of recasting a bell."

## SMEETON-WESTERBY.

CHRIST'S CHURCH.                                    2 BELLS.

Two small bells in an inaccessible turret.   They were founded in 1849.

## SNARESTON.

S. BARTHOLOMEW.                                    2 BELLS.

1.  JOHN O NEWBOLD O CHAPPEL O WARDEN O 1718.
    ( Diam. 19 in.  Coins of Wm. III. )
2.  GOD [ 13 ] SAVE [ 13 ] HIS [ 13 ] CHVRCH [ 13 ] 1721.
    ( Diam. 22 in.  Cracked. )

## SNIBSTONE.

S. MARY.                                             1 BELL.

1.  W + BROOKE BROMSGROVE MADE MEE ˙1739.
    [ Diam. 12 in. )

## SOMERBY.

ALL SAINTS.                                         3 BELLS.

1.  JOHN ADCOCK C W THOMAS HEDDERLY FOUNDER
    NOTM. 1767.
2.  ALL GLORY BEE TO ꓷOD ON HIGH 1664.
3.  WILLIAM BULL CH WARDEN 1813.

In 6 Edward VI. there were " iij bells wᵗʰ a sanctus bell."

## SOUTH  CROXTON.

S. JOHN BAPTIST.                                    4 BELLS.

1.  GOD [ 9 ] SAVE [ 9 ] THE [ 9 ] kING [ 9 ] 1636 [ ∪ 1. ]
    ( Diam. 26¼ in. )

2 N

2.  IH'Ƨ : NAZARENVS [9] REX : IVDEORVM [9] FILI : DEI
    [9] MISERERE : MEI [9] 1636 [ Ʊ 1. ]
    (Diam. 31¼ in.)

3.  The same.
    (Diam. 32¼ in.)

4.  The same, dated 1637.
    (Diam. 35 in.)

At the death-knell three tolls are given for a male, two for a female, both before and after the knell.

Nichols says these bells "are pretty tunable songsters, cast by the same hand as cast S. Margaret's ancient six, the celebrated Mr. Watts, as appears by his signature."

## SOUTH KILWORTH.

S. Nicolas.                                                    4 Bells.

1.  GOD ƧAVE HIƧ CHVRCH 1659.
2.  JHESVS BEE OVR ƧPEED 1659.
3.  IHƧ NAZARENVS REX. G. OLDFIELD 1659.
4.  ALL GLORY BEE TO GOD ON HIGH 1659.

A daily-bell is rung at 1 p.m. The Pancake-bell is rung on Shrove-Tuesday. In gleaning time a bell is rung at 8 a.m. For this latter duty the ringer receives a *toll* of one halfpenny from each household.

There is a tradition that there were formerly five bells, but one being cracked, was sent to the foundry to be recast; the inhabitants, however, being poor, were unable to pay the cost, and so lost their bell, which was purchased by the inhabitants of North Kilworth. This tradition is said to be strengthened by the perceptible disproportion between the weight and tone of the 3rd and 4th bells of the present ring. One of the first peals upon this ring would in all probability be in honour of the Restoration of the Royal family in 1660.

At the death-knell all the bells are tolled in order, beginning with the treble, thrice for a male, and twice for a female.

## SPROXTON.

S. BARTHOLOMEW.                                    3 BELLS.

1. [ + 55 ] LEVS [ □ 59 ] TIBI [ □ 59 ] DOMINE
2. [ + 55 ] IHESVS [ □ 59 ] NAZARENVS
   [ □ 59 ] REX [ □ 59 ] IVDEORVM
   and round the bell under the canons
   [ + 54 ] IHOHANNES [ □ 56 ] DE [ □ 56 ]
   YORKE [ □ 56 ] ME [ □ 56 ] FECIT
   [ □ 56 ] IN [ □ 56 ] HONORE [ □ 56 ]
   BEATE [ □ 56 ] MARIE [ □ 56 ]
3. Huius Sci Rychardi [ □ 19 ] [ ▽ 63 ]

A Pre-Reformation ring of bells. The 1st and 2nd are by the same founder—John of York—whose name appears in very small Gothic capitals, the same height as the engraved cross, round the haunch of the 2nd bell.

In 6 Edward VI. there were "iij bells in y⁴ stepyll."

The bells have not been rung, only chimed, for many years; their condition is considered unsafe, and the approach to them is difficult.

The Gleaning-bell is sounded during harvest time.

A sanctus bell formerly hung near the south window: it is said to have been stolen and carried off in the night.

## STANTON-UNDER-BARDON.

There was formerly a chapel here which possessed two bells. These were purchased by Thomas Boothby, Esq., of Tooly, when he gave a new ring to the parish of Peckleton, in 1714.

## STAPLEFORD.

S. MARY MAGDALENE.                                 6 BELLS.

1. THE GIFT OF THE Rt. HON. EARL HARBOROUGH
   EDWd. ARNOLD LEICESTER FECIT 1785.

2. OMNIA FIANT AD GLORIAM DEI.    SIR   PHILIP
   SHERARD GAVE THIS BELL 1652 RECAST 1754.
3. CELORVM CHRSTE PLATIAT TIBI REX SONVS ISTE
   1615 [ ▽ 1. ]
4. GLORY BE TO GOD AND (*sic*) HIGH. JOHN KITCHINGS
   C. W. 1757 THO. HEDDERLY FOUNDER
   ( Near the canons are four fleur-de-lis, each on a lozenge. )
5. IH'Ƨ : NAZARENVS REX : IVDEORVM FILI : DEI
   MISERERE : MEI 1617 [ ▽ 1. ]
6. [ + 34 ] ᴆᴏꜱ ꜱᴠᴍᴠꜱ ᴄᴏᴆꜱᴛᴚᴠᴄᴛɪ
   ᴁᴆ ᴌᴁᴠᴆᴇᴍ ᴆᴏᴍɪᴆɪ 1611 [ ◻ 8. ]

In 6 Edward VI. there was no mention of bells.

Previous to 1785, when the church was rebuilt, there were only five
bells.   The 4th was formerly inscribed "God save his chvrch."

The tenor bell only can be rung : the rest are chimed by means of a
key-board, levers and hammers, hence in the local rhyme already quoted:

> Brentingby pancheons
> And Wyfordby pans ;
> Stapleford *organs*
> And Burton ting-tangs.

There are chimes, but they are out of order.


# STAPLETON.

S. Martin.                                             1 Bell.

1. REVᴅ. G. METTAM M.A. RECTOR J. BEALE & J. H.
   FOX CHURCHWARDENS 1848.   J. TAYLOR & SON
   FOUNDERS.

There were formerly two bells here.

## STATHERN.

S. GUTHLAC.                                                  4 BELLS.

1.  GOD [ 12 ] SAVE [ 12 ] HIS [ 12 ] CHVRCH [ 12 ] THO.
    BARNET WARDEN 1730.
                    ( Diam. 30 in. )

2.  𝕴 sweetly · toling · men · do · call · to · tuste · on · ments · that ·
    feeds · the · soole · 1607 [ □ 8. ]
                    ( Diam. 32 in. )

3.  𝕲𝕷𝕺𝕽𝖄 𝕭𝕰 𝕿𝕺 𝕲𝕺𝕯 𝕺𝕹 𝕳𝕴𝕲𝕳
    1613 [ □ 8. ]
                    ( Diam. 37 in. )

4.  my roaring sounde doth warning geve that men cannot heare allways lybe
    1607 [ □ 8 ]
                    ( Diam. 40 in. )

In 6 Edward VI. there were "j sanctus bell . . . iij bells."
The 1st was previously inscribed " Jhesus be our speede."


## STAUNTON HAROLD.

HOLY TRINITY.                                                 8 BELLS.

1, 2.  SIR ROBERT SHIRLEY BARR. DONER HEREOF
       DYED THE 28 NO. AN DOM 1656 [ □ 11 ] 1669.

3.   ( The bells are so crowded that it is impossible to get a rubbing, or
     clear reading, of this: it appears to record that " Robt. Earl
     Ferrers donor died in 1717.")

4, 5, & 6.  Blanks.

7, 8.  SIR ROBt. SHIRLEY BARt. DONOR HEREOF DIED
       NOVr. 28TH, 1656. T. MEARS OF LONDON FECIT.
       RECAST ANNO DOMINI 1831 AT THE EXPENSE
       OF THE RIGHT HONble. WASHINGTON EARL
       FERRERS.

For a full account of the Donor and his family see *Nichols' Leicester-shire* under Staunton Harold.

## STOCKERSTONE.

S. PETER.                                         3 BELLS.

1. THOMAS BURTON MILES ET BARONETTA DOMINUS
   MANERII 1630.
2. JOHN TAYLOR FOUNDER LOUGHBOROUGH 1842.
3. IH'S : NAZARENVS [9] REX : IVDEORVM [9] FILI : DEI
   [9] MISERERE : MEI [9] 1634 [ ∪ 1. ]

## STOKE GOLDING.

S. MARGARET.                                      4 BELLS.

1. BRYANVS ELDRIDGE ME FECIT 1656.
   (Diam. 28 in.)
2. GOD [9] SAVE [9] THE [9] kING [9] 1634 [9] [ ∪ 1.]
   (Diam. 29 in.)
3. [ + 34 ] JESVS BE OVRE SPEDE
Under which are two ornate Gothic letters �𝔥 . 𝔇 [ □ 37 and 38 ]
   the C being placed upside down to make a D.
   (Diam. 33 in.)
4. JOHN RUDHALL GLOUCESTER FECT 1825 . .:. .
   (Diam. 36¾ in.)

The Charity Commissioners in their Report (1837), p. 178, mention
a parcel of land, called "Eight o'clock Bell Land," in the parish of
Higham-on-the-Hill, the rent of which was stated to them to have been
formerly paid to the parish of Stoke for ringing the eight o'clock bell.
It was comprised in certain bequests made by Thomas Daville, Esq., in
1714. The Commissioners say no Curfew had been rung for forty years
or more, neither could they trace any account of such bequest.

## STONESBY.

S. PETER.                                         3 BELLS.

1. [ + 21 ] OMNIA FIANT AD GLORIAM DEI 1626.

2. Ħæ Ĉampana Ƀeata Ꞩacra Ꞇrinitate Ƒiat.
3. JOHN SMITH CHURCHWARDEN. THOMAS HEDDERLY
    FOUNDER NOTTM 1761.

In 6 Edward VI. there were "iij bells of a corde."
The 3rd was previously inscribed "Tobie Norris cast me 1671."

## STONEY STANTON.

S. MICHAEL.                                           6 BELLS.

1. JOHN SANKEY RECTOR HENRY TOWNSHEND ESQR.
    C. W. JOHN ORTON W ORTON JAMES ORTON
    C ORTON G ORTON J. PEGG T. HIGGINSON.
2. OMNIA FIANT AD GLORIAM DEI 1842. J. TAYLOR
    FECIT.
3. OMNIA FIANT AD GLORIAM DEI 1842.
4. J. TAYLOR FECIT 1842.
5. J. TAYLOR (PILGRIM) BELLFOUNDER 1842.
6. J. TAYLOR BELLFOUNDER 1842. JEHOVAL JIREH.
        ( Weight 8 cwt.   Key G sharp. )

Previous to the year 1842 the ring consisted of three bells
inscribed :—

1st. "Omnia fiant ad gloriam Dei. Tho. Eayre Kett. fecit Benjᵃ.
Everard C. W. 1744."

2nd. "Be yt knowne to all that doth me see that Newcombe of
Leicester made mee 1609."

The 3rd. "IH'Ƨ Nazarenvs Rex Judeorvm Fili Dei miserere mei 1625."

Nichols says that John Orton of Kidderminster, Innholder, on 26 May
1790, assigned to the minister churchwardens and overseers of the poor
of Stoney Stanton for the time being, for ever, the sum of £25, upon
trust ( among other things ) to pay a certain portion [ of the proceeds
thereof] equally to and amongst four poor boys, belonging to the parish,
and being between the ages of nine and seventeen years, who do not
receive any parish pay, and who can and shall ring four peals upon

Stoney Stanton bells upon the 5th day of January (being old Christmas Day); the same to be paid to them upon the said 5th day of January for ever.

This payment has not been made within memory. Mr. John Orton was the great promoter of the present ring. He, his brothers and the other gentlemen whose names appear on the 1st bell, subscribed £10 each towards the cost. The Ortons were all skilful ringers.

## STONTON WYVILLE.

S. DENYS.                                            1 BELL.

1. JONATHAN WADE CHURCHWARDEN 1768.

In 6 Edward VI. there was "j bell" which was recast by Joseph Eayre of St. Neots as above.

There is a tradition that bells were sent from this parish to Deene in Northamptonshire.

A morning bell is rung on Sundays at 8 a.m.

## STOUGHTON.

B. V. MARY.                                          4 BELLS.

1. THOMAS BEAVMONT KNIGHT
   [ ▽ 1. ]
2. RICE    CHAPMAN    CHURCHWARDEN   ·:·   1739   ·:·
   OMNIA FIANT AD GLORIAM DEI : T : EAYRE ·:·
3. Feare god and obey the prince unon domini 1612 (?) [ ▽ 1. ]
4. CELORVM CHRSTE PLATIAT TIBI REX SONVS ISTE
   ና191 [ ▽ 1. ]

This Sir Thomas Beaumont, Knight (second surviving son of Sir Nicholas Beaumont of Coleorton), became possessed of Stoughton Grange and Manor with its members in right of his wife Catharine, daughter and heir of Sir Thomas Farnham of that place, Knight.— *Nichols.*

## STRETTON MAGNA.

S. GILES.                                     1 BELL.

1. WILLIAM HOBSON CHURCHWARDEN EDWD. ARNOLD
   LEICESTER FECIT 1791.


## STRETTON PARVA.

S. . . . . .                                  1 BELL.

1. EDWD. ARNOLD ST. NEOTS FECIT 1781.


## SUTTON CHENEY.

S. . . . . .                                  4 BELLS.

1. GOD [ 12 ] SAVE HIS [ 12 ] CHVRCH [ 12 ] 1724.
   ( Diam. 27 in. )
2. RICHARD ROBERTES RICH-
   ARD SWINFEN 1593 [ ▽ 1. ]
   ( Diam. 30 in. )
3. GOD [ 9 ] SAVE [ 9 ] THE [ 9 ] kING [ 9 ] 1635 [ ▽ 1. ]
   ( Diam. 33 in. )
4. IH'2 : NAZARENVS REX IVDEORVM FILI DEI MISE-
   RERE W MATHEW C WARDEN 1678.
   [ 14 ] T M E S [ 14 ]
   (close to the mouth of the bell) W N [ + 25 ]
   ( Diam. 36 in.  Cracked and unhung. )

See Pedigree of Robertes in *Visitation of Leicestershire* 1619 (issued by
Harleian Society) p. 117. The tenor bell, with ancient cross, is from
the Nottingham foundry. The first part of inscription is in letters
formerly used by Hugh Watts of Leicester.

2 O

## SWEPSTONE.

S. Peter.　　　　　　　　　　　　　　　　　　4 Bells.

1. GOD [14] SÁVE [14] THE [14] kING [14] 1664.
2. GOD SAVE HIS CHVRCH 1711.
3. IH'Ƨ : [12] NAZARENVS [12] REX : IVDEORVM [12] FILI [12] DEI [12] MIƧERERE [12] J D WARDEN 1696.
4. 𝕮𝖄𝕸 [9] 𝕮𝖄𝕸 [9] 𝕬𝕹𝕯 [9] 𝕻𝕽𝕬𝕴𝕰 [9] 1634 [▽ 1.]

In 6 Edward VI. there were "foore belles one of them a saunce bell."
A morning-bell is rung on Sunday at 8 a.m.

## SWINFORD.

All Saints.　　　　　　　　　　　　　　　　　4 Bells.

1. [+44] 𝕵𝕳𝕰𝕾𝖄𝕾 𝕭𝕰 𝕺𝖀𝕽 𝕾𝕻𝕴𝕯 𝕬𝕹𝕺 𝕯𝕺𝕸𝕴𝕹𝕴 1598 [▽ 1.]
   (Diam. 30¾ in.)
2. IH'Ƨ : NAZARENVS [9] REX : IVDEORVM [9] FILI : DEI [9] MISERERE : MEI [9] 1631 [▽ 1.]
   (Diam. 32¼ in.)
3. 𝕲𝕺𝕯 𝕾𝕬𝖁𝕰 𝕺𝖀𝕽 𝕼𝖀𝕰𝕰𝕹𝕰 1599 [▽ 1.]
   (Diam. 35 in.)
4. 𝕬𝕭𝕯𝕯 [□ *] 𝕰𝕱𝕲𝕳𝕴 [□ †] 𝕂𝕷𝕸𝕹𝕺𝕻.
   (Diam. 38 in.)

   [ * A Portcullis with its chains, ensigned by the Tudor crown.
   † A Tudor Rose ensigned in the same way.  This bell I
   believe to be from the Nottingham foundry.]

At the Death-knell thrice three tolls are given for a male, and thrice
two for a female, both before and after the knell.
A morning-bell is rung on Sundays at 7 a.m.

# SWITHLAND.

S. LEONARD.        6 BELLS.

1 & 2. THE GIFT OF SIR JOHN DANVERS BART. 1760.

3. THE GIFT OF SIR JOHN DANVERS BART. EDWARD
     ARNOLD LEICESTER FECIT 1793.

4 & 5. THE GIFT OF SIR JOHN DANVERS BART. 1760.

6. THE GIFT OF SIR JOHN DANVERS BART. 1760. LET
     EVERYTHING THAT HATH BREATH PRAISE THE
     LORD. JOSEPH EAYRE St. NEOTS.
                ( Weight 8 cwt. )

Sir John Danvers died 21 September, 1796. For an account of him, his family, and a magnificent monument erected to his memory during his lifetime, see *Nichols' Leicestershire* under Swithland.

# SYSONBY.

S. . . . . .        1 BELL.

1. [ + 20. ] IN : HONORE : SANCTI
     LEONARDI
           ( Diam. 18 in. )

# SYSTON.

S. PETER.        6 BELLS.

1. GOD [ 12 ] SAVE [ 12 ] QUEEN [ 12 ] ANNE [ 12 ] 1704 [ 12 ]
           ( Diam. 32 in. )

2. GOD [ 12 ] SAVE [ 12 ] HIS [ 12 ] CHVRCH 1704.   W
     NORTH [ 12 ] J WHATTOFF CH. WARDENS.
           ( Diam. 34 in. )

3. WILLIAM PARR THOMAS
     ADCOCKE C. ANNO DMI
     1634 [ 9 ] [ ᴜ 1. ]
           ( Diam. 35½ in. )

4. [ + 42 ] AVE [ □ 43 ] MARIA [ □ 43 ] GRA̅
   [ □ 43 ] PLENA [ □ 43 ] DN̅S [ □ 43 ]
   TECVM
          ( Diam. 37 in. )

5. IH'S : NAZARENVS [ 9 ] REX : IVDEORVM [ 9 ] FILI :
   DEI [ 9 ] MISERERE : MEI [ 9 ] 1628 [ ▽ 1. ]
          ( Diam. 40¾ in. )

6. The same dated 1619.
          ( Diam. 45¾ in. )

The Pancake-bell is rung on Shrove-Tuesday at noon.   On Sundays
one bell is rung at 7 a.m.; two bells at 9 a.m.   At the Death-knell three
tolls are given for a male, two for a female, on all the bells, beginning
with the treble.


# THEDDINGWORTH.

ALL SAINTS.                                        5 BELLS.

1. PRAISE THE LORD 1595.
          ( Diam. 33 in. )

2. CELORVM CHRSTE PLATIAT TIBI REX SONVS ISTE
   1615 [ ▽ 1. ]
          ( Diam. 34 in. )

3. [ + 42 ] S [ □ 43 ] PG [ □ 43 ] FG [ □ 43 ] [ ▽ 6. ]
          ( Diam. 37 in. )

4. NOS SUMUS CONSTRUCTI AD LAUDEM DOMINI : ·
   LAUDATE ILLUM CYMBALIS SONORIS † A D 1757.
          ( Diam. 40 in. )

5. + J. TAYLOR & Co LOUGHBOROUGH 1873 + LAUS
   DEO
          ( Diam. 48 in. )

Until 1873, when the present fine tenor bell was purchased by subscription, there were only four bells.

The Pancake-bell is rung on Shrove-Tuesday.

# THORNTON.

S. Peter. 3 Bells.

1. IH'S : NAZARENVS [9] REX : IVDEORVM [9] FILI :
   DEI [9] MISERERE : MEI [9] 1626 [ ▽ 1. ]
   (Diam. 32 in.)
2. SERVE GOD HONOVR THE KING 1663.
   (Diam. 35 in.)
3. FOR CHVRCH AND KING WE ALLWAYS RING 1757
   M. PAYNE C. WARD : THOMAS HEDDERLEY
   FOUNDER.
   (Diam. 39 in.)


# THORPE ACRE.

No Dedication. 1 Bell.

A new church with a small bell in an external turret.


# THORPE ARNOLD.

S. Mary. 3 Bells.

1. 𝕮𝖀𝕸 𝕮𝖀𝕸 𝕬𝕹𝕯 𝕻𝕽𝕬𝖞 1597 [ ▽ 1. ]
2. IH'S [12] NAZARENVS [12] REX [12] IVDEORVM [12]
   FILI [12] DEI [12] MISERERE 1685.
3. [ + 3 ] 𝕾 𝕮𝕺𝕽𝕹𝕰𝕷𝕴 [ ▽ 6. ]

In 6 Edward VI. there were "iij bells and a saunce bell."

The 2nd bell is from the Nottingham foundry, but the letters are those previously used by Hugh Watts of Leicester.

The dedication of the 3rd bell is a rare one.

## THORPE LANGTON.

S. Leonard.                                    3 Bells.

1.  𝔊𝔒𝔐 𝔄𝔑𝔇 𝔓𝔯𝔞𝔠 [▽ 1.]
        (Diam. 24 in.)
2.  GOD [9] SAVE [9] THE [9] kING [9] 1630 [▽ 1.]
        (Diam. 28 in.)
3.  IH'S : NAZARENVS [9] REX : IVDEORVM [9] FILI :
        DEI [9] MISERERE : MEI [9] 16 ? [▽ 1.]
        (Diam. 32 in.)

## THORPE SATCHVILLE.

S. Michael.                                    1 Bell.

1.  J. TAYLOR & Co. 1872.

## THRUSSINGTON.

Holy Trinity.                                  3 Bells.

            𝔍.𝔍.𝔠.
1.  [ + 45 ]  𝔄𝔙𝔈 : 𝔐𝔄𝔯𝔦𝔄 : 𝔊𝔯𝔞𝔠𝔦𝔄 :
            𝔓𝔩𝔢𝔫𝔞 : 𝔇𝔬𝔪𝔦𝔫𝔲𝔰 : 𝔗𝔢𝔠𝔲𝔪
2.  GOD [14] SAVE [14] THE [14] KING  M WELLES
        W SKILLINGTON WARDENS 1677.
3.  [ + 83 ] 𝔄𝔟𝔢 𝔐𝔞𝔯𝔦𝔞 𝔊𝔯𝔞𝔠𝔦𝔞 𝔓𝔩𝔢𝔫𝔞 𝔇𝔬𝔪𝔦𝔫𝔲𝔰 𝔗𝔢𝔠𝔲𝔪.

## THURCASTON.

All Saints.                                    3 Bells.

1.  CELORUM CHRSTE PLATIAT TIBE REX SONUS ISTE
        1614 [▽ 1.]
2.  R. HEYCH W. THORNTON WARDENS. GOD [12] SAVE
        HIS CHVRCH 1701.

3. 𝕴𝕹 [ □ 24] 𝕿𝕳𝕰 [ □ 29 □ 28] 𝕹𝕬𝖄𝕸 [ □ 73]
   𝕺𝕱 [ □ 19] 𝕴𝕳𝕾 [ □ 29 □ 28] 𝕾𝕻𝕰𝕯 [ □ 73.]
   𝕸𝕰 [ ▽ 51.]

In 6 Ed. VI. there were "three belles and a saunce belle."


## THURLASTON.

ALL SAINTS.                                          3 BELLS.

1. OMNIA FIANT AD GLRIAM DEI ·∴· GLORIA DEO
   SOLI ·∴· T ∶ EAYRE ·∴· A ∶ D ·∴· 1746.
   (Diam. 32 in.)
2. [ + 71 ] 𝖂𝕾𝕯𝕮𝕰𝕳 [ □ 62 ] [ + 71 ] 𝖂𝕾𝕯𝕮𝕰𝕳𝕴𝕺𝖄
   [ + 71 ] 𝖂𝕾𝕴𝕯𝕳𝕯𝕮 𝕽 (grotesque animals and
   fleur-de-lis thrice repeated.)
   (Diam. 35½ in.)
3. SOLI DEO GLORIA PAX HOMINIBUS 1653  I M.
   (Diam. 38 in.)

See *Nichols' Leicestershire* iv. part 2, p. 997, for some curious and
learned attempts to read the inscription on the 2nd bell. It is simply
an "alphabet bell" with the letters upside down.


## THURMASTON.

S. MICHAEL.                                          5 BELLS.

1. JNo TAYLOR & SON FOUNDERS LOUGHBOROUGH
   1848.
2. IH'Ƨ ∶ NAZARENVS [9] REX ∶ IVDEORVM [9] FILI ∶
   DEI [9] MISERERE ∶ MEI [9] 1627 [ ▽ 1. ]
3. + 𝕹𝖔𝖒𝖊𝖓 𝕾𝖚𝖓𝖈𝖙𝖊 𝕵𝖊𝖘𝖚 𝕹𝖔𝖘 𝖘𝖊𝖗𝖚𝖆 𝖒𝖔𝖗𝖙𝖎𝖘 𝖆𝖇 𝖊𝖘𝖚
   JOHN TAYLOR & SON FOUNDERS OF LOUGH-
   BOROUGH A.D. 1848.

4. IHS NAZARENUS REX JUDEORUM FILI DEI MISERERE MEI RECAST BY J TAYLOR & SON OF LOUGHBRO' A.D. 1848. DATE OF OLD BELL 1625.

5. IHƧ : NAZARENVS [9] REX : IVDEORVM [9] FILI : DEI [9] MISERERE : MEI [9] 1625 [ ▽ 1. ]

## THURNBY.

S. LUKE.                                                    5 BELLS.

1. THIS BELL GIVEN BY O : V : HUNT 1872 J : TAYLOR & Co. FOUNDERS LOUGHBOROUGH.

2. J. GUDE & J. GODDARD CHURCHWARDENS O EDWARD ARNOLD LEICESTER FECIT 1794 O O O

3. WILLIAM UNDERWODD CHURCH WARDEN O JOSEPH EAYRE St. NEOTS FECIT 1765.

4. CVM · SONO · SI · NON · VIS [9] VENIRE [9] NVN-QVAM · AD · PRECES [9] CVPIES · IRE [9] 1631 [9] [ ▽ 1. ]

5. IH'Ƨ : NAZARENVS [9] REX : IVDEORVM [9] FILI : DEI [9] MISERERE : MEI [9] 1631 [9] [ ▽ 1. ]

The Pancake-bell on Shrove-Tuesday is only recently discontinued.

There is a tradition that the tenor bells of Thurnby and Humberstone, being both recast at the same time, were exchanged by a blunder of the founder.

## TILTON-ON-THE-HILL.

S. PETER.                                                    4 BELLS.

1. PRAISE THE LORD [ ▽ 1. ]

2 and 3. IH'Ƨ : NAZARENVS [9] REX : IVDEORVM [9] FILI : DEI [9] MISERERE : MEI [9] 1638 [ ▽ 1. ]

4. The same dated 1640.

# TUGBY.

S. Thomas à Becket.                                                4 Bells.

1. + A : RIGBY : MADE : ME : 1702 : WILLIAM : PAR-
   TRIDGE : CH : W.
   ( Diam. 26¼ in. )
2. THOMAS MEARS & SON OF LONDON 1809.
   ( Diam. 27¼ in. )
3. CVM CVM AND PRAC 1602 [℧ 1.]
   ( Diam. 29 in. )
4. ABC DEF GHIK [℧ 1.]
   ( Diam. 31 in. )

# TUR-LANGTON.

S. Nicolas.                                                        1 Bell.

1. EDWARD ARNOLD LEICESTER FECIT 1794.
   ( Diam. 23 in. )

# TWYCROSS.

S. . . . . . .                                                    3 Bells.

1. GOD SAVE HIS CHVRCH J. W. J. O. WARDENS 1691.
2. T. MEARS OF LONDON FECIT RECAST 1814 Wm.
   CLARE CHURCHWARDEN.
3. THOMAS MEARS LONDON RECAST 1814.

# TWYFORD.

S. Andrew.                                                        3 Bells.

1. [+ 22.] NEWCOMBE · OF · LEICESTER · MADE · ME · 1604.
   ( Diam. 30 in. )
2. IH'S : NAZARENVS [9] REX : IVDEORVM [9] FILI :
   DEI [9] MISERERE : MEI [9] 1602 [9] [℧ 1.]
   ( Diam. 31¾ in. )

2 P

3. 𝕽𝖊𝖈𝖆𝖘𝖙 𝖇𝖞 𝕵𝖔𝖍𝖓 𝕿𝖆𝖞𝖑𝖔𝖗 𝖆𝖓𝖉 𝖘𝖔𝖓 𝖔𝖋 𝕷𝖔𝖚𝖌𝖍𝖇𝖔𝖗𝖔𝖚𝖌𝖍 1853.
           ( Diam. 36 in.    Weight 7 cwt. )

Mr. Higgs writes :—" The inscription on the previous Tenor bell
was 'cvm cvm and pray 1600.' Perhaps I may be permitted to add
that it was principally by my own exertion that the old cracked bell was
recast, and the church clock—*the old Leicester Exchange clock*—purchased
in 1853, having raised by subscription for both purposes a sum of
between £80 and £90."

## WALTHAM-ON-THE-WOLDS.

S. Mary Magdalene.                                          5 Bells.

1.  SURGE · AGE : HENRY · PENN : MADE · ME : 1726.
2.  OMNIA FIANT AD GLORIAM DEI THO : EAYRE · :·
        · KETT :· · FECIT · : A : D. 1744.
3.  OMNIA FIANT AD GLORIAM DEI. . : CAST : · 1744 : ·
4.  [+21] GOD · :· SAVE · :· THE · :· CHVRCH · :· OVR
        · :· QVEENE · :· AND REALME · :· AND · :·
        SEND · :· VS · :· PEACE · :· IN · :· CHRIST
        · :· AMEN [ □ 8. ]
5.  OMNIA FIANT · AD GLORIAM · DEI · :· GLORIA ·
        PATRI · FILIO · ET SPIRITUI SANCTO · :· ANNO ·
        DOM · ·:· · 1744 · · · · ·

In 6 Edward VI. there were " iiij belles and a lyttle bell."
There is a piece of land called the " Bell-close " which forms an
endowment for ringing a bell at 4, 5, or 6 o'clock (according to the time
of year) in the morning, and the Curfew at 8 o'clock in the evening,
excepting on Saturday evening, when it is rung at 7 o'clock.  After the
ringing of the Curfew (the 3rd bell) the number of the day of the month
is tolled on another bell.  (See *Report of Charity Commissioners for Leicestershire* 1837, page 455.)
The Gleaning-bell (4th) is rung during harvest.

There is a tradition that there were here, formerly, six bells, and that the tenor was appropriated by a neighbouring parish. There is no evidence in support of this.

## WALTON ISLEY.

ALL SAINTS. 2 BELLS.

1. [ + 39 ] 𝔸𝕍𝔼 : 𝕄𝔸ℝ𝕀𝔸 : ℙ𝕃𝔼ℕ𝔸 : 𝔾ℝ𝔸ℂ𝕀𝔸 : 𝔻ℕ̄𝕊 : 𝕋𝔼ℂ𝕌𝕄

( Diam. 18 in. )

2. [ + 41 ] 𝕄 𝔸 ℝ 𝕀 𝔸

( Diam. 21 in. )

In 6 Edward VI. there were "tow belles (small) in the steple."

## WALTON-LE-WOLDS.

S. BARTHOLOMEW. 3 BELLS.

1. GOD SAVE THE CHVRCH ROBERT BLUNT 1656 [ ☐ 11. ]
2. John Taylor & Son of Loughborough founders 1853.
3. J PALMER AND JOHN BRYANT HERTFORD FECERUNT 1807 REVᴅ PHILIP STORY RECTOR J SHUTTLE-WOOD C. W.

( Weight 7 cwt. )

## WANLIP.

S. NICOLAS. 3 BELLS.

[ ☐ 62 ]

1. Sacet Nomen Magdalene Campana.

[ ▽ 1 ]

2. [ ☐ 80 ] [ + 55 ] [ ☐ 80 ] Sancte Nicolane Ora Pro Nobis.
3. [ + 3 ] GEVE [ + 3 ] THANKES TO [ + 3 ] GOD.

In 6 Edward VI. there were "thre greate bells and a saunce bell tow hand bells."

# WARTNABY.

S. MARTIN.                                                    2 BELLS.

1.  GOD SAVE HIS CHURCH 1731.  ED. GVI CH.WARDEN.
        ( Diam. 24 in. )
2.  JOHN TAYLOR & SONS LOUGHBOROUGH 1857.
        ( Diam. 25 in. )

# WELBY.

S. . . .                                                      1 BELL.

1.  [ + 3 ]  𝔄 𝔅𝔈 𝔇𝔈 𝔉𝔊 𝔥.𝔦.
        ( Diam. 24 in. )

In 6 Edward VI. there were " ij bells."

The second bell is said to have been removed many years ago from the church to a farmhouse in the parish, on the occasion of a wedding, and instead of being returned, to have been broken up and sold for old metal.

# WELHAM.

S. ANDREW.                                                   2 BELLS.

        𝔗 [ □ 67 ]  𝔖 [ □ 67 ]  𝔯 [ □ 67 ]  𝔫.
1.  [ + 72 ] MVLTI [ □ 67 ] VOCATI [ □ 67 ] PAVCI [ □ 67 ]
        ELECTI [ □ 67. ]
        𝔊𝔳𝔩𝔦𝔢𝔩𝔪𝔳𝔰 : 𝔥𝔞𝔳𝔣𝔬𝔯𝔡𝔢
        𝔞𝔯𝔪𝔦𝔤𝔢𝔯 1604 [ + 72 ]
        ( Diam. 31 in. )

[ □ 52 ]

2. ℭelorum xɾe placeat tibi rex sonus iste

[ ▽ 32. ]          [ □ 75. ]          ○ ○ ○

(Diam. 35 in.)

There were formerly three bells here: the ancient second, which is said to have borne the letters S PAℭEGT, was cracked about the year 1820, when it was very improperly taken out of the church, and disposed of, for what purpose is unknown, as there is no entry in the parish books respecting it (see *Hill's Hist. of Langton, &c.*, p. 328).

William Halford, Esq., was the owner of Welham by purchase before 1590. His grandson and heir, William Halford of Welham, was High Sheriff in 1617, and died in 1628.

The Rev. Assheton Pownall, F.S.A. (a member of the London Numismatic Society) kindly informs me that the three coins on the present 2nd bell are *certainly* fifteenth century groats, and *probably* those of Henry VI.

## WHATTON (LONG).

All Souls.                                                3 Bells.

1.  [ + 70 ] ⊕ℜℭℜ [ □ 49 ] Ⅎ [ + 70 ] ⊕ℜℭℜ [ □ 49 ] Ⅎ
    (Diam. 32 in.)
2.  [ + 21 ] GOD SAVE OVR CHVRCH [ □ 8. ]
    (Diam. 35 in.)
3.  ALL YOV THAT HEAR MY MOVRNFUL SOVND REPENT
    BEFORE YOV LYE IN GROVND   J. STEVENSON
    G. PEAT C. W. 1756.
    (Diam. 40 in.   Cracked.)

In 6 Edward VI. there were "three belles wythe a small bell."

## WHETSTONE.

S. Matthew.                                              4 Bells.

1.  THOMAS MEARS OF LONDON FOUNDER 1834.

2. IH'S : NAZARENVS [9] REX : IVDEORVM [9] FILI :
   DEI [9] MISERERE : MEI ⌊9⌋ 1640 [ ⊽ 1. ]
3. The same dated 1623.
4. T. MEARS OF LONDON FECIT 1824.

The ringing of the Curfew is lately discontinued.

## WHITWICK.

S. JOHN BAPTIST.                                4 BELLS.

1. GOD SAVE THE kING 1628 [ ⊽ 1. ]
                 ( Diam. 32 in. )
2. CELORVM CHRSTE [9] PLATIAT TIBI [9] REX SONVS
   ISTE 1628 [ ⊽ 1. ]
                 ( Diam. 34 in. )
3. IH'S : NAZARENVS [9] REX : IVDEORVM [9] FILI :
   DEI [9] MISERERE : MEI [9] 1628 [ ⊽ 1. ]
                 ( Diam. 38 in. )
4. The same.
                 ( Diam. 41 in. )

In 6 Edward VI. there were "three belles a saunce bell and a hand
bell."

## WIBTOFT.

ASSUMPTION OF OUR LADY.                         1 BELL.

1. WILLIAM : BALLARD : C W THOMAS HEDDERLY
   FOUNDER NOTTM. 1758.
                 ( Diam. 16¼ in. )

## WIGSTON-MAGNA.

ALL SAINTS.                                     6 BELLS.

1. CUM · SONO · SI · NON · VIS · VENIRE · NUNQUAM ·
   AD · PRECES · CUPIES · IRE. [ ▢ see below ] JOHN
   TAYLOR & CO. FOUNDERS LOUGHBOROUGH 1874.

2. IH'S : [ 12 ] NAZARENVS [ 12 ] REX [ 12 ] IVDEORVM [ 12 ]
   FILI [ 12 ] DEI [ 12 ] MISERERE [ 12 ] R. B. T. D.
   WARDENS 1682.
3. IH'S : [ 12 ] NAZARENVS [ 12 ] REX [ 12 ] IVDEORVM [ 12 ]
   FILI [ 12 ] DEI [ 12 ] MISERERE 1702.
4. T. MEARS OF LONDON FECIT 1824. JOHN RAGG
   ESQ. THOMAS WILSON CHURCHWARDENS.
5. J. BRIANT CORT & CO. FECERUNT 1804 HERTFORD.
   J. LANGHAM AND J. HUNST C. W.
6. GOD SAVE HIS CHVRCH. R. BREWIN T. DAVEN-
   PORT WARDENS 1632.

The 1st bell was the gift of Thomas Ingram, Esq., of Hawthorn-field
in this parish : it bears his crest, a Forget-me-not, and the motto
" 𝔚𝔞𝔱𝔠𝔥 𝔞𝔫𝔡 𝔚𝔬𝔯𝔨."

The 2nd and 3rd bells bear the letters previously used by Hugh
Watts, of Leicester, showing that his foundry gear passed into the
hands of the Nottingham founders. The tenor bell is also from
Nottingham.

Unfortunately the Churchwardens' Accounts, which were ancient
and full of interest, have, I understand, passed into private hands.
They ought to be restored to the parish. Nichols gives a few extracts,
from which the following are quoted :—

" Extract from earliest Register beginning 1569 :—

1682. New Bells a free gift; from the married men £43 ; from the
batchelors £12.

Extracts from Churchwardens' Accounts 1591—1660 :—

| | £. | s. | d. |
|---|---|---|---|
| 1591. A bell new cast at Leicester. | | | |
| 1597. Fore and great bell cast. | | | |
| 1601. Paid for casting the third bell metal ............... | 5 | 19 | 0 |
| 1613. Paid Ringers on St. James day ..................... | 0 | 0 | 8 |
| 1620. Paid Ringers on Coronation day .................... | 0 | 2 | 6 |
| 1634. Gave the Ringers when the King & Queen came | 0 | 1 | 8 |

Extracts from more modern Account Books :—

| | | £. | s. | d. |
|---|---|---|---|---|
| 1763. | Paid Mr. Hacket court charges on account of bells | 2 | . 3 | 10 |
| 1764. | Paid Cornelius Parker for carriage of third bell to St. Neots ................................................. | 3 | . 3 | . 0 |
| | Paid Mr. Eayre for casting third bell and tuning the other ................................................. | 17 | . 1 | 10 |

At the death-knell three tolls are given for a male ; two for a female.

## WIGSTON-MAGNA.

S. Wolstan.                                                    No Bell.

## WIGSTON-PARVA.

Assumption of our Lady.                                    1 Bell.

1.  1758.

(Diam. 15¾ in.)

## WILLOUGHBY WATERLESS.

S. Mary.                                                    4 Bells.

1.  THOS. PERKINS CH. WARDEN 1818.
(Diam. 25 in.)

2.  IHS NAZARENE REX IUDEORUM FILI DEI MISERERE MEI ANNO 1730.
(Diam. 29 in.)

3.  [ + 69 ] SANCTE LAVRENCI ORA PRO NOBIS
(Diam. 31 in.)

4.  HENRY [9] EARLE [9] OF [9] STANFORD [9] GAVE [9] THIS [9] BELL [9] ANO [9] DMI 1632 [9] TR [9] IK [9] JP [9] [ ꓵ 1. ]
(Diam. 33 in.)

# WISTOW.

S. Wistan. 3 Bells.

1. GOD [9] SAVE [9] THE [9] kING [9] 1625 [9] [▽ 1.]
2. The same dated 1631.
3. [ + 3 ] 𝕴 𝕳 𝕰 𝕾 𝖄 𝕾 [▽ 6]

# WITHCOTE.

S. . . . 1 Bell.

1. T. EAYRE A.D. 1744.

# WITHERLEY.

S. Peter. 5 Bells.

1. OMNIA FIANT AD GLORIAM DEI : · THOs. EAYRE
   FECIT . ˙. RICHARD FARMER . ˙. C. W. 1744.
2. OMNIA FIANT AD GLORIAM DEI · : · GLORIA DEO
   SOLI · : · THOs. EAYRE FECIT 1744.
3. [ + 22 ] BE · YT · KNOWNE · TO · ALL · THAT · DOTH
   · ME · SEE · THAT · NEWCOMBE · OF · LEICESTER
   · MADE · MEE 1609.
4. IH'S NAZARENVS [9] REX : IVDEORVM [9] FILI :
   DEI [9] MISERERE : MEI [9] 1619 [▽ 1.]
5. [ + 55.] 𝕵𝕰𝕾𝖄𝕾 𝕹𝕬𝖅𝕬𝕽𝕰𝕹𝖄𝕾 [ □ 59.]
   𝕽𝕰𝖃 [ □ 59.] 𝕴𝖄𝕯𝕰𝕺𝕽𝖄𝕸 [ □ 59.]

Nichols relates the following anecdote in connection with the casting
of the two first bells, and with Mr. Farmer, whose name appears upon
the 1st. "In the year 1743 there were but four bells at Witherley, and
the fourth was cracked; upon which Mr. Farmer of Witherley, being a
great ringer, wished it to be recast into two smaller ones, to make five of
them: but Mr. King opposed him, wanting it to be recast of the same

2 Q

size, and not to alter the number of them. The contention running high, Mrs. Beet, a near neighbour, said to Mr. King, 'If I had your fortune, I would turn Mr. Farmer's red waistcoat wrong side outwards,' but after being at law for some time, Mr. King gave it up, and it was cast into two."

## WOODHOUSE.

S. MARY.                                                              5 BELLS.

1.  1818.
2.  J. TAYLOR & CO. LOUGHBOROUGH 1868.
            (Weight 3 cwt. 3 qrs. 5 lbs.)
3.  JOHN SIMPSON JOSEPH BESTON CHURCHWARDENS
        1814. T. MEARS LONDON FECIT.
4.  T. MEARS OF LONDON FECIT 1814.
5.  J. TAYLOR & CO. LOUGHBOROUGH 1868. HENRY
        HUMPHREYS CHURCHWARDEN.
            (Weight 6 cwt. 3 qrs. 11 lbs. Diam. 32 in. Note C.)

In 6 Edward VI. there were "tow belles." Nichols says there were two bells in 1800. They were inscribed, 1st "1590" 2nd "God save the King 1619." He also says that previous to the year 1617 the Woodhouse people buried their dead at Quorndon, in return for which they gave a bell to the church there, and provided it with a rope.

The Pancake-bell is rung on Shrove-Tuesday.

## WOODHOUSE EAVES.

S. PAUL.                                                              1 BELL.

1.  THOMAS MEARS OF LONDON FECIT 1837.
            (Diam. 25 in.)

## WOODVILLE.

S . . . . .                                                          1 BELL.

A modern bell weighing 4 cwt. founded by Messrs. J. Taylor and Co., Loughborough.

# WORTHINGTON.

S. MATTHEW.                                                    1 BELL.

1. ( Blank. )

In 6 Edward VI. there were " tow belles in the steple."

# WYFORDBY.

S. MARY.                                                       2 BELLS.

1. [ + 82 ] 𝔸𝕍𝔾 : 𝔐𝔸ℝ𝕀𝔸 : 𝔾ℝ𝔸𝔾𝕀𝔸 : ℙ𝕃𝔼

2. ᵫ    ᵫᵵ    ᵯᵫ    ᵳᵢ    ᵫ    [ ∪ 63 ].

In 6 Edward VI. there were " ij bells."

For local doggerel on these and other neighbouring bells see p. 284.

In 1402 John Woodford of Brentingby bequeathed ten marks to the church of Wyfordby towards the maintenance of the fabric and the bells *(Nichols).*

# WYMESWOLD.

S. MARY.                                                       6 BELLS.

1. INTACTUM SILEO PERCUTE DULCE CANO 1795. THOMAS OSBORN DOWNHAM NORFOLK FOUN-DER 1795.
   ( Diam. 29 in. )

2. CUM VOCO VENITE 1795. THOMAS OSBORN FECIT.
   ( Diam. 28 in. )

3. THOMAS OSBORN FOUNDER DOWNHAM NORFOLK 1795.
   ( Diam. 31 in. )

4. BEG YE OF GOD YOUR SOULS TO SAVE BEFORE I CALL YOU TO THE GRAVE.
   T. OSBORN DOWNHAM NORFOLK FOUNDER 1795.
   ( Diam. 33½ in. )

5. OUR VOICES SHALL WITH JOCUND SOUND
MAKE HILLS AND VALLIES ECHO ROUND 1795.
T. OSBORN DOWNHAM NORFOLK FECIT 1795.
(Diam. 37 in.)

6. T. OSBORN DOWNHAM NORFOLK FECIT 1795.
(Diam. 41¼ in.)

In 1783 there were only four bells, which were much injured when the spire was struck by lightning.

The ring was increased to six bells in 1795.

A daily-bell rings at five o'clock a.m. during the summer months, and at six o'clock in the winter: also at six p.m. Tradition says the parish clerk formerly received the proceeds of a close of land for performing this duty. It was called "the forty acre," or rather—it being less than an acre in extent—"the faulty acre." He now receives £1. 10s. 0d. per annum in lieu.

The bells and belfry have been both put into excellent order by the present vicar—the Rev. R. Walker—who obliged me with an inspection of an agreement dated 4th Aug. 1742, between Thomas Hedderley of Nottingham, Bellfounder, and the churchwardens of the parish. Thomas Hedderley undertook to recast the 3rd bell and "uphold the same sound and tuneable" for a year and a day, for a payment at the rate of 20s. per cwt. for every cwt. the bell should weigh.

# WYMONDHAM.

S. Peter.                                                    6 Bells.

1. GOD [9] SAVE [9] THE [9] KINGE [9]
   1611 [ ʊ 1. ]

2. SIR [9] HENR₂ [9] BERKLE [9]
   BARANETT [ + 22 ] AND LADY
   KATHEREN HIꙅ WIFE GAVE MEE AND MOVLDED
   VS ALL 1611 [ ʊ *arms.* ]

3. 𝕾𝕴𝕽 [9] . 𝕳𝕰𝕼𝕽𝖞 [9] 𝕭𝕰𝕽𝕶𝕷𝕰 [9] 𝕭𝕬𝕽𝕬𝕼𝕼𝕰𝕿 1611 [9] [ + 44 ] [ ▽ *arms.* ]

4. The same.

5. [ ▽ *arms* ] 𝕾𝕴𝕽 [9] 𝕳𝕰𝕼𝕽𝖞 [9] 𝕭𝕰𝕽𝕶𝕰𝕷𝕰𝖟 [9] [ ▽ *arms* ] 𝕭𝕬𝕽𝕽𝕺𝕼𝕰𝕿 [9] 𝕳𝕮𝕼 [9] 𝖇𝕮𝕼 [9]

6. THIS BELL IS DEDDECATED TO THE HOLY TRINITY 1755. THOs. BVLIVANT CHVRCHWARDEN THOMAS HEDDERLY FOVNDER.

In 6 Edward VI. there were " iij greitt beylles."

The arms placed upon the bells as indicated are:—Quarterly 1 and 4 a chevron between ten cinquefoils, *Berkeley:* 2 and 3 a lion rampant crowned, *Hamelin;* impaling a lion rampant between five fleur de lys, *Beaumont.*

Thomas; second son of Thomas Lord Berkeley of Coston, obtained Wymondham by marriage with the daughter and heiress of Sir John Hamelin early in the fourteenth century. His descendant, the donor of the above bells, Sir Henry Berkeley Baronet, was Lord of the Manor of Wymondham in 1611. He was the first, and (dying without issue) the only baronet. He married Catherine, daughter of Nicholas Beaumont, of Coleorton, Esqre.

The Gleaning-bell (the 1st) is rung during harvest at 8 a.m. and at 6 p.m.

The Pancake-bell (the 5th) is rung on Shrove-Tuesday.

The death-knell is rung very fast for five minutes; then slowly: three tolls are given for a male, two for a female.

# GOD'S

## APPOINTMENT

### IS MY

## CONTENTMENT.

*Plate I.*

2

3

4

I

5

6

I

*Plate II.*

7

8

9

10

11

*Plate III.*

12

13

14

*Plate IV.*

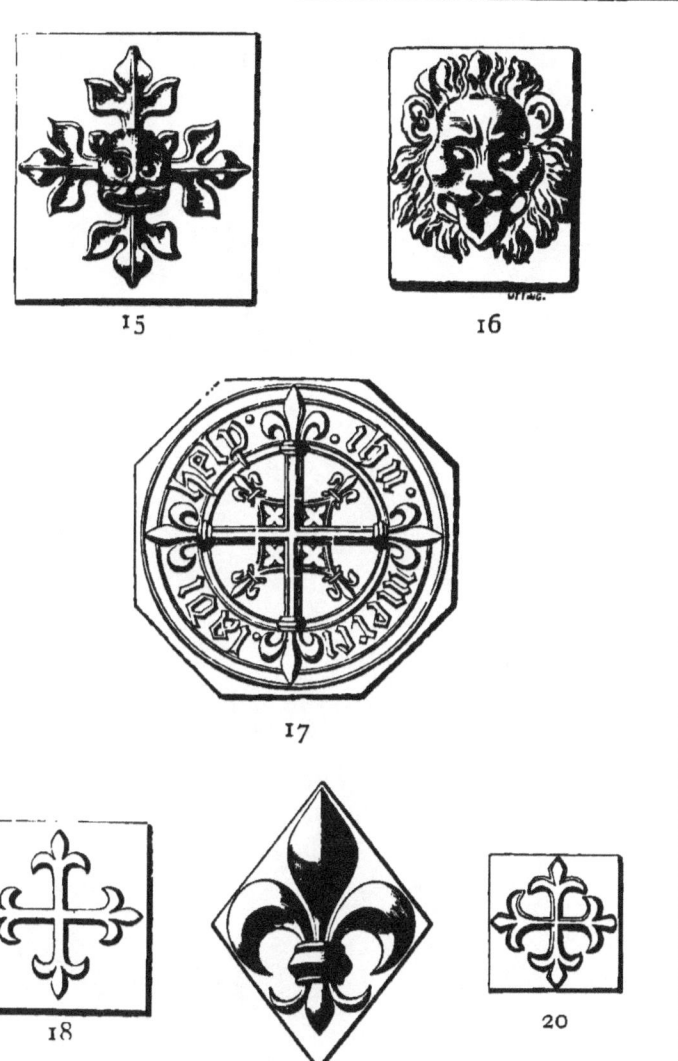

15

16

17

18

19

20

*Plate V.*

21

22

23

24

25

26

*Plate VI.*

27

28

29

30

31

32

*Plate VII.*

33

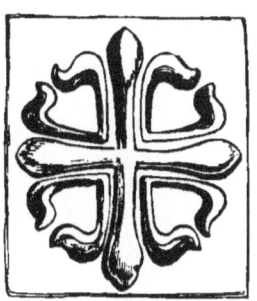

34

35

36

*Plate VIII.*

38

41

40

37

39

Plate IX.

42

43

44

45

46

*Plate X.*

49

47

48

50

*Plate XI.*

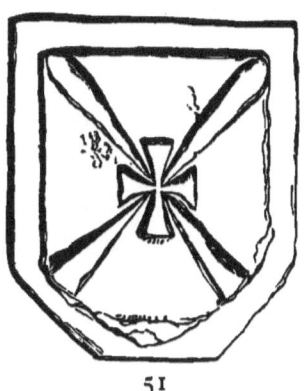

51

51a

52

53

*Plate  XII.*

54

55

56

57

58

59

60

*Plate XIII.*

61

62

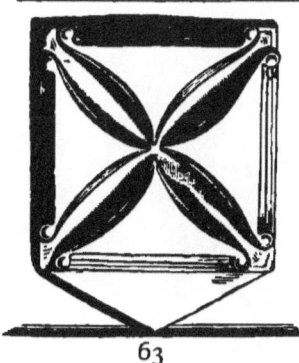

63

64

*Plate XIV.*

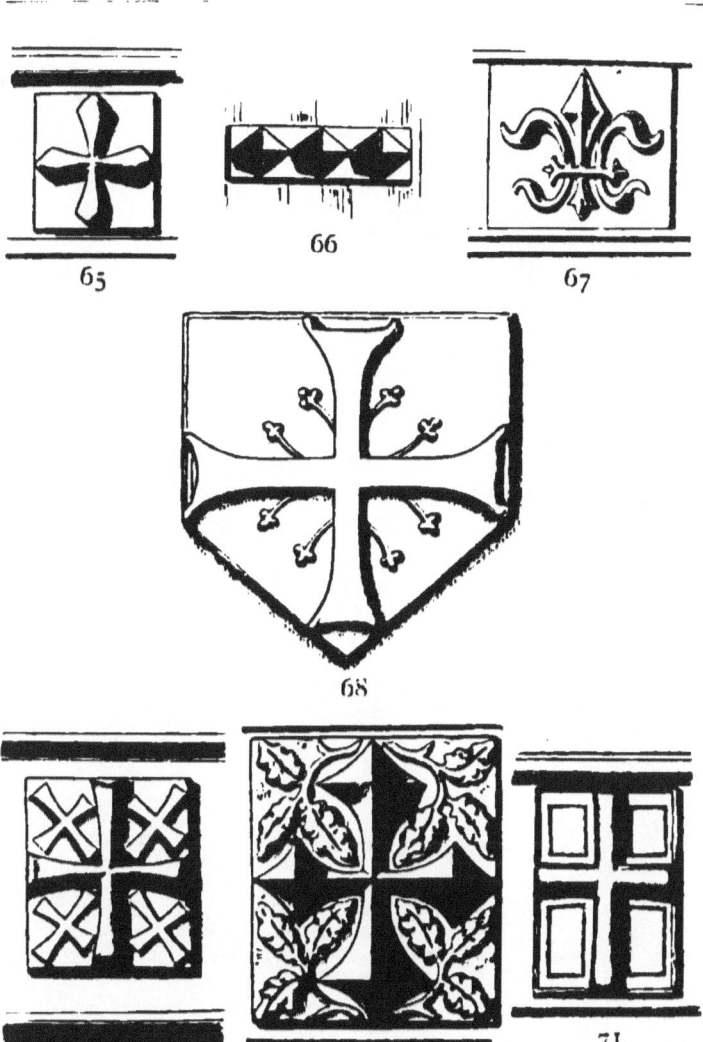

65

66

67

68

69

70

71

*Plate XV.*

72

73

74

75

*Plate XVI.*

76

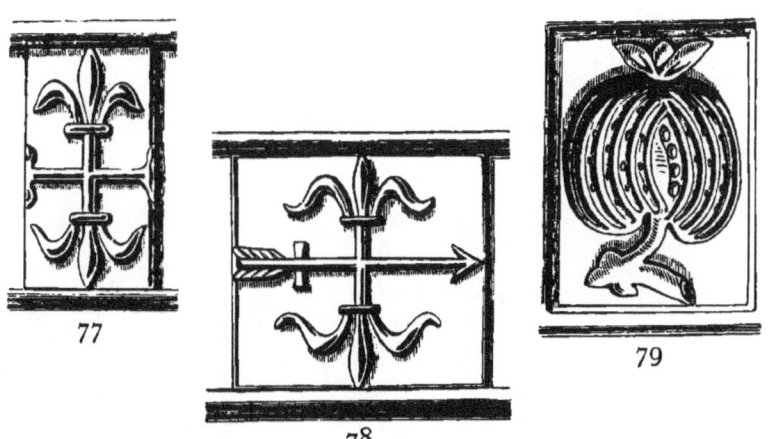

77

78

79

80

81

82

83

*Plate XVIII.*

84

85

86

87

# INDEX.

2 R

*Printed by* SAMUEL CLARKE, *Leicester.*

# ERRATA.

P. 91, line 14, *for* " bear " *read* " bears."
P. 106, line 6, *strike out* " Lutterworth."
P. 133, line 4, *for* " Commissioners " *read* " Commissioners'."

explains the ancient ritual of the church, the furniture, and the ornaments of the fabric and of the officiating clergy, and the origin and history of the Town Guilds · · · · which does not, however, consist of dry details, such as we have indicated, but is made up, independently of these, with pleasant discussions and with much information on matters which just now are assuming importance."—*The Churchman.*

"Mr. North · · · · has done really good service to archæology by the publication of his present work, which is, without exception, the best of the kind we have seen · · · · his volume is not only one of local but general interest, and one which serves in an important degree to illustrate the general history of the Church and of those its most troublous and trying times."—*The Reliquary.*

"Local histories possess an interest and do good far beyond the original circles for which they were intended. So we welcome and commend Mr. North's Chronicle of the church of S. Martin, at Leicester."—*Ecclesiastic.*

"Mr. North has successfully attempted to place before the reader 'A Chronicle of the Church of St. Martin in Leicester,' · · · · and his narrative naturally shows, to a great extent, the progress of the Reformation in that parish, as exemplified in the changes made in the furniture of the church, and the accessories of the worship, and by the abrogation of local customs and peculiarities · · · · his book is a valuable addition to our local histories and ecclesiological literature. It is well printed and illustrated with five curious engravings."—*Church Review.*

"· · · · carefully compiled and valuable work · · · · There is a great deal of curious matter connected with the various changes in religious worship which occurred during the years over which the before-mentioned Churchwardens' Accounts range, and a good index furnishes a ready means of reference to any item to which the reader may desire to turn. · · · · "—*Church Times.*

"Mr. North · · · · has done his work carefully and judiciously. He has produced a book abounding in interesting memories of past times."—*Leicester Advertiser.*

"All who would encourage the preservation of a knowledge of the past, whether as a beacon to guide us in the future, or as a subject of pleasing retrospect, will find Mr. North's book a record complete and faithful, as far as it proposes to go, of the matters to which it relates, and is worthy a place in the library for perusal now and hereafter."—*Leicester Chronicle.*

"Mr. North · · · · then passes on to elucidate all the conditions affecting the church above-named, its chapels, appointments, furniture, vestments, vessels, altars, processions, relics, obits, images, plays, books of office, customs and usages, guilds, &c. Of these and many other matters, his work, beautifully printed and illustrated, is a veritable storehouse of information, showing the state of things prior to, and during the progress of the Reformation. · · · · We would strongly recommend Mr. North's book to the archæological world, as one in which they will find great store of information, well-digested and arranged, and presented in a most attractive form."—*Worcester Herald.*

"· · · · The whole work we find carefully authenticated with references, and it possesses a copious index; it is amusing for the drawing room; a thoroughly furnished handbook for the ecclesiologist; and precious to the conservator of parish memories . . "—*Leicester Journal.*

"· · · · a very trusty and instructive monograph he places before us, throwing light and interest over a transition period of English history. It is of much more than parochial value. It illumines the broad story of our country."—*Newcastle Daily Chronicle.*

"· · · · enough has been shown to satisfy the lovers of Archæology that Mr. North's book abounds in interesting and valuable matter."—*Northampton Mercury.*

www.ingramcontent.com/pod-product-compliance
Lightning Source LLC
Chambersburg PA
CBHW021712110726
47902CB00005B/1159